T0305123

Developing Next Generation Leaders for Transgenerational Entrepreneurial Family Enterprises

THE SUCCESSFUL TRANSGENERATIONAL ENTREPRENEURSHIP PRACTICES SERIES (STEP)

Series Editor: Pramodita Sharma, *University of Vermont and Babson College, USA*

The success of passing a family business from one generation to another depends not only on instilling business ideas and leadership in future generations, but also on engendering the entrepreneurial spirit in those business leaders to come; this is the practice of transgenerational leadership. Successful Transgenerational Entrepreneurship Practices, more commonly known as the STEP Project, was put in place to help facilitate family enterprising. An innovative research initiative that spans the globe, it offers insight, partnership and solutions for current and future family leaders. As part of the STEP Project, academic experts in entrepreneurship and business collaborate with prosperous multigenerational family businesses to explore and identify those practices that will help family businesses grow and prosper. The project focuses on three key tenets: venturing (launching new businesses), renewal (revitalizing existing businesses), and innovation (introducing new products and processes). By creating a stream of powerful practices and cases that empower families to build their entrepreneurial legacies, the members of the STEP Project are rapidly moving their discoveries from research into practice.

Current STEP Affiliates

Europe
Antwerp Management School, Antwerp, Belgium
Dublin City University, Dublin, Ireland
EMLYON, Écully, France
ESADE Business School, Barcelona, Spain
Jönköping International Business School, Jönköping, Sweden
Lancaster University Management School, Lancaster, England
RANEPA of the President of Russia, Institute of Business Studies, Moscow, Russia
Università Bocconi, Milan, Italy
Università della Svizzera Italiana, Lugano, Switzerland
Universität St. Gallen, St. Gallen, Switzerland
Universität Witten-Herdecke, Witten, Germany
University of Edinburgh, Edinburgh, Scotland
Windesheim University, Zwolle, the Netherlands

Latin America
Fundação Dom Cabral, Belo Horizonte, Brazil
Instituto de Estudios Superiores de Administración (IESA), Caracas, Venezuela
Universidad Interamericana de Puerto Rico (UIPR), San Germán, Puerto Rico
Tecnológico de Monterrey, Mexico City, Mexico
Universidad Adolfo Ibáñez, Santiago, Chile
Universidad de Los Andes, Bogotá, Colombia
Universidad de Piura, Piura, Perú
Universidad Icesi, Cali, Colombia
Universidad San Francisco de Quito, Quito, Ecuador

Asia Pacific
Bangkok University, Bangkok, Thailand
Bond University, Gold Coast, Australia
China Europe International Business School, Shanghai, P.R. China
Chinese University of Hong Kong, Hong Kong
Indian School of Business, Hyderabad, India
National Sun Yat-Sen University, Kaohsiung, Taiwan
Singapore Management University, Singapore
Universiti Tun Abdul Razak, Kuala Lumpur, Malaysia
Waseda University, Tokyo, Japan
Zhejiang University, Hangzhou, P.R. China

North America
Babson College, Massachusetts, USA
Baylor University, Texas, USA
Dalhousie University, Nova Scotia, Canada
HEC-Montreal, Quebec, Canada
Northwestern University, Illinois, USA
Oregon State University, Oregon, USA
Stetson University, Florida, USA
University of Vermont, Vermont, USA
Utah State University, Utah, USA
Worcester Polytechnic Institute, Massachusetts, USA

Africa
Nelson Mandela Metropolitan University, Port Elizabeth, South Africa

Developing Next Generation Leaders for Transgenerational Entrepreneurial Family Enterprises

Edited by

Pramodita Sharma

University of Vermont, USA

Nunzia Auletta

Instituto de Estudios Superiores de Administración (IESA), Venezuela

Rocki-Lee DeWitt

University of Vermont, USA

Maria José Parada

ESADE Business School, Spain

Mohar Yusof

Universiti Tun Abdul Razak, Malaysia

THE SUCCESSFUL TRANSGENERATIONAL
ENTREPRENEURSHIP PRACTICES SERIES

 Edward Elgar
PUBLISHING

Cheltenham, UK • Northampton, MA, USA

Published by
Edward Elgar Publishing Limited
The Lypiatts
15 Lansdown Road
Cheltenham
Glos GL50 2JA
UK

Edward Elgar Publishing, Inc.
William Pratt House
9 Dewey Court
Northampton
Massachusetts 01060
USA

A catalogue record for this book
is available from the British Library

Library of Congress Control Number: 2015943185

This book is available electronically in the **Elgar**online
Business subject collection
DOI 10.4337/9781784717872

ISBN 978 1 78471 786 5 (cased)
ISBN 978 1 78471 787 2 (eBook)

Typeset by Servis Filmsetting Ltd, Stockport, Cheshire
Printed and bound in Great Britain by TJ International Ltd, Padstow

Contents

Figures

Tables

Contributors

Nunzia Auletta is a Full Professor at the Centre of Entrepreneurship, Instituto de Estudios Superiores de Administración (IESA), Venezuela. Her current research is mainly focused on business innovation, sustainability, and entrepreneurial orientation in family firms. She coordinated the research teams for the Global Entrepreneurship Monitor (GEM) and the Successful Transgenerational Entrepreneurship Practices (STEP) in Venezuela, since 2009. She earned her PhD at the Universidad Simón Bolívar, Venezuela.

Barjoyai Bardai is a Professor at the Graduate School of Business, Universiti Tun Abdul Razak, Malaysia. He is a Chartered Accountant, obtained a PhD in Taxation from University College London, the University of London in 1991. Has been teaching Accounting, Finance, Taxation, Entrepreneurship, Creativity and Innovation in Business and Islamic Banking and Finance since 1975 at Universiti Kebangsaan Malaysia, Universiti Teknoloji Malaysia, Universiti Malaya, UNIRAZAK, MUST, Al-Medinah International University, UNISEL, INCIEF, UTAR, UITM and TAYLOR Universities. Has been involved in business and entrepreneurship development including venture capital activities in the Silicon Valley since 1997 and listed four companies successfully in the Toronto and Montreal Stock Exchange. He is still active in technology venture development in Malaysia and the region. Has been researching on small business and entrepreneurship development in the State of Pahang, Trengganu, Kelantan, Selangor, Wilayah Persekutuan, Negeri Sembilan and Malacca in Malaysia. Has written two books in entrepreneurship, published by the national publisher Dewan Bahasa dan Pustaka in the year 2000. He has supervised over 50 PhD students in the areas of Entrepreneurship, Accounting, Taxation and Innovation.

Patrick Bender graduated from Jönköping International Business School (JIBS), Sweden in 2014 with a master's degree in Business Administration and Economics. He works in the financial department of the family business. He administers one of the smaller companies and supports the CFO of the consolidated family business in specific projects. His academic research has mainly focused on successions of family businesses.

Navneet Bhatnagar is a research associate at the Thomas Schmidheiny Centre for Family Enterprise of the Indian School of Business, India. He has an MBA from the Institute of Management Studies, Indore and received his master's degree in Economics from Barkatullah University, Bhopal. He is pursuing a doctoral degree at the Department of Management Studies, Indian Institute of Technology Madras, India.

Frank H. Bos holds a master's degree in Business Administration from the University of Groningen, the Netherlands. He works at Windesheim University of Applied Sciences, the Netherlands, both as lecturer and as a researcher within the Windesheim Family Business Research Center. He is a PhD candidate at the University of Groningen. His PhD research focuses on family firm top management teams. He is interested in questions relating to the effect of family involvement on managerial practices and professionalization of top management teams within the family business context.

Mara Brumana is Research Fellow at the University of Bergamo, Italy. She is also a member of the Research Center for Young and Family Enterprise (CYFE). As a visiting scholar, she has been at the Alberta School of Business (Canada), the Johannes Kepler University and the WU Vienna University (Austria). Her research interests lie at the intersection of entrepreneurship, organization theory and international business, with a particular focus on family firms' entreprencurial initiatives, institutional-bound strategic change and power relationships within multinational corporations.

Lucio Cassia is a Full Professor in Strategic Management and Entrepreneurship at the University of Bergamo, Italy. He teaches strategic management, corporate strategy, competition and growth and entrepreneurial strategy in graduate, postgraduate and PhD programs. He is currently leading research, education and consulting on entrepreneurship, business strategy and family business. Main interests are in technology-based start-ups, high-tech companies, innovation tools and patterns of growth of small and medium enterprises. With particular focus on the topics of youth entrepreneurship, growth of family businesses, managerial succession and generational change, Lucio promoted and founded the Research Center for Young and Family Enterprise (CYFE). Lucio has published ten books and over 150 papers in academic and professional journals.

J.P. Coen Rigtering holds a master's degree (cum laude) in Policy, Communication and Organization from the VU University in Amsterdam and a PhD in Corporate Entrepreneurship from the Utrecht University School of Economics (USE), the Netherlands. Currently, he works as an

Assistant Professor at USE specializing in corporate entrepreneurship, organizational theory and entrepreneurship. His work is published in several academic journals such as: *Review of Managerial Science, International Entrepreneurship and Management Journal*, and *The Service Industries Journal*. In 2012 he was named the USE PhD student of the year. His primary research interests are in the field of corporate entrepreneurship, intrapreneurship, and strategic management in family businesses.

Alfredo De Massis is a tenured Full Professor who holds the Chair in Entrepreneurship and Family Business at the Lancaster University Management School, UK and is Director of the School's Centre for Family Business. He served as Global Board Member and Chairman of the European Leadership Council of the Global STEP Project for Family Enterprising, and is a member of the Academic Advisory Board of the Institute for Family Business (IFB) Research Foundation. Alfredo's family business research has been published widely in leading academic and professional journals. He serves on the Editorial Boards of *Entrepreneurship Theory and Practice, Strategic Entrepreneurship Journal, Family Business Review* and *Journal of Family Business Strategy*, and has been Editor of seven special issues on family business research in leading entrepreneurship, strategy and innovation journals.

Rocki-Lee DeWitt, PhD (Columbia University) is a Professor of Management in the School of Business Administration at the University of Vermont, US. Her current research examines intergenerational innovation, the role of non-family members in family business success, socially responsible succession planning, and the role of family businesses in industry emergence and evolution. She is a member of the Editorial Board of *Family Business Review*, the former Chairperson of the North American Council of STEP, and is currently affiliated with the UCESI STEP team.

Luis Díaz Matajira is Assistant Professor at the School of Management Universidad de los Andes, Colombia where he serves as Director of the Undergraduate Program. His research interests are in the fields of family business strategy, public management and corporate social responsibility. He has been part of the STEP project since 2006. He holds a BA in Economics from Universidad Nacional de Colombia, a master's in Development Studies from the London School of Economics and a master's in Management from Tulane University. He is also a PhD student in Management from Tulane University, New Orleans.

Allan Discua Cruz, PhD, is a lecturer in Entrepreneurship at the Institute for Entrepreneurship and Enterprise Development (IEED) in the Lancaster

University Management School, UK. He is a third generation member of a family in business and his professional background is on industrial analysis and manufacturing management. He is also a member of the Centre for Family Business at IEED. He has published in entrepreneurship and family business journals as well as book compilations. His current research focuses on entrepreneurial dynamics by families in business and social contexts of entrepreneurship.

Alberto Gimeno is an Associate Professor of Strategy and General Management at ESADE Business School, Spain. He is the Director of the ESADE International Family Business Lab and the CEMS Master in International Management. A member of the Global Board of the STEP Project (Successful Transgenerational Entrepreneurship Practices), he is a fellow of the Family Firm Institute (FFI). An active international speaker in academic and business meetings, Alberto is a Board Member in different family businesses and a senior partner of Family Business Knowledge (FBK), an international family business consultancy. His research is focused on the application of the theory of complexity to family business management, in domains such as succession, professionalization, communication, governance and identity creation.

Gustavo González Couture is Full Professor at the School of Management Universidad de los Andes, Colombia. His research interests are in the fields of virtue ethics in entrepreneurial families, business ethics, and workplace spirituality. He holds a PhD in Philosophy, has been Provost of Universidad de los Andes and has served on STEP's Regional Council and Global Board.

Denize Grzybovski is a Professor of Organizational Theories and coordinator of the postgraduate management programme at the Passo Fundo University (UPF), Brazil. She is a Guest Professor at the Master in Development Programme at Regional University of the Northwest of the State of Rio Grande do Sul (UNIJUÍ) and the General Secretary of the Brazilian Association for Studies on Entrepreneurship and Management of Small Businesses (ANEGEPE). Professor Grzybovski holds a doctorate in management from the Lavras Federal University (UFLA).

Margré Heetebrij-van Dalfsen holds a master's degree in Business Administration, more specifically in Organizational and Management Control, from the University of Groningen, the Netherlands. Currently she works as a researcher and a lecturer at Windesheim University of Applied Sciences, the Netherlands. In her role as lecturer she specializes in business economics in general and more specifically in strategic management, finance and management control. In her research she focuses on the relationship between values and managerial practices in family businesses. Being a junior researcher this chapter is her first work being published.

Hiro Higashide is Professor of Entrepreneruship, Creativity and Family business at the Graduate School of Commerce, Waseda University, Japan. He received an MBA and a PhD in Entrepreneurship at Imperial College, University of London. Before his degrees, he had been involved in property development in the UK and continental Europe. His current focus is on the impacts of creativity, various 'intelligences', death and religion, ego and freedom, and individual capabilities, on the happiness of stakeholders. He has presented his work in such conferences as the Babson conferences, AOM, BAM and Global Entrepreneurship Research Conference and has published articles in such journals such as *Journal of Business Venturing*, *Journal of Management* and *Japan Ventures Review*.

Naomi Kozono is a business consultant specializing in formulating business strategies, standardizing operating procedures, and optimizing business systems for global companies. She received an MBA from the Graduate School of Asia-Pacific Studies, Waseda University, Japan. Her family runs their family business. While she attended graduate school, she studied and conducted research on longevity and succession in family businesses. After obtaining the MBA, she worked for a foreign consultancy firm. Currently, she works as an independent consultant.

Christian Lechner is currently Full Professor of Strategy and Entrepreneurship at the Free University of Bolzano, Italy. He is the Director of the PhD program in Economics and Management on Organisational and Institutional Outliers. He held previously, for 12 years, a position at Toulouse Business School where he was involved in entrepreneurship activities, the launch of an incubator and the coaching of small firms. He received his PhD in Business Administration from the University of Regensburg, an MBA from the University of Georgia, a university degree in Business Administration from the Ludwig-Maximilians-University, and international business studies at the Università degli Studi di Firenze. His research interests are inter-firm and inter-personal networks, habitual entrepreneurship, organizational configurations of new firms and growth, the resource-based view and family business management.

Ilse A. Matser is Professor of Family Business Management at Windesheim University of Applied Sciences, the Netherlands. She received her PhD in Family Business Management from the Utrecht University School of Economics. She is also the Director of the Dutch Centre for Family Business, an expertise center for family firms. Her primary research interests are in the field of ownership, governance and transgenerational entrepreneurship. Her work is published in several academic journals such as: *Family Business Review* and *Journal of Family Business Management*.

Tommaso Minola is co-founder and Director of the research Center for Young and Family Enterprise (CYFE) of the University of Bergamo, Italy, where he is Lecturer in the fields of Technology Management, Entrepreneurship and Strategy. He is TOFT Visiting Professor at Jönköping International Business School (Sweden). His research and teaching is focused on entrepreneurship, family business, technological innovation, technology transfer. His work is published in several academic journals such as: *R&D Management, The Journal of Technology Transfer, International Journal of Entrepreneurial Behaviour & Research*. He is member of several academic and professional associations on entrepreneurship and family business, and reviewer for major international journals in the field. He has also been Technology Manager and Director of Technology Incubator at Politecnico di Milano.

Leilanie Mohd Nor is an Assistant Professor at the Bank Rakyat School of Business and Entrepreneurship, Universiti Tun Abdul Razak, Malaysia. Her specialization is in entrepreneurship, focusing on family business theories and models, decision-making process, venture creation, and portfolio entrepreneurship. Leilanie is the team leader for STEP (Successful Transgenerational Entrepreneurship Practices) Malaysia since 2009. She was the STEP Asia Pacific Leadership Council (Chair) for five years from 2010 to 2014, and currently sits on the STEP Global Board. She has also been involved in the Global Entrepreneurship Monitor (GEM) study since 2009. In addition, her more than 15 years managerial experience in large companies contributes to her capabilities and competencies as a consultant and trainer. Leilanie holds a BA from Michigan State University and her PhD focused on the venture creation decision-making process within family businesses.

Angelica Nilsson graduated from Jönköping International Business School (JIBS), Sweden in 2014 with a master's degree in Business Administration and Economics. Today Angelica works in the accounting department of the family firm. She also develops new projects together with the CFO. One of her greatest interests is leadership and related challenges that occur in family firms. Her research is focused on the leadership of next generation in family firms.

Maria José Parada is lecturer of Strategy and Family Business at the Department of Strategy and General Management in ESADE Business School, Spain, and Co-Director of the ESADE Family Business Lab. She holds a PhD from Jönköping International Business School (JIBS),

Sweden. She obtained a Master of Research and an MBA from ESADE and a Family Business Advising certificate from FFI. She has been Visiting Researcher of the INSEAD Global Leadership Center, France, and Visiting Scholar at HEC, Paris. Her research focuses mainly on the development of governance structures, professionalization, values transmission and change, and entrepreneurship in family businesses.

Kavil Ramachandran, a permanent faculty of the Indian School of Business (ISB) since its establishment in 2001, is the Executive Director of the Thomas Schmidheiny Centre for Family Enterprise at ISB. Professor Ramachandran received his PhD in Business Management from Cranfield University (UK) in 1986. For the next 15 years he served as professor at the Indian Institute of Management, Ahmedabad. His areas of specialization are family entrepreneurship and strategic management. He has been a consultant to the World Bank, International Labour Organization, Swiss Development Agency, Department for International Development (UK), various state governments and development banks in India.

Marcela Ramírez-Pasillas is an Assistant Professor and Project Manager of PRME (United Nations Principles of Responsible Management Education) at the Jönköping International Business School (JIBS), Sweden. She serves as a Chair of the STEP European Leadership Council of the Global STEP Project for Family Enterprising. Her research is related to entrepreneurship and branding in family businesses and entrepreneurship in international trade fairs and cluster networks, and is published in book chapters and academic journals. She is a faculty member of the Master in Managing in a Global Context. She is interested in entrepreneurial phenomena that are socially based triggering different responsible entrepreneurship(s).

Maria Teresa Roscoe is a Professor of Development of Shareholders, Family Companies, Governance, Management by Processes and Organizational Restructuring at Fundação Dom Cabral (FDC), Brazil. She has coordinated the Partnership for the Development of Shareholders Programme (PDA) at FDC for seven years. Professor Roscoe holds a master's in Business Administration from the Pontifical Catholic University of Minas Gerais (PUC-MG) and an MBA from FDC.

Pramodita Sharma is the Sanders Chair and Professor for Family Business at the School of Business Administration, University of Vermont, US. She holds an honorary doctorate from the University of Witten/Herdecke, Germany. Her research on succession processes, governance, innovation, next generation commitment and entrepreneurship has been honored with several international awards. She is among the most frequently cited scholars in family business studies. In addition to seven co-authored books, she has published over 50 scholarly articles and book chapters on family business studies. She is the Editor of the *Family Business Review* and is a recipient of the prestigious Barbara Hollander award of the Family Firm Institute.

Adriane Vieira is a Professor and researcher in the Faculty of Management of Health Services at the Universidade Federal de Minas Gerais (UFMG), Brazil. She is also guest researcher at Fundação Dom Cabral (FDC) and has worked with family-owned businesses over the last eight years. Professor Vieira is a psychologist with a doctorate in administration from UFMG.

Siri Roland Xavier is currently the Deputy Dean of Bank Rakyat School of Business and Entrepreneurship at Universiti Tun Abdul Razak, Malaysia. He is also the Programme Director of the Entrepreneurship programmes in collaboration with Babson College, Boston, USA. Prior to academia he started his career with Andersen Consulting providing consultation services to the local banking industry. His working experience (spanning 20 years) has included senior managerial positions in sales, marketing, production and distribution in a NYSE listed company, Asia Pulp & Paper. In research he is the National Team leader (since 2009) for the Global Entrepreneurship Monitor (GEM), project leader for GEM ASEAN entrepreneurship research funded by IDRC and a member of the National Successful Tran-Generational Entrepreneurship Practices (STEP) family business research program. He is a Board Member of the Global Entrepreneurship Research Association (GERA) since 2011. He was appointed 'Subject Matter Expert' for Entrepreneurship, New Venture Development and Marketing Strategy (since 2007) to the OPEN University Malaysia (OUM). Roland has conducted training and consultancy for many financial and academic institutions both local and international including being a keynote speaker globally.

Katsushi Yamaguchi is a research student and PhD candidate at the Graduate School of Commerce, Waseda University, Japan. He received a master's degree in Commerce from the Graduate School of Commerce, Waseda University. Between 2011 and 2013, he served as a Research Associate at the Research Institute of the Faculty of Commerce, Waseda University. He is a member of the International Family Enterprise Research Academy (IFERA). His research interests include succession and development of successor, and entrepreneurship in family firms.

Mohar Yusof is an Associate Professor at the Bank Rakyat School of Business and Entrepreneurship, Universiti Tun Abdul Razak, Malaysia.

His specialization and research interest are in the field of entrepreneurship, family business, and strategy. He has been involved in the Global Entrepreneurship Monitor (GEM) study and the Successful Transgenerational Entrepreneurship Practices (STEP) project on family business since 2009. He has a PhD in Management (by Research) in which he studied the organizational antecedents of academic entrepreneurship. In addition, he holds the Malaysian Institute of Management – Certified Professional Intellectual Property Manager (MIM-CPIPM) certification and he is also a Certified Financial Planner (CFP).

1. Developing next generation leaders

**Rocki-Lee DeWitt, Nunzia Auletta,
Maria José Parada, Mohar Yusof and
Pramodita Sharma**

INTRODUCTION

Transgenerational entrepreneurship is defined as the 'processes through which a family uses and develops entrepreneurial mindsets and family influenced capabilities to create new streams of entrepreneurial, financial, and social value across generations' (Habbershon, Nordqvist, and Zellweger, 2010: 1). Developing next generation leaders lies at the heart of transgenerational entrepreneurship as it squarely focuses attention on those individuals – family or non-family members – who alone, or in collaboration, are responsible for the success and longevity of a family enterprise. This book aims to understand the pathways used by enterprising families around the world to develop next generation leaders. We set out to explore how leadership becomes an enduring source of advantage that is less dependent upon who is in a formal role and relies more upon the process by which the family's core values shape and build the next generation of leaders. When leadership development is considered as an underlying process, generational transitions become less rigid and episodic, thereby potentially less disruptive. Continuous shifting of roles and ongoing development of the current and next generations becomes an enduring source of advantage.

In practical terms, our interest was to understand how the next generation members are introduced to the business and what it stands for. How do they become aware of the key decisions and defining moments of the past and the influences of those decisions on current practices? How do they become involved in entrepreneurial activities and decision-making of their family business? What opportunities – inside and outside the business – prove useful in their development and growth as responsible owners? These are but a few of the types of research questions explored in this book.

Scholars affiliated with the Successful Transgenerational Entrepreneurship Practices (STEP) project were invited to develop chapters to enhance our understanding of the development of the next generation of family and non-family entrepreneurial leaders, and their role in creating sustained value for family enterprises. Following the format adopted in the previous volume in this series: *Exploring Transgenerational Entrepreneurship: The Role of Resources and Capabilities* (Sharma et al., 2014) each chapter starts with a mini-case – a dilemma related to the development of next generation leaders. The chapter, then, closely examines the available literature and one or more case studies to draw pragmatic conclusions of how the dilemma might be resolved. Theoretical and practical implications are discussed.

Longitudinal case studies of 27 family firms in nine different countries spread across the three continents of Asia, Europe and South America, provide a rich, global selection of leadership development insights. Operations of the businesses studied range from a focused commitment to a single industry and a local market, to geographic diversification spanning multiple industries and continents. While the youngest firms were transitioning from first to second generation, the oldest 192-years-old Japanese sake business was focused on the sixteenth and seventeenth generations. This diversity of cases and chapters summarized in Table 1.1 provides a rich foundation for insight into the pathways currently in use to develop the next generation leaders.

The contributors examine the role of values, professionalization, leadership style and contingent factors centering their discussions on what helps next generations develop their leadership styles and their entrepreneurial attitudes. The findings suggest the importance of focusing on leadership as a shared capability, the transmission of specific values to maintain an entrepreneurial culture, the fit between professionalization and values to increase transgenerational potential, the need to address the structure of the business to provide with entrepreneurial opportunities, and the focus on parenting to develop next generations.

In the next section, we examine the three major themes that emerge from the nine chapters: (1) From a Leader to a Leadership Capability, (2) Familial Values and Professionalization, and (3) Structure and Next Generation Leader Preparation. While some chapters fit squarely in one theme, others spill-over into multiple themes. Nevertheless, for the sake of parsimony, we classified each chapter under one broad theme. After discussing the chapters briefly and offering some insights for each section, this introductory chapter concludes with a brief discussion of possible future research with a potential of practical implications.

Table 1.1 An overview of the chapters

	Chapter	Authors	Context	Approach	Research Question(s)
From a Leader to a Leadership Capability	2	Ramírez-Pasillas, Bender, and Nilsson	Sweden 1st to 2nd generation Single industries	Multiple cases	How do successors experience their socialization? How do successors engage in the entrepreneurial activities of their family business?
	3	González Couture and Díaz Matajira	Colombia 2nd to 3rd generation Single industry and diversified corporations	Multiple cases	What pathways are adopted to prepare the next generation for responsible ownership?
	4	Ramachandran and Bhatnagar	India 1st to 2nd generation Diversified corporation	Single case informed by other cases	How can the transition from collective decision-making to collective leadership be managed?
Familial Values and Professionalization	5	Brumana, Cassia, De Massis, Discua Cruz, and Minola	Italy 1st to 2nd generation Diversified corporation	Single case Multiple informants	What skills and entrepreneurial attitudes distinguish generations and how is this related to professionalization?
	6	Matser, Bos, Heetebrij-van Dalfsen, and Coen Rigtering	Netherlands 1st to 2nd generation Single industry	Single case Multiple informants	How can a focus on family values help the firm remain competitive and facilitate transgenerational potential? What are the limits of professionalization?
	7	Yamaguchi, Kozono, and Higashide	Japan 16th to 17th generation Single industry	Single case Single informant	What is most important to pass on to the next generation?

Table 1.1 (continued)

	Chapter	Authors	Context	Approach	Research Question(s)
Structure and Next Gen Leader Preparation	8	Mohd Nor, Lechner, Yusof, Bardai, and Xavier	Malaysia 1st to 2nd generation Diversified corporation	Single case Multiple informants	How does trust affect a family business' diversification decisions? How is competence-based trust developed?
	9	Roscoe, Vieira, and Grzybovski	Brazil 2nd to 3rd generation Diversified corporation	Single case Multiple informants	What is the influence of family social capital on transgenerational learning and entrepreneurship? How should you respond to a child's interest in joining the family business?
	10	Gimeno and Parada	Spain Baby boomer to Gen X Unknown	Multiple cases	How do parenting styles impact the development of flexibility and cohesion in next generation family members?

LEADERSHIP DEVELOPMENT IN FAMILY BUSINESS

For each of the three major emergent themes, we share an overview, a brief chapter summary, and close with integrative insights.

From a Leader to a Leadership Capability

The first three chapters suggest pathways to help family enterprises evolve from a focus on the individual leader to readying the individual/s to be part of a leadership capability. While a focus on 'a leader' rather than 'leadership' may serve the family enterprise well in its foundational and early stages, as the business and/or the controlling family becomes more complex such singular focus on one individual leaves it vulnerable to one viewpoint, limits expansion which is requisite to sustainability and growth, thereby increasing the risk of disruptions.

Chapter Summaries

'The process of becoming: entrepreneurial leadership transition to the second generation' by Ramírez-Pasillas, Bender and Nilsson

Based upon the point of view of eight second generation family business CEOs in Sweden, the analysis focuses on their recollections of how they became successors. Three elements were identified. First, successors were socialized into their families' approaches, through their families' expectations regarding their future roles, and, beginning at an early age, their own experiences with their family businesses' work-lifestyle. Second, successors were groomed into developing entrepreneurial self-concepts through gradual involvement in practicing an entrepreneurial orientation, bringing in new ideas for the business and through external training. Third, successors experienced the transition into entrepreneurial leaders' roles by developing mentor-type relationships with the older generations and learning to make decisions, delegate tasks, and admit mistakes. These strong relationships between generations appear to give rise to a pool of entrepreneurial ideas that can be informed by the transfer of knowledge from incumbents to successors.

'The next generation: pathways for preparing and involving new owners in Colombian family businesses' by González Couture and Díaz Matajira

Using evidence from five Colombian entrepreneurial family businesses, the authors examine the pathways adopted to prepare next generation members for responsible ownership. In contrast to the classic studies of readiness for managerial leadership, this chapter focuses on how third generation family members are prepared to assume leadership roles in governance bodies, like companies' boards and family councils. This is especially relevant for transitions that occur beyond the second generation, where the number of family members involved grows and they do not expect to be entitled to the 'right to work' in the family business. The analysis suggests that it is important to pay attention to how the practices of entrepreneurial learning were implemented following two different pathways. One is related to achieving intra-family management leadership; the other is focused on creating communities of practice that fostered entrepreneurial identities conducive to responsible ownership. When the expectations that the next generation will play an active management role are reduced, a responsible ownership perspective can engender long lasting interest in wealth and legacy. Thus, preparing the next generation implies not only a set of clear rules, such as a family protocol, but also a leadership meta-system, linking subsystems of the family unit, the business entity and the individual family members, to form a dominant coalition and support a shared vision.

'Challenges of collective leadership' by Ramachandran and Bhatnagar
Collective leadership, sharing the highest leadership position, is the focus in the case of KPRT, an Indian diversified group, whose founder was faced with the dilemma of anointing a single successor or paving the road for a successful collective leadership mechanism. KPRT's leader was able to drive effective collective leadership by establishing a formal structure for joint decision-making that involved three potential successors. This collective process was facilitated by four factors. First, a high degree of cohesion among family members that was further reinforced by support mechanisms for joint decision-making. Second, an active founder and co-founder who promoted collective functioning from early in the business' history. Third, a capacity to anticipate areas of potential conflict among family members and evolve effective forums to prevent them. Fourth, a collectivist culture instated in the family DNA, and reinforced thanks to the strong interpersonal bonds among members of the leadership team. Comparisons to other examples of collective leadership evidence that the practice is not limited to the KRPT case. The successful implementation of collective leadership was further complemented by assigning responsibilities based on family members' proven expertise and competences in specific business areas.

Integrative insights
Chapters in this section help us evolve from a leadership perspective that emphasizes development of an individual to an intergenerational

transition aimed to develop a shared leadership capability. The recognition that the leadership demands of a family business can evolve in a variety of ways as they pursue entrepreneurial opportunities – committing to a single industry, remaining in an industry and pursuing geographic expansion, or going to the extreme of diversification into a portfolio of seemingly unrelated businesses – draws our attention to the importance of understanding leadership development as both individual development of new skills and abilities and taking a more expansive notion of leadership development as a dynamic capability that informs and is informed by the scope of the family business.

In the Swedish chapter, multiple cases of the 'father to son' transition from the perspective of the son evidence the role that successor's experience in their own entrepreneurial endeavors plays in readying them for the leadership role. Working alongside the father shows leadership becoming a shared capability. In the case of the Colombian businesses, multiple family members become involved in leadership, with leadership expanding to consider both managerial and owner-leader roles and practices. Selection of those best suited to the managerial leadership role requires explicit consideration to the future of the business from an ownership perspective with attention given to leadership capabilities required for managerial roles. Those who are not working within the family business need to be prepared to lead from the owner's vantage. In the Indian chapter, shared and collaborative leadership with multiple members of the second generation working together evolves into a potential for collective leadership. Decision-making processes give voice to all members of the top management team and consensus is the criteria for the pursuit of new directions.

The integrative insight that comes out of these first three chapters is that as family businesses become more complex, it becomes more important to have the prospect of new opportunities be accompanied by a more systematic and consistent evaluation of the choices facing the family business.

Familial Values and Professionalization

Chapters in this section highlight the different pathways that enterprising families adopt in an attempt to balance the maintenance of core family values and the professionalization needs of their enterprise as they prepare the next generation leaders.

Chapter Summaries

'Transgenerational professionalization of family firms: the role of next generation leaders' by Brumana, Cassia, De Massis, Discua Cruz and Minola
Based on the case of Persico, a second generation, diversified Italian family business, analysis shows how transgenerational professionalization enhanced the entrepreneurial attitudes and behaviors of next generation leaders of family firms. Two factors appear to positively impact transgenerational professionalization: transgenerational learning and an organizational structure that accommodates the family structure. Notably, strong overlap of ownership and management potentially constrains the transfer of leadership. Moreover, the effect of these factors could be enhanced by the presence of internal firm growth and external industry challenges, when the first generation has a high entrepreneurial orientation or in case of high levels of emotional involvement.

'The re-establishment of family values as a driver of transgenerational potential' by Matser, Bos, Heetebrij-van Dalfsen and Coen Rigtering
In a study of a second generation Dutch family business, the limits of professionalism and bureaucracy on transgenerational potential are explored. Analysis of the role of family values in helping the family firm remain competitive and realize transgenerational potential is undertaken. The case examines the founder's key challenges to pass the family business to the next generation, while restoring family values within the context of a more formal business structure. Unwanted side effects resulting from professionalization efforts within the business are identified. They appear to be related to a detachment between family values and professional non-family managers' values and were considered a threat to transgenerational potential. The re-establishment of family values helped the company reinvent its managerial practices and had a positive impact on the family's perceptions of their business' social and entrepreneurial performance.

'What should be passed on to the successor? The case of a long-standing Japanese family-owned small sake brewery' by Yamaguchi, Kozono and Higashide
The case of Tamura Sake Brewery, a small but long-standing family business in Japan, poses the question of what values should the incumbent pass over to his successor. Drawing upon the 16th generation incumbent's recollections of key incidents addressed by the 15th generation, evidence is provided about the influence of role models and respect for rules and traditions. Two key insights are evident. The case shows that the

company culture was imbued with human-oriented values such as treating employees with respect and building trust in the community, placing strong emphasis on personal characteristics of the successor, rather than the tactical knowledge or competencies in doing business. The case also shows that the family wanted to preserve long-term orientation in decision-making. That means to make a decision based on anticipation of its consequences in the future generations. The respect of this tradition, along with the presence of a non-family member, who assisted in transmitting the values by giving meaningful feedback, has ensured smooth transitions and preserved the family business core.

Integrative insights
Whether the entrepreneurial prospects brought by the next generation precede professionalization efforts or professionalization has already been established, the use of professionalization implies a systematic approach that is intended to enhance coordination and link the allocation of resources to the family business' goals and objectives, both financial and socio-emotional (Gomez-Mejia et al., 2007; Miller and Le Breton-Miller, 2014). The codification of decision-making should increasingly embed leadership as part of the family business, freeing up the time of the individuals who are in leadership roles to engage in more exploratory undertakings. The chapters that cover the Italian and Dutch business offer strong corroboration of the ideas presented by Stewart and Hitt (2012) that professionalization needs to be seen within the context of the family business' values and culture and aligned accordingly, on a recurrent basis. The significance of values and culture are also illustrated in the Japanese chapter. In highlighting the lessons learned from a long-standing business (16th to 17th generation), values and the trusted counsel of a long-lived non-family member appears to be a distinguishing factor in creating a transgenerational legacy.

Structure and Next Generation Leader Preparation

Structure, at work and at home, has a reinforcing capacity to develop the value based leadership in next generation. In the chapters from Malaysia and Brazil, this reinforcing capacity of the triumvirate of values, trust and social capital, is brought forth. The Spanish chapter suggests that the availability of family talent, namely the next generation's interest in the family business and its readiness begins with the parenting structure and style.

Chapter Summaries

'Family's decision in venture creation for next generation leaders: the role of trust across two generations in the case of diversification' by Mohd Nor, Lechner, Yusof, Bardai and Xavier

The case of the Mofaz Group, in Malaysia, uncovers the role of trust in the decision-making process of a successful and diversified entrepreneurial family enterprise and how the motivation for the second generation family members and leaders to create and lead or manage new ventures became a critical component of the process. The ability of the founder to foster trust in the family and among the employees leads to faster decision-making in venture creation. The primary motive for venture creation was finding a place for the family that was aligned with their interests, and not focused on growth per se. The top priorities for the founder in creating ventures were the hope that the next generation will take over the business, and the dream of having a continuously harmonious family institution.

'Family social capital, transgenerational learning and transgenerational entrepreneurship' by Roscoe, Vieira and Grzybovski

Analysis of the case of Braile Biomedica, a Brazilian diversified health products and services business, offers insight to a founder's intention to effect a generation-skipping leadership transition. Unexpected health problems of the founder accelerated the transition to the second generation, whose main role was not to assume the family business leadership, but to preserve its legacy for the grandchildren. The grandchildren were chosen by the founder to perpetuate 'traces of his passage'. The grandchildren were imbued with the family legacy at a young age through content delivery strategies adopted by their grandfather, and their career choices and entrepreneurial mindset were influenced by him. While the third generation and future business leaders were set free to pursue their own learning process both through strong family ties and formal education, the second generation was focused on smoothing the transition for the third generation. Business professionalization, with a special regard to financial outcomes and innovation, was a method to ensure the company's profitable future in a competitive business environment, while the family was set on developing family social capital and preserving their organizational identity.

'Parenting and next gen development' by Gimeno and Parada

A multi-case analysis of nine Spanish family businesses focuses on the role of different models of parenting styles in developing flexibility and cohesion in next generation family members. A variety of situations – the firms differ in size, industry, and generation in charge – provides the basis for exploration of how younger generations are raised and developed and how parenting affects both the company and the individual members of the family. It is argued that an authoritative parenting style develops a better capacity for the family members to arrive at functional agreements to address family business demands that require both relational and instrumental competence. In contrast, a permissive parenting style allowed the next generation to develop social skills and a greater degree of freedom, but did not necessarily contribute to the development of the instrumental competence and maturity so relevant in family business. This is especially important when the elder generation losses its capacity for maintaining the direction of the company. These results highlight the heterogeneity of family businesses and suggest that the way business families exercise their parenting role may be one of the fundamental aspects for understanding families' behaviors toward their businesses.

Integrative insights
The diversified corporation is a mechanism for creating room for the entrepreneurial interests of the next generation. The structure of roles and the use of meetings and protocols for reviewing progress create a more formal discipline for addressing the increased complexity that accompanies growth in the family and growth in the business; it helps focus attention on the family business' business. The sequencing of the next generation's progression through responsibility for increasingly more difficult and complex situations provides a proving ground for readiness and establishes the family member as a credible leader in the eyes of non-managerial family owners and non-family managers and employees. All of the aforementioned are structural solutions for leveraging talent.

As suggested by the chapter from Spain, a mix of the parenting styles of warmth and control, evidenced in developing children through conversations, is best suited for readying the next generation to realize cohesion and flexibility. From those formative experiences of having an opportunity to tell coupled with the expectation of listening and conducting oneself within the family's moral strictures, the reinforcement of those linked behavior-positive effect moments inside and outside the family likely provide the readiness to learn and eventually lead. Whether that next generational leadership will be realized within the family's business or within their own entrepreneurial venture is heavily dependent upon both individuals seeing themselves as capable in those roles and others seeing them as capable.

Familiarity with the family business, inculcation of family and business values, and experience with entrepreneurial decision-making underpin the leadership development process. Consideration of the interface of these leadership building blocks with structures that apply next generation talent in a variety of contexts can provide insight to how individual role development, professionalization, and scope of the family business inform the contingent nature of leadership development.

PRACTICAL RESEARCH IMPLICATIONS

Three perspectives on leadership are especially useful in informing our understanding of what a family business leader is expected to do, and consequently, what contributes to developing readiness for the role. Continuing with the three identified themes, in this section we share a few ideas for research that are likely to lead to usable knowledge for enterprising families in preparing next generation leaders.

From a Leader to a Leadership Capability

In family businesses, leaders exhibit a set of entrepreneurial, ownership, and managerial behaviors that involve others when family and business demands warrant growth in leadership capacity. Studies place attention on the activities undertaken and the manner, or style, with which those activities are carried out. More significant attention has been placed on leadership as the set of classic entrepreneurial behaviors that involve founding the firm and the related managerial behaviors that involve planning, organizing, staffing, directing, and controlling (Koontz and O'Donnell, 1972).

As shown in the Swedish chapter, father to son linkages occur early on. This suggests that it is incumbent upon the first generation to prepare family leaders early on, so that they feel responsible for maintaining the family legacy in the following generations. This could be done through transgenerational learning and entrepreneurship which have been found to be key facilitating factors in next generation leadership selection and development. These facilitating factors become more apparent when elements of socio-emotional wealth and family social capital are born in the family generational system and radiate across the organization and the community, affecting the dynamics between the family business and its internal and external stakeholders. Emphasis is given to leadership as 'leader-member' exchange, both as 'family to family' and 'family to non-family' exchange and its role in establishing and building trust and social capital (Steier and Muethel, 2014). 'Leader-member' exchange can be observed when children in the next generation show interest and are keen to take a leadership role in the family business, learning from family and non-family keypersons alike.

Contingency approaches draw attention to person-situation fit. The underlying argument is that different situations require different types of leaders and different leadership processes. Situations vary in the type of perspectives, demeanor and knowledge required to be effective. Comprising top management teams and diverse boards of directors are mechanisms for overcoming the limitations of a single leader's capability. In studies of non-family businesses, the emphasis is often on replacing the leader as opposed to changing the approach to leadership and/or modifying the situation to leverage the leadership resource. In family businesses, greater consideration is given to leveraging individual capabilities alone and in concert with others. As the family business grows, leadership effectiveness is less about what the individual knows and more about the individual's ability to bring the expertise of others to bear on a situation, alone and in combination with others (Sorenson, 2000).

Growth in size of the enterprise and its leadership demands creates a juncture at which either the approach of the leader needs to change (the leader him/herself has to develop) or a leadership capability that is less reliant on the capability of a single individual needs to be developed. The family offers a potential resource for addressing that aspect and the founder's desire to keep the family in the business provides the motive.

Shared leadership may need to evolve to effect the next level of collaboration required by diversification. Decision-making structures may be useful to address business-related issues, but, shared leadership may go beyond the business dimension and be beneficial and effective in addressing family and ownership-related matters as well, as illustrated by the Indian chapter. It would be interesting to further examine the antecedents and outcomes of shared or collective leadership. Culture, family size and multigenerational intentions may be important influences on shared leadership and its role in creating business legacies across several generations.

Familial Values and Professionalization

As an individual who influences others, family business leaders establish a 'tone at the top' of the business. Values are established within the family and transcend the family system to affect the values and culture of the family business (Sorenson, 2014). Founders are especially influential in establishing the family business' values (Dyer, 1986). Exhibiting and promulgating moral values (Rokeach, 1973) that evidence a duty of care and duty of loyalty characterize a leader as ethical (Trevino, Brown and Hartman, 2003). When these types of leadership values are evidenced in leadership behaviors, leaders are perceived as increasingly trustworthy (Sundaramurthy, 2008). In sum, a leader's values help establish the standards by which the family business will conduct itself, establish a lens through which leaders, their family, and subordinates view situations, and establish a standard against which a leader's conduct is assessed.

Two of the chapters are especially helpful in expanding our understanding of the importance of values and the sharing of values in leadership's influence on a family business' behavior and transgenerational entrepreneurship. In Chapter 7 by Yamaguchi, Kozono, and Higashide, the importance of transmitting certain values from one generation to the next, as a source to guide their actions and influence others' in relation to the family business is highlighted. This chapter also sheds light on how these values are transmitted via conversations, by example, and by receiving feedback from non-family top executives. Matser, Bos, Heetebrij-van Dalfsen and Coen Rigtering (Chapter 6, this volume) also note how founder's values have served as the guiding principle to manage the family business. However, despite the transference of these values to the next generation, the non-family leaders' efforts conflicted with those of the family, leading to a less efficient organization. The family saw the need to re-establish specific values to change managerial practices into a more dynamic and less bureaucratic approach.

In both the Japanese sake business and the Dutch automotive carpet business, the capacity to deal with circumstances that could not have been anticipated or the use of overly formalized standards, respectively, necessitated a more enduring and flexible basis for judgment. Notably, in both chapters, the application of values complement established policies and practices, and, trusted non-family members contribute to leadership. The policies and practices underpin operating legitimacy, a requisite for success in the family business' competitive markets. But, it appears when situations can be viewed through a common values lens by multiple individuals, family businesses establish greater capacity to establish cohesion and accommodate variation. This suggests that values play an important role in familiness as a resource and that non-family members can contribute to or detract from the development of familiness and its contribution to leadership as a capability.

The fact that values play a key role in developing next generations and the way they lead the family business presents an important avenue for future research. Mixed results can be found in the literature regarding the permanence of values over time. Most studies suggest that values need to be transmitted, as do these two chapters in the book. Other studies however, suggest that certain values need to be changed for family businesses to survive over time (e.g. Parada, Nordqvist, and Gimeno, 2010).

Understanding better which values should be transferred and which values may be changed may shed light on the role values play in the sustainability of the family business and the development of next generations.

Whereas Yamaguchi et al. (Chapter 7, this volume) suggest that values can be transferred via non-family managers' feedback, Matser et al. (Chapter 6, this volume) note that non-family managers, as they come with different values, may erode the family values. In light of this contradicting argument, it would be interesting to understand what role non-family managers play in the transmission of values to the next generation and how non-family managers are exposed to and embrace family values.

In drawing attention to the consideration of professionalization of the family business, an emphasis on agency theory logic suggests important distinctions between the manager's role and the owner's role and the establishment of standards and procedures for both roles. The family business becomes more formal and professionalized for purposes of coordination of activity and oversight, albeit with a number of alternatives for doing so (Stewart and Hitt, 2012).

The chapters based on an Italian firm and on a Dutch family business offer interesting insights about professionalization. Brumana, Cassia, De Massis, Discua Cruz and Minola (Chapter 5, this volume) show how the process of professionalizing the family business influences the entrepreneurial attitudes of next generation leaders. Shifts in education and knowledge from more intuitive and tacit leadership to a more formal, analytic approach and the increase in felt responsibility for the family business as a result of the next generation's involvement in the management of the business occur in tandem with professionalization. This suggests that the way family businesses deploy their professionalization affects how next generations will behave with regards to entrepreneurial activities. Chapter 6 by Matser et al. also tackles professionalization, but points out that professionalization efforts may endanger organizational culture and management style. The implications of both chapters are that family businesses need to carefully work on their professionalization; the manner in which the business is professionalized can positively impact the entrepreneurial capabilities of next generations, but it may also slow down decision-making and negatively affect the family business' competitive edge.

While traditionally research has addressed how the family's failure to professionalize the business limits its future, it is also important to consider how professionalization can be initiated and managed so that it does not become a threat to the organization's culture. A possible avenue is to clarify the importance of hiring people who share the family values that the family business wants to preserve over time (Parada et al., 2010). Interestingly, the possibility that professionalization may change the organizational values may also open opportunities for family business to drive change in the organization when needed.

Structure and Next Generation Leader Preparation

Understanding that professionalization has an effect on the development of entrepreneurial attitudes may necessitate proactive consideration by business families about the organizational structure they want to create and its relation to transgenerational learning opportunities. Further research about the types of structures used and their relationship to business complexity and entrepreneurial attitudes and outcomes would inform greater precision in choice of approach to professionalization (Stewart and Hitt, 2012). Additionally, exploration of how transgenerational learning for the next generation may need to encompass the complementary development of formal and analytical education and the development of intuitive skills is warranted.

When the leader (the incumbent or founder) is able to develop interpersonal trust and competence based trust by welcoming and being open to others, as evidenced in the Malaysian chapter, whether it is intentional or unintentional, with the latter based upon values and principles towards life, it is evident that the leader feels and exercises responsibility for family and non-family members beyond the immediate family. This may lead to the leader giving everything he can to achieve outcomes to reciprocate the efforts of others, which in turn, builds a broader construal of familiness and attachment to the family business as a resource (Habberson and Williams, 1999). Trust as a personal value becomes trust as a resource (akin to social capital) when values inform behavior and do so in a consistent and recurrent manner. Without followership, it is hard to have leadership. In this context, the family business fosters institutional trust and gain benevolence, integrity, consistency based trust and competence based trust (Steier and Muethel, 2014).

In multiple chapters, we observe that situations involving subsequent generations are shaped to take advantage of the emergence of talented family members. Diversification of the family business provides an opportunity to benefit from the family resource and further develop the leadership capability. When businesses expand and diversify, the tangible and intangible resources and capabilities within the business will also need to grow. When this business situation accompanies an increase in family size and members, common to evolution from the founder to the next generation and forward, we can expect a bigger pool of family capital with regards to leadership, management and knowledge capabilities and competencies. The family business' structure can be modified to address and manage the increased complexity in decision-making, socio-emotional wealth and relationships. Family members may become functional specialists or emerge into roles as leaders of business units. But eventually, especially if the family retains ownership and managerial control, solutions to develop shared or even collective leadership both intragenerationally and intergenerationally will be needed.

The diversified business structure can provide opportunities to utilize and further develop family leaders and leadership. Five chapters evidence some form of diversification as a mechanism for leveraging family interests; idiosyncratic family interests better explains the unrelatedness of diversification. Only in the case of the geographically diversified Dutch family business, does economic logic, likely introduced by the non-family managers that bridged the first and second generations, appear to prevail as an explanation for expansion.

In closing, we believe that the chapters in this book are path breaking in their exploration of the ways in use to develop the next generation entrepreneurial leaders of family enterprises. We hope you enjoy reading these pioneering insights and find yourself drawn to conceptualize and implement innovative ways to develop next generation leaders of family firms.

REFERENCES

Dyer Jr., W.G. (1986). *Cultural Change in Family Firms: Anticipating and Managing Business and Family Transitions*. San Francisco, CA: Jossey-Bass.

Gomez-Mejia, L.R., Haynes, K.T., Nunez-Nickel, M., Jacobson, K.J.L., and Moyano-Fuentes, H. (2007). Socioemotional wealth and business risk in family-controlled firms: evidence from Spanish olive oil mills. *Administrative Science Quarterly*, 52(1): 106–137.

Habbershon, T.G. and Williams, M.L. (1999). A resource-based framework for assessing strategic advantages of family firms. *Family Business Review*, 12: 1–25.

Habbershon, T.G., Nordqvist, M., and Zellweger, T.M. (2010). Transgenerational entrepreneurship, in Nordqvist, M. and Zellweger, T.M. (eds), *Transgenerational Entrepreneurship: Exploring Growth and Performance in Family Firms Across Generations* (Chapter 1). Cheltenham, UK and Northampton, MA, USA: Edward Elgar Publishing.

Koontz, H. and O'Donnell, C. (1972). *Principles of Management: An Analysis of Managerial Functions*. New York, NY: McGraw-Hill.

Miller, D. and Le Breton-Miller, I. (2014). Deconstructing socioemotional wealth. *Entrepreneurship Theory and Practice*, 38(4): 713–720.

Parada, M.J., Nordqvist, M., and Gimeno, A. (2010). Institutionalizing the family business: the role of professional associations in fostering a change in values. *Family Business Review*, 23: 355–372.

Rokeach, M. (1973). *The Nature of Human Values*. New York, NY: The Free Press.

Sharma, P., Sieger, P., Nason, R.S., Gonzalez L., A.C., and Ramachandran, K.

(2014). *Exploring Transgenerational Entrepreneurship: The Role of Resources and Capabilities*. Cheltenham, UK and Northampton, MA, USA: Edward Elgar Publishing.

Sorenson, R.L. (2000). The contribution of leadership styles and practices to family and business success. *Family Business Review*, 13(3): 183–200.

Sorenson, R.L. (2014). Values in family business, in Melin, L., Nordqvist, M. and Sharma, P. (eds), *The Sage Handbook of Family Business* (463–479). London: Sage Publications.

Steier, L. and Muethel, M. (2014). Trust and family businesses, in Melin, L., Nordqvist, M. and Sharma, P. (eds), *The Sage Handbook of Family Business* (498–513). London: Sage Publications.

Stewart, A. and Hitt, M.A. (2012). Why can't a family business be more like a non-family business? Modes of professionalization in family firms. *Family Business Review*, 25(1): 58–86.

Sundaramurthy, C. (2008). Sustaining trust within family businesses. *Family Business Review*, 21(1): 89–102.

Trevino, L.T., Brown, M., and Hartman, L.P. (2003). A qualitative investigation of perceived ethical leadership: perceptions from inside and outside the executive suite. *Human Relations*, 55: 5–37.

PART I

From a leader to a leadership capability

2. The process of becoming: entrepreneurial leadership transition to the second generation

Marcela Ramírez-Pasillas, Patrick Bender and Angelica Nilsson

MINI CASE STUDY: SUCCESSORS OF THE FIRST-, SECOND- AND THIRD GENERATION: NEW WINE IN OLD BOTTLES?

My name is Matthias and I am 23 years old. I just completed my master's degree in business administration and joined the marketing department within the family business. I started my employment the day after my graduation ceremony. It is an exciting time! In the long run, I aim for a top management position in the family business, preferably the CEO. It excites me to have the possibility to change something for the better. I began to work in the family business during summer breaks from elementary school and continued to do so until I started my full-time employment. My family never said that I had to work in the family business, but it was definitely something that my father and grandfather thought was very positive. As a result, I switched to a new position each summer to learn a bit about everything in the organization, and then I was able to discuss different aspects of the business with my father and grandfather. Switching positions gave me the opportunity to get to know many of the employees, and they also got to know me. Building a relationship with employees is a resource that has benefitted my father a lot as a CEO.

During my high school years, my brother and I started our first business together with two friends. My father was very supportive during the entire process! He asked us useful questions and helped us to reflect on what we were doing. Our primary activity consisted of buying IT equipment that we modified and installed as media centers with a helpdesk service. We continued with this business as a side activity until I graduated. One year after graduation, we started our first limited company. We got the idea for the business while traveling around the United States. We noticed a product that we had never seen in our country and got interested in selling similar products. Instead of taking our vacation, we rented a car and visited a manufacturer to learn more about the product. The manufacturer granted us exclusivity for its product in the Nordic countries! Shortly after that, my brother and I came back home to Sweden and started our company. Our new company challenged me to find solutions to everyday problems. These problems could be anything from fixing an electrical error with a motor to easing customers' concerns. This experience was very different from working within the family business; I discovered what I personally needed to develop. Giving and receiving feedback between family members was one thing that I worked on. When my brother and I joined the family business, we put the company on hold because we no longer had the time for it.

The transition from working in my own company to being part of the family business has been easy. Instead of being an independent entrepreneur, I consider myself to be a corporate entrepreneur. I like corporate entrepreneurship because I focus on my own projects within the family business. In our independent business, we worried a lot about overall business development. So far, my ideas have been met with excitement by my family, which is really fun! For instance, I updated our ERP system (i.e. enterprise resource planning system) to collect information from our suppliers' shipments. I had to go through a lot of data to build a database of our suppliers' shipments. After a while, I got bored doing the same steps over and over again, and I looked for alternative ways to automate the process in my spare time. I created a program that did the same work a lot faster. I was able to do other things while my program processed the data. My father was surprised to learn how I created resources to do this work. He became more interested in my ideas, and we spent more time discussing them.

My father was always interested in the family business. He worked in different departments and is knowledgeable about the production process. When he joined the family business, he took on responsibility for new projects; it could be everything from launching a new raw material to entering a new market. This experience gave him a lot of insight and prepared him for his role as a family CEO; it also gave him a better foundation to lead the business. Many external CEOs of large publicly listed companies lacked this type of knowledge. Because my father had an interest in taking over the business, he became the natural choice for the CEO position. The succession process was developed gradually, relying on mentoring. My grandfather coached my father particularly on aspects related to entrepreneurship. There were a few decisions where they had major differences, but they usually found a solution that both were comfortable with even if it took time. These solutions were often characterized by 'out of the box thinking', which is one of their greatest strengths! Many of these ideas were created after the working hours; thus their way of working together and thinking about the firm led to these 'out of the box ideas.' Living with the firm seems to be important to our family business, and it has enabled us to expand greatly in the last decade. Nowadays, my father and my grandfather generally discuss major decisions with each other and give updates on the business. When my brother and I joined the business, we agreed that we would have meetings to discuss family business issues. We prioritize creating a harmonious relationship between all of us.

During my studies, I spent time reflecting on how to become an entrepreneurial leader in a family business. I talked with my father about the right path to follow in terms of external and internal training. If I leave the family business now, it will be easier to create a broad network and build my own professional identity. By choosing this path, I could choose whether to develop as an independent entrepreneur or to work in the industry. However, if I stay in the family business, I will be restricted to corporate entrepreneurship as long as we expand the business. Staying in the family business could magnify the risk of inheriting the same mindset of my family, and I wonder if this would be good or bad in terms of my own entrepreneurial development. What would you do if you were me and wanted to become CEO of the family business? Is it the same being a potential successor in the first-, second- and third generation?

Problem Statement

The development of the successor positively influences the perception of opportunities in the context of the family business (Sardeshmukh and Corbett, 2011). Still, even though a majority of firms in today's global economy are family businesses, there is limited research on the entrepreneurial leadership development of the next generation (cf. Lansberg, 2007; Le Breton-Miller, Miller, and Steier, 2004; Dawson, Irving, Sharma, Chirico, and Markus, 2014). The successor's leadership development is important because CEOs worldwide believe that their company's performance could decrease due to the next generation's insufficient leadership qualities and skills (Economist intelligence unit, 2008).

Research on the next generation leadership development processes in family businesses from the point of view of the successors is gaining interest but it is still limited (cf. Salvato and Corbetta, 2013). Traditionally, literature on succession seldom focuses on specific generations (cf. except Handler, 1990, 1992; García-Álvarez, López-Sintas, and Saldaña-Gonzalvo, 2002); rather leadership succession is studied including different generations in the samples (cf. Lambrecht, 2005; Cadieux, 2007; Cater and Justis, 2009).

This literature assumes that incumbent senior generation leaders just relinquish their position and thereby allocate their power and trust to a successor (Miller, Steier, and Le Breton-Miller, 2003; Cadieux, 2007; De Massis, Chua, and Chrisman, 2008). Therefore, literature on succession recognizes the importance of leadership development as series of milestones (Lambrecht, 2005; Cater and Justis, 2009) or as a process (Salvato and Corbetta, 2013). To ensure that the next generation members are suitable for a leadership transfer, this literature emphasizes the development of successors' knowledge and skills by incorporating the next generation of family entrepreneurial leaders into the firm at an early age and/or once they obtain training outside of the family business (Lambrecht, 2005; Chirico, 2008; Sardeshmukh and Corbett, 2011). Recent literature on succession shows also that advisors play a key role in building successors' leadership roles and modulate the relationship with the incumbent senior generation (Salvato and Corbetta, 2013). Yet, when the senior manager of the first generation passes the baton to the next without relying on advisors, we know little about how successors work together with the senior generation to gradually assume an entrepreneurial leadership role. Since first- and second generation of family businesses involve on average in more entrepreneurship than in later-generation family businesses (Cruz and Nordqvist, 2012; Miller, Le Breton-Miller, Lester, and Canella Jr., 2007) investigating the process of becoming entrepreneurial leaders during these successions is important. The first- and second generation of family businesses build the entrepreneurial legacy that is passed on to later generations (Jaskiewicz, Combs, and Rau, 2015).

Entrepreneurial leaders create scenarios for potential opportunities given the resource constraints of the firm and are able to access the necessary resources to realize these opportunities (Gupta, MacMillan, and Surie, 2004). By means of internal training, future successors *and entrepreneurial leaders* interact with the business and reach a cultural understanding (Hall and Nordqvist, 2008). By working in a non-family business, they build networks and a reputation in the industry (Lambrecht, 2005; Cater and Justis, 2009). However, there is scarce knowledge regarding how potential successors become entrepreneurial leaders who are able to create opportunities by utilizing their internal and external training to build a new role identity.

Thereby, the aim of this chapter is to explore the process of becoming an entrepreneurial leader from the point of view of successors in the second generation. To explore this process, we have conducted eight case studies with family CEOs of Swedish family businesses that carried out an insider succession from the first- to the second generation. We focus on the perceptions of the next generation because research on successors' views, opinions and experiences is limited. Our study contributes to the literature on insider successions by building theory at the intersection of succession and entrepreneurship to advance our understanding of the development of the next generation of entrepreneurial leaders.

THEORETICAL BACKGROUND

Ensuring entrepreneurial leadership prior to and during leadership succession is important to sustaining the family business across generations. Entrepreneurial leadership integrates the concepts of entrepreneurship (Schumpeter, 1934), entrepreneurial management (Stevenson, 1983), and entrepreneurial orientation (Lumpkin and Dess, 1996) with leadership. Entrepreneurial leaders create scenarios of potential opportunities given the resource constraints, convince followers and stakeholders, and obtain the resources needed to realize these opportunities (Gupta et al., 2004). Entrepreneurial leadership in a family business is complex because succession is related to many different aspects of leadership development including the change of roles, mastering new jobs and building relationships (Salvato and Corbetta, 2013) while simultaneously developing an entrepreneurial orientation (Habbershon, Nordqvist, and Zellweger, 2010). The literature on leadership succession has two dominant approaches. The first approach addresses leadership succession as a set of steps that must be fulfilled to become a successful leader or a family CEO. The second approach considers leadership succession to be an outcome of a socialization process in which the next generation is introduced to knowledge and practices that make them suitable for a leadership role. While both of these approaches somehow recognize the importance of formal education, prior experience in start-ups and entrepreneurial activities, they downplay the importance of entrepreneurial leadership. Entrepreneurial leadership is important for the pursuit of new family visions that include an insightful understanding of the business (Kansikas., Laakkonen, Sarpo, and Kontinen, 2012). In the following subsections, we discuss the two approaches, indicating the role that entrepreneurship plays in the leadership succession.

Leadership Succession as a Series of Steps Followed by the Next Generation

The literature on leadership succession addresses generation change as a series of steps or milestones by which leadership is nurtured and transferred (for a review, see Le Breton-Miller, Miller, and Steier, 2004). In this literature, leadership succession is not studied as a process of becoming an entrepreneurial leader; rather, leadership is handed over. Successions from the first- to the second generation are commonly addressed as transitions from the owner-manager to a son or from the owner-manager to a sibling partnership (Ward, 2004). Leadership succession is a process initiated by a trigger event (i.e. mandatory retirement ages, unanticipated incidents, decision, death, etc.) that requires replacing the incumbent senior leader for a successor (Gersick, Lansberg, Desjardins, and Dunn, 1999). The literature on leadership succession acknowledges the transition processes that take place when a family business changes ownership structure (Gersick et al., 1999; Murray, 2003). However, specific features and capabilities of entrepreneurship and/or leadership of successions from the first- to the second generation are absent in the milestones defined in this literature. The development of the successors in different generations of family businesses is elaborated by simply adding milestones to the leadership succession models. For instance, Lambrecht (2005) models interpreneurship as studies, formal internal education, external experience, climbing the company ladder, and writing a plan, and making agreements in multigeneration successions. While interpreneurship is a key element of the leadership succession, it is restricted to an internal training process for transferring knowledge, management values, and entrepreneurial characteristics of the family and the family business at an early age. Entrepreneurial characteristics linked to an entrepreneurial orientation (Habbershon et al., 2010) are not discussed and the consideration of external experiences does not include launching a business (cf. Turner Foster, 1995; Gersick et al., 1999; Murray, 2003; Lambrecht, 2005). Both of these features and activities are central to pursuing business opportunities in the family business. Although a focus on leadership succession as an outcome of milestones captures the requirements of successors, it falls short on presenting entrepreneurial leadership as a dynamic process of preparation, formation and development through interaction and activities. The steps or milestones represent checkpoints that are or are not followed. Once the successor is incorporated into the family business, the literature emphasizes the importance of giving freedom to the successor to take responsibility and ask for advice from the older generations. While these aspects are important to becoming an entrepreneurial leader, the literature on leadership succession based on steps does not explore how the second generation works with the older generation as proposed by Le Breton-Miller et al. (2004) to support entrepreneurial leadership.

Advancing previous studies, other literature addresses the development of successors from followers to leaders by focusing on the changes in the roles of the incumbent senior manager and the future successor (Handler, 1990; Cadieux, 2007; Cater and Justis, 2009). An important feature of this literature is that leadership succession moves from an individual approach (i.e. something the successor or incumbent does), to a dyadic approach (i.e. something between incumbent and successor), to a collective approach (i.e. something among all relevant parties). This literature helps to recognize the importance of developing a spirit of cooperation between generations, of the mentor role played by the incumbent senior manager and of the acceptance of employees and family members. Although this literature is important to understanding how incumbent senior managers and future successors build positive relationships and how the roles of leader and follower shift over time, it does not study the process of utilizing self-reflection, feedback, and insight in assimilating the new CEO role. Furthermore, this literature identifies leadership succession as a challenging event since the first generation might experience issues to 'let go' and allow the next generation to take over the business. This literature misses to examine that the incumbent senior managers run the business while they give space and resources to the next generation to implement entrepreneurial ideas (Jaskiewicz et al., 2015).

Leadership Succession as the Socialization of the Next Generation into the Family Business

Literature on leadership succession as a socialization process emphasizes the influence of family and stakeholders in the formation of successors. It is a process for building a relationship between the organization's past and present (Miller, Steier, and Le Breton-Miller, 2003). Socialization is the exposure of individuals to the world of society. Even though leadership succession is introduced as the outcome of a socialization process representing the 'how we do things' in the family and in the family business over time, this view does not recognize that leadership and *entrepreneurial leadership* is a process of mutual influences and construction (Day, 2001). The 'how we do things' is so deeply internalized in the family business that it becomes taken for granted because of the socialization processes (Berger and Luckmann, 1966). Thus, the issue of how entrepreneurial leadership develops by means of socialization is central, but it is not addressed in, for instance, building an entrepreneurial orientation. An entrepreneurial orientation promotes a decision-making style that is proactive, risk-taking and innovative when second generation successors pursue opportunities (Cruz and Nordqvist, 2012).

The literature distinguishes two stages of socialization: primary socialization and secondary socialization (Berger and Luckmann, 1966) or family socialization and business socialization (García-Álvarez et al., 2002). Primary/family socialization includes the acquisition of values and knowledge that makes it possible to interact and build relationships. During this type of socialization, the older generation members often try to form their successors according to their own image and values (Handler, 1994), or they try to influence their career choices (Le Breton-Miller et al., 2004). They also encourage successors to set up their own businesses, which might or might not be merged with the family firm (García-Álvarez et al., 2002). In secondary/business socialization, successors develop their personality and identity (Hogg, Terry, and White, 1995) and recognize the roles of significant others. Although socialization is central to understanding leadership succession as embedded in daily practice (Haag, 2012), it does not highlight how successors can be socialized into entrepreneurial leaders. Successors become entrepreneurial leaders by developing an entrepreneurial role and adopting an entrepreneurial orientation (Cruz and Nordqvist, 2012) that results from training, own choices and acceptance of the new role. This role is an outcome of individual decisions and multiple interactions with the context.

In summary, we argue that the existing two approaches on leadership succession do not systematically address entrepreneurial leadership. Although these theories were not developed to target the specific case of entrepreneurial leadership in second generation successions, they provide a point of departure for exploring this phenomenon. Because these perspectives provide knowledge regarding the different elements of the leadership succession process, they should not be seen as separate. Rather they are complementary; socialization is present as successors experience each milestone. Thereby these perspectives will be used to investigate the relevance and process of becoming an entrepreneurial leader by examining how successors experience their socialization, if and how prior start-ups influence their formation, and how successors engage in entrepreneurial activities in their family firms.

RESEARCH METHODOLOGY

This chapter uses interpretivist and abductive case study research to explore the entrepreneurial leadership development process of second generation successors in eight Swedish family businesses. Case study research is particularly useful at the early stages of theory development when key themes and categories need to be identified using content analysis (Gioia and Pitre, 1990). This chapter followed the recommended procedures for conducting case study research (Gioia and Pitre, 1990; Miles and Huberman, 1994). In line with Chua, Chrisman, and Sharma (1999: 25), we define a family firm as '*a business governed and/or managed with the intention to shape and pursue the vision of the business held by a dominant coalition controlled by members of the same family or a small number of families in a manner that is potentially sustainable across generations of the family or families.'*

Data Collection

To explore the entrepreneurial leadership development process, we gathered the recollections of second generation members with regard to how they became CEOs for eight cases. We considered several dimensions when selecting our cases. First, we chose intergenerational successions from fathers to sons from the first- to the second generation. Because we focus on entrepreneurial leadership development of second generation successors, we included family CEOs that had started, developed and matured in their position. Our selected next generation members had worked as family CEOs from 2 to 19 years. They ranged in age from 28 to 58 years old. With the exception of two CEOs, all of our successors had both internal and external experience. Second, we selected firms varying in size and active in different industries (machinery, hoses, trailers, farming, real estate, kitchen design and manufacture, and concrete manufacture). Third, the families had similar features. With the exception of one case, the incumbent senior manager and the successor had a harmonious relationship. During these leadership successions, the incumbent-senior manager acted as a mentor for the next generation. In all of our cases, successors were allowed to develop entrepreneurial activities in the business. In summary, these dimensions allowed us to contrast the eight cases considering entrepreneurial leadership processes prior and during succession. Our study was anchored in the relevant perceptions of the second generation in terms of their becoming an entrepreneurial leader. We prepared interview guidelines, which included questions that allowed us to compare successions, leadership and entrepreneurship experiences. We conducted 12 interviews with the family CEOs of the eight family businesses. We first conducted eight interviews lasting between 40 and 85 minutes and a field visit to the companies. Before each interview, we studied the family business websites and their annual reports to obtain a better understanding of the businesses. We conducted four follow-up interviews as we proceeded with our analysis. Table 2.1 presents our cases.

Data Analysis

Utilizing content analysis (Gioia and Pitre, 1990; Miles and Huberman, 1994), we conducted multiple readings of the data to develop a data

Table 2.1 Background of next generation members in our study

CASE			CEO FEATURES				BUSINESS FEATURES			
No.	Age	Years as CEO	Internal training FB: Positions occupied in FB before becoming CEO	External training: education and positions occupied in prior employment in FB	Ownership transition	First leadership role (internal)	Founding year	Industry	No. of employees	Generations currently involved
1	29	4	Different tasks since childhood: economic assistant, warehouse worker, factory worker, adviser	University degree related to FB Driving tractors, working with machinery Started a business	No	CFO	1980	Machine industry	56	2
2	28	2	Different tasks since childhood: carpenter, administration	University degree related to FB Summer jobs in different industries Electronics store seller	No	CFO	1980	Real estate industry	3	2
3	32	2	Different tasks since childhood: administration, maintenance	University degree related to FB Broker, toy store seller, waiter, auto parts seller Started two businesses	Yes	CFO	1990	Real estate industry	15	2
4	44	10	Different tasks to learn the business	Unfinished university degree related to FB Tobacco store accountant, petroleum worker Started a business	Yes	CEO	1990	Trailer industry	6	2

5	54	9	Worked since 9th grade during the summers Computer systems, economics, administration, product line, pallets manufacture	University degree related to FB Computer systems manager, consultant, joined army Started a business	Yes	IT Manager	1925	Kitchen design and manufacture industry	300	2
6	55	15	Helped when FB needed it since early age Farmer	Unfinished university degree related to FB Took courses related to FB Contract worker, CEO of shipping company Started a business	Yes	CEO	1960	Farming industry	7	1
7	56	19	Line worker, line manager, truck driver, administration	Unfinished university degree related to FB Took courses related to FB	Yes	Line Manager	1965	Concrete manufacture industry	500	3
8	58	10	Different tasks since childhood: counting screws, economic assistant, adviser, personal seller	University degree not related to FB Road constructions manager	Yes	Sales Manager	1945	Machine industry	15	1

structure. We created tables with the relevant excerpts from interviews under specific recurring themes. We discussed emerging themes back and forth among us and further specified them into seven themes as first order categories. We concluded that these themes needed to be related to each other by means of three dimensions. After several discussions, we named these dimensions as follows: being socialized into family approaches, developing an entrepreneurial self-concept and becoming an entrepreneurial leader. Figure 2.1 introduces our themes and the structure of our data. We present the first order data using excerpts from our interviews, leading to the second order data. The second order themes result from a combination of our data with the relevant literature, which we then aggregate into dimensions that serve as a basis for a model of the entrepreneurial leadership process. Figure 2.1 is a process-based model; thus, we see these dimensions as processes that the next generation in our cases go through to assume a leadership position in the family business. These processes are not exclusive; some can occur concurrently. In Table 2.2 we include additional representative excerpts from our interviews.

Findings

The iterative process between data analysis, interpretation, and writing resulted in a model for the entrepreneurial leadership transition process to the second generation (see Figure 2.1). On Dimension 1 (in Figure 2.1), entrepreneurial leaders are socialized into family approaches; they are born with certain expectations and are gradually introduced to the family business work style. Next, successors develop an entrepreneurial self-concept (Dimension 2 in Figure 2.1) by working in the family business, building a professional and entrepreneurial role identity, and practicing their entrepreneurial orientation. By taking their first leadership role, successors become an entrepreneurial leader (Dimension 3 in Figure 2.1). They experience a role transition when shifting from being a follower to being a leader. They also rely on the incumbent senior manager as a mentor and build familiarity with their new leadership role. In the following, we discuss our dimensions and themes based on our interviews.

Dimension 1. Being Socialized into Family Approaches

The second generation of CEOs expressed that they had been introduced to the family business at an early age. In an indirect manner, successors became aware of the business and their families' expectations (1a. Born with expectations) as well as becoming acquainted with the overlap between family and business (1b. Introducing the family business work-lifestyle).

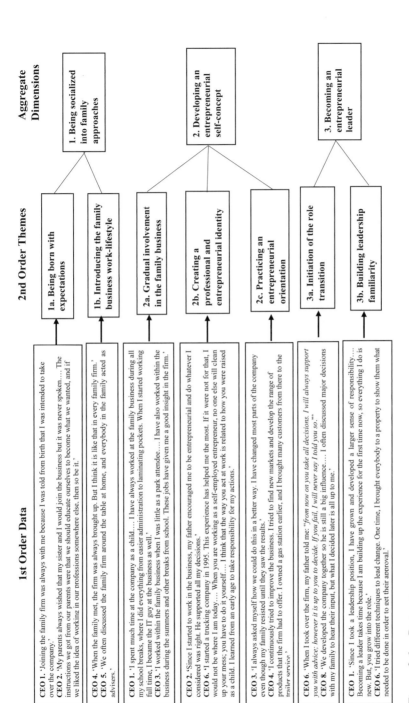

Figure 2.1 Data structure

Table 2.2 Additional data supporting 2nd order themes

Second order theme	Representative first order data
1a. Being born with expectations	**CEO 2**. 'I have been at the company since I was a child, and there was never anything else that interested me.' **CEO 5**. 'Even though my father never asked me to come home, I felt that they wanted me and needed me to come home.' **CEO 6**. 'The characteristic of the firm came naturally to me since I have grown up with it.' 'I always had the choice not to do it. . . . I think that the way you act at work is related to how you were raised as a child. I learned from an early age to take responsibility for my actions.'
1b. Introducing the family business work-lifestyle	**CEO 1**. 'Even the family gatherings at someone's birthday felt work related.' **CEO 2**. 'I usually played around in the warehouse as a child, even though I was not really aware of what was happening around me.' **CEO 6**. 'We did not talk about it much if I did not bring it up. It was one of my largest interests.' **CEO 8**. 'Even while working outside of the family firm, I still took part in the discussions and gave advice. Because of this, it was easy to start working within the company again, as you already knew everything.'
2a. Gradual involvement in the family business	**CEO 2**. 'The office of the firm was next to our house, so I played there when I was younger, although, I did not understand what was going on there.' **CEO 6**. 'I spent much time at the firm as a child driving tractors and such. I got to do many different tasks, but machinery was the most interesting.' **CEO 7**. 'Both my father and I thought it would be a good idea to start working within the company; he needed the help and I was interested. . . . I have been working at almost every part of the company, I started at the bottom and worked my way up. That way I understand the problems the guys face in the production line, for example.' **CEO 8**. 'I started working within the business when I was five, counting screws. After that, I also worked there during breaks with different tasks. . . . Later I started to work as a salesman, and after that it just happened.'

| 2b. | Creating a unique professional and entrepreneurial role identity | CEO 3. 'I started two companies as class projects during my school years. . . . Besides attending university, I worked with properties at another company, and after I finished my degree, I started to work at a property agency for a year. . . . I have also worked at a value transporting business, in a toy store, in a restaurant, by selling styling to cars and as a broker. All of these experiences have helped me when entering my family firm. . . . It is easier to question things if you have other (external) knowledge on how to handle things. . . . I would have been eaten alive if I did not have external experience when I entered my family business. . . . As a broker, you work independently. Such experience and my own desire made me question and change things today.'

CEO 4. 'I have three years in high school, and joined the army for a year after that. . . . I got an internship where I learned to deal with economics and I got a large responsibility. . . . I started at a gas station, Statoil, which gave me much experience, and many of our current customers come from that industry.'

CEO 8. 'I am educated in road and water engineering, which helped me during my time outside of the business. . . . I did not go directly from school to the family firm when I was finished, but was out on the public market for four years. I have to say that this experience actually helped me when entering the family firm. It mainly gave me a broader view and different perspectives and insights from other directions.' |
|---|---|---|
| 2c. | Practicing an entrepreneurial orientation | CEO 1. 'I was often introduced to new suggestions that I tried out, and I had a free hand to come up with new innovative ideas. . . . The company has to keep up with the market needs and develop with the market.'

CEO 2. 'I started to build databases about our real estate. With the databases, I retrieved information quickly when I needed it. My dad usually took hours to do the same work.'

CEO 6. 'I changed the administrative part because it was old. I swapped all the old machines and replaced them with new modern, more efficient ones.'

CEO 8. 'I brought new customers from the network I gained outside the family business.' |
| 3a. | Initiation of the role transition | CEO 1. 'The process of succession was gradual, and we worked together for many years. He knows the firm and the market better because he has grown with it. . . . We complemented each other well. He has worked within the business his whole life, so I tended to ask him for advice. He knew how similar experiments went. But, for example, I came up with new things that I learned from school, which he |

35

Table 2.2 (continued)

Second order theme	Representative first order data
3a. Initiation of the role transition	might not have thought about. . . . Dialogues with the staff helped me also to identify ideas that could be taken into consideration or could be further developed.' **CEO 2.** 'In the past, we had our own labor force but instead we started to hire other firms for specific projects.' **CEO 5.** 'My dad was still around for some time after he stepped down, so I got some help from him. . . . I got support from both my brother and my father during the succession. . . . I felt that the ownership within the company gave me some sort of legitimacy together with my experiences of the company in the production and IT departments.' **CEO 6.** 'I started a business many years ago, but I sold it when I became CEO of the family firm because it became too much managing both businesses.'
3b. Building leadership familiarity	**CEO 2.** 'I took more and more responsibility as time passed and it felt natural. I have more confidence and know what I can do and cannot do when having a leadership position. . . . I do not take risks, which might be negative with my leadership style. I only make decisions on solid grounds.' **CEO 6.** 'You have to trust yourself! There is a difference to owning the business and acting as an employee. If you screw up, you have to fix it yourself. . . . I continuously try to improve the business by finding new markets and ways to develop the product range that the firm offers.' **CEO 8.** 'I always tried to delegate some of the important work to empower the employees; I think that skill is what I developed the most during my time as a leader. . . . I always knew where I wanted my company to be in the future.'

Theme 1a. Being born with expectations

The second generation CEOs expressed a variety of expectations deriving from their families and the family business. Some of the interviewed CEOs indicated that their family had expected them to take over the company in the future:

> Joining the family firm was always with me because I was told from birth that I was intended to take over the company. (CEO 1)

In some cases, parents gave their children the freedom to choose their professions even though they conveyed a different message in non-verbal ways. Parents' expectations created an awareness of being needed and provided a sense of belonging:

> Even though my father never asked me to come home, I felt that they wanted me and needed me to (start working in the family business). (CEO 3)

In other cases, expectations were part of a continuous dialogue between the two generations. These dialogues shaped the views and decisions of the second generation:

> Both my father and I thought it would be a good idea to start working within the company; he needed the help, and I was interested. (CEO 7)

In the analyzed interviews, being born with expectations directly or indirectly influenced the professional choices of the second generation members. The business was often present in the background and also often strongly embedded in the daily life or thoughts of the next generation.

Theme 1b. Introducing the family business work-lifestyle

Introducing the family business work-lifestyle meant that second generation members became socialized into the overlap between family and business at an early age. Interviewed family CEOs considered the family business work-lifestyle to have been a feature in their lives since an early age. This perception was conveyed by a family CEO:

> When the family met, the firm was always brought up. But I think it is like that in every family firm. (CEO 4)

Another aspect of the overlap between family and business was that this overlap was accepted to a point in which the second generation CEOs became the ones starting business conversations and bringing business decisions at home. Second generation members took part in these discussions whether or not they were active in the family business. In this way, they kept open the possibility of working in the family business:

> Even while working outside of the family firm, I still took part in the discussions (about it) and gave advice. Because of this, it was easy to start working within the company again, as you already knew everything. (CEO 8)

Dimension 2. Developing an Entrepreneurial Self-concept

Developing an entrepreneurial self-concept implied that the second generation members nurtured their self-concept by working in different jobs at the family business (2a. Gradual involvement in the family business), attending to university education and obtaining their own professional and entrepreneurial experiences (2b. Creating a unique professional and entrepreneurial role identity) and developing an entrepreneurial mindset by continuous practice (2c. Practicing an entrepreneurial orientation).

Theme 2a. Gradual involvement in the family business
Gradual involvement in the family business entailed that the second generation developed a business relationship with the family business as a child, teenager and young adult. The second generation indicated that working during schools breaks as teenagers was a regular activity both in the family business and/or in other non-family businesses. Summer break jobs provided a general overview of different areas within the business. Two CEOs shared the following:

> I worked within the family business when I was little as a park attendee . . . I have also worked within the business during the summers and other breaks from school. These jobs have given me a good insight in the firm. (CEO 3)
> I have always tried to work elsewhere on summer breaks to gain as much experience as possible. (CEO 6)

The interviewed family CEOs agreed that their initial jobs created a natural transition to a full-time job in the family business:

> I spent much time at the company as a child. . . . I have always worked at the family business during all my school breaks, where I did everything from easier administration to laminating pockets. When I started working full time, I became the IT guy at the business as well. (CEO 1)

Theme 2b. Creating a unique professional and entrepreneurial role identity
With the exception of one case, seven of the second generation members interviewed expressed different types of experiences including working at

a non-family firm, starting a company and working in the family business. All of our interviewed CEOs studied at university. Thus, they relied on their external training when they engaged in the family business:

> Neither my mom nor dad had an (university) education within that area, which gave me an edge. (CEO 2)

Some of the interviewed second generation members created alternative roads for developing business skills and knowledge of their industries. They took internships in other companies, obtained their first jobs and/or started their own businesses. Starting their own businesses gave them the experience and insight to develop the family business:

> I started a trucking company in 1995. This experience has helped me the most. If it were not for that, I would not be where I am today. (CEO 6)

Some of the interviewed second generation members stated that they had preferred to work in a business other than the family business upon graduation from university. They gained different perspectives from that of the family and the family business, and they built a professional identity in the industry:

> I am educated in road and water engineering, which helped me during my time outside of the business. . . . I did not go directly from school to the family firm when I graduated. I was out on the public market for four years. I have to say that this experience actually helped me when entering the family firm. It mainly gave me a broader view and different perspectives and insights from other directions. (CEO 8)

The second generation members mastered their work and became acquainted with their industries, which allowed them to build their unique way of performing and handling activities in the family business:

> It is easier to question things if you have other (external) knowledge on how to handle things. . . . I would have been eaten alive if I did not have external experience when I entered my family business. . . . As a broker, you work independently. Such experience and my own desire made me question and change things today. (CEO 3)

Theme 2c. Practicing an entrepreneurial orientation
The interviewed second generation members indicated that when they worked in the family business, they brought new ideas or materialized family ideas to apply their knowledge to the business:

> I was often introduced to new suggestions that I tried out, and I had free hands to come up with new innovative ideas. . . . The company has to keep up with the market needs and develop with the market. (CEO 1)
> I started to build databases about our real estate. With the databases, I retrieved information quickly when I needed it. My dad usually took hours to do the same work. (CEO 2)

In some cases, developing the entrepreneurial orientation was naturally incorporated into the family's way of working and in other cases, it led to tensions between the incumbent senior and the second generation:

> We (my father and I) developed a whole new system for production. We integrated all of the different parts into the system. (CEO 5)
> I always asked myself how we could do this or that in a better way. I have changed most parts of the company even though my parents resisted until they saw the results. (CEO 3)

Dimension 3. Becoming an Entrepreneurial Leader

Becoming an entrepreneurial leader occurred through a role transition in which the second generation took a leadership position and learned to rely on others (3a. Initiation of the role transition) and themselves (3b. Building leadership familiarity).

Theme 3a. Initiation of the role transition
The interviewed second generation members experienced a role transition when they assumed a leadership position in the family business, and the older generation provided support when needed. The interviewed second generation members developed a professional- and mentor-type relationship with the older generation. This relationship helped the second generation to work jointly in the best possible way. The second generation expressed their complementarity with the older generation:

> The process of succession was gradual, and we worked together for many years. He knows the firm and the market better because he has grown with it. . . . We complemented each other well. He has worked within the business his whole life, so I tended to ask him for advice. He knew how similar experiments went. But, for example, I came up with new things that I learned from school that he might not have thought about. (CEO 1)

The second generation developed their own ideas and intentions with the business, which eventually differed from those of their parents:

> Both my father and I had many different experiences. There is a rapid pace in development that makes it hard sometimes for the older generation to adapt; they are used to a certain way. (CEO 6)

Another aspect in the role transition was the perception of developing the business together. This inclusion eased communication between generations:

> We developed the company together, so he is still a big influence. . . . I often discussed major decisions with my family to hear their input, but what I decided later is all up to me. (CEO 7)

Theme 3b. Building leadership familiarity

The second generation members agreed that becoming an entrepreneurial leader took time because they needed to grow into their new role. As part of their new role, the interviewed second generation members learned to make decisions, delegate tasks, and admit mistakes. A family CEO expressed the following:

> Since I took a leadership position, I have grown and developed a larger sense of responsibility. . . . Becoming a leader takes time because I am building up the experience for the first time now, so everything I do is new. But, you grow into the role. (CEO 1)

To grow into a leadership role, the next generation learned to trust themselves. When they made mistakes, they recognized them, reflected on them, and moved forward:

> It is up to the leader to reach a decision after discussions with employees. A leader needs to take the command and say: let us do that! If it does not work, let us try another way. You should never be afraid to admit that you were wrong. (CEO 1)

The second generation members expressed the importance of allowing themselves to try different approaches to leadership:

> I tried different techniques to lead change. One time, I brought everybody to a property to show them what needed to be done in order to get their approval. (CEO 3)

DISCUSSION

In this chapter, our focus was on exploring the perceptions of family CEOs regarding their process of becoming an entrepreneurial leader in the family business. We termed this opening stage the 'entrepreneurial leadership transition' because we limited it to becoming a CEO in the family business as an initial stage in insider successions from the first- to the second generation. Three dimensions integrate our entrepreneurial leadership transition model: *being socialized into family approaches, developing an entrepreneurial self-concept* and *becoming an entrepreneurial leader*. Because these dimensions are processes, they advance our understanding of leadership succession. Previous literature views leadership succession as steps and did not consider that such milestones are activities used by potential CEOs to develop entrepreneurial leadership based on their interests, preferences, and family backgrounds (cf. Gersick et al., 1999; Murray, 2003; Lambrecht, 2005). Through primary and secondary socialization and their own will, potential CEOs became entrepreneurial leaders over time. We elaborate our three dimensions as follows:

- *Being socialized into family approaches*
  Being socialized into family approaches comprised that children became self-aware of the culture into which they were born through socialization. Lambrecht (2005) called this process 'interpreneurship' (p. 276). Children internalize the world of their parents and made it their own through a deep and interactive process (Berger and Luckmann, 1966). In children of parents owning and managing a family business, socialization has different dimensions due to the overlap between family, business and ownership (García-Álvarez et al., 2002). *Being born with expectations* implied that throughout socialization, different generations were connected (cf. Haag, 2012) to expectations and approaches forming certain skills and knowledge suitable to their family (cf. Lambrecht, 2005). Because expectations were introduced directly or indirectly, the second generation became acquainted with the family values and perceptions about entrepreneurship and the family business from an early age. Overall, successors felt needed by their families, which encouraged them to develop a sense of responsibility for the family and thus to make a contribution in the business (cf. Birley, 1986). *Being introduced into the family business work-lifestyle* was important because successors perceived that they were influenced long before the transfer of power in the business: this influence existed throughout the history of these entrepreneurial leaders (Miller et al., 2003). To prepare for the future, they had an awareness of the knowledge and skills that they needed to develop in order to make a difference in their family businesses.

- *Developing an entrepreneurial self-concept*
  Developing an entrepreneurial self-concept was a product of *gradual involvement in the family business, the development of a professional and entrepreneurial role identity* and *practicing an entrepreneurial*

orientation. The *gradual involvement in the family business* corresponds to a 'secondary socialization' (Berger and Luckmann, 1966: 150) or a business socialization (García-Álvarez et al., 2002) that stimulates the acquisition of role-specific knowledge through a variety of jobs in the family business. Gradual involvement in the family business was affected by experiences from childhood, the teen years and early adulthood. To complement this internal experience, most next genera-tion members also opted for external training in the form of practical training courses, university education, start-up experience, internships, jobs at non-family businesses (cf. Chirico, 2008) or military experience. University education was particularly relevant in our cases to build a unique area of expertise that was useful in the development of the business. It gave second generation successors an ability to analyze markets in order to engage in entrepreneurial activities (cf. Cruz and Nordqvist, 2012). Once successors joined the family business, they were encouraged to act entrepreneurially. During this time, the next generation members related to the business from different perspectives. The *development of a professional and entrepreneurial role identity* is linked to the construction of their 'role identities' (Hogg, Terry, and White, 1995: 256). Role identities imply that people come to know who they are through social interactions, which in turn provide meaning to these individuals (Hogg et al., 1995). Professional and educational experiences influenced the perceptions and the self-conceptualization of the second generation's members. These 'own' experiences provided them with a broader understanding of their area of specialization and improved their judgment (cf. Miller et al., 2003); further, these experiences offered them industry contacts and customers. Another important aspect of developing a professional and entrepreneurial self-concept was the entrepreneurial orientation (Habbershon et al., 2010). *Practicing an entrepreneurial orientation* implies using perceptions and interpretations of the competitive environment to allow next genera-tion members to make decisions and materialize ideas in a proactive, risk-taking and innovative manner (Cruz and Nordqvist, 2012). The entrepreneurial leaders developed own initiatives or ideas generated by the family, and some worked, while others failed. Still, by exercis-ing their entrepreneurial orientation regularly, the second generation members acquired, improved or maintained the entrepreneurial spirit of the family once in the CEO role.

- *Becoming an entrepreneurial leader*
  Becoming an entrepreneurial leader included a *role transition* and *building leadership familiarity*. The *role transition* corresponded to

a work-role-transition occurring between the senior manager in the first generation to the successor in the second generation (cf. Salvato and Corbetta, 2013). A work-role-transition is a process of adjustment that includes changes in values, skills and dispositions due to a new employment status (Nicholson, 1984) and a new family status. Succession implied developing an appropriate relationship between past and future, and a different relationship between the founder/prior CEO and the successor/new CEO (Handler, 1990; 1992; Cadieux, 2007). The interviewed CEOs initiated their role transition by working together with the older generation for several years (cf. Cater and Justis, 2009). As new leaders, they recognized the support of the older generation at their 'backs' and activated it if needed. This support was central to take decisions conducive to the business growth. The experience of being an (independent or corporate) entrepreneur and of having worked themselves up to the position created a different relational dynamic with the older generation. The older generation assumed thereby a mentor role from one leader to another (cf. Cadieux, 2007). *Building leadership familiarity* meant that successors built acquaintance with the meaning and activities of their leadership role. Familiarity with the leadership role results as a process of learning, applying and developing leadership techniques through work-interactions (Atwood, Mora, and Kaplan, 2010). Thus, familiarity focuses on the new CEO's degree of comfort and confidence with ideas and activities of the different responsibilities at hand. It suggests that leadership behaviors changes when some degree of familiarity with the new role is achieved (Kaplan, 1999). Once in the new position, the entrepreneurial leaders deepened their self-awareness to advance their leadership skills. They also continued to learn their jobs and started building trust in themselves.

Limitations and Future Research

There are several limitations to our study. First, we focused on successions from the first- to the second generation with families having two children. While this delimitation allowed us to concentrate on the same phenomenon with relatively similar dynamics among siblings, these cases did not include the dynamics among siblings. Future research can study family dynamics on leadership succession when there are several siblings interested in becoming the CEO. This focus will allow us to understand how siblings agree on the next family CEO and how roles and positions change during succession. Second, we selected male-to-male succession. Thus, we were not able to capture dynamics between father-to-daughter successions.

Future research can address leadership transitions for father-to-daughter successions and advance our knowledge on how daughters build competencies as CEOs that allow them to succeed in male dominated industries. Third, we only investigated the perceptions of the next generation to study the entrepreneurial leadership transition process. While we considered that there was a lack of studies emphasizing the perceptions of successors, this study did not combine them with the perceptions of the first generation. Future research can combine the perceptions of different generations to provide a holistic understanding of how incumbents grow into the new role while the second generation also takes on a new role. Fourth, we concentrated on the first experience in a leadership position of successors in the family business. Future research could take a closer look into the role transition and leadership familiarity. Role transition is particularly important to understand the interactions between the entrepreneur leader and the older generations, and between the entrepreneurial leader and his/her employees (cf. Cater and Justis, 2009). Future research on the role of leadership familiarity during and post succession can help us predict positives changes in behaviors and skills of new CEOs.

CONCLUSIONS

Practitioners as well as the family business literature confirmed the importance of becoming a leader that makes a difference. Prior literature acknowledged that different requirements along with socialization are needed to become a CEO in a family business. Traditionally, the literature distinguished these aspects through two separate approaches to leadership succession. In this chapter, we linked these two approaches and added entrepreneurial elements in a model for entrepreneurial leadership transition from the first- to the second generation. This model showed how the successor's own choices and the family influence supported the development of entrepreneurial leaders prior to and during succession. Infusing an entrepreneurial shift to leadership succession, not only supported the second generation's development, but also assisted successors as future CEOs on their subsequent contribution to the family business. Understanding the influence and role of entrepreneurship in leadership successions is central for building a legacy that is transferred to future generations (Jaskiewicz et al., 2015). The process of becoming an entrepreneurial leader was shaped through interactions with relevant stakeholders, working inside and/or outside of the firm, obtaining a university education, and engaging in entrepreneurial activities (often launching a company). As a result, successors built an entrepreneurial self-concept; the family business provided a playground for building such entrepreneurial self-concept. Entrepreneurial leaders exercised their decision-making in order to exploit opportunities with the family support prior to and during succession. Thereby, these families fostered transitions that did not result in failure (cf. Miller et al., 2003) or claims of nepotism (Salvato, Minichilli, and Piccarreta, 2012).

There are several practical implications for future entrepreneurial leaders such as Matthias and their families. Leadership succession literature approaches generational changes as a process in which new wine is put into old bottles, our model of entrepreneurial leadership transition sees succession as a process in which new wine is poured into improved bottles. Our model added an entrepreneurial dimension to the leadership succession process. In successions from the first- to the second generation, entrepreneurial experiences in the form of launching an independent business or committing to entrepreneurial activities in the family business were important to build an entrepreneurial self-concept. Potential CEOs developed their entrepreneurial identity and practiced an entrepreneurial orientation in relatively controlled situations. A self-perception as an entrepreneurial leader was key to growing into a CEO that is willing to make a difference. The entrepreneurial leaders in our cases stated that the experiences of starting a business and of working with new projects were more important than their other types of experiences. Once the next generation members created a company, they communicated with incumbent senior managers from one entrepreneur to another. Thus, encouraging next generation members to start a business is an important element in the formation of potential CEOs. When the next generation members carried out entrepreneurial activities, the support of the older generation was central to launch new products, enter new markets, or introduce processes. In conversations with the older generation, potential successors can learn from their mistakes. Thus, the support of the older generation helps future successors to act courageously and develop individually. Successors feel more motivated to advance the business with solutions outside the box.

REFERENCES

Atwood, M.A., Mora, J.W., and Kaplan, A. (2010). Learning to lead: evaluating leadership and organizational learning. *Leadership and Organization Development Journal*, 31: 576–595.

Berger, P.L. and Luckmann, T. (1966). *The Social Construction of Reality: A Treatise in the Sociology of Knowledge*. Garden City, NY: Anchor Books.

Birley, S. (1986). Succession in the family firm: the inheritor's view. *Journal of Small Business Management*, 24: 36–43.

Cater, J.J., III. and Justis, R.T. (2009). The development of successors from followers to leaders in small family firms: an exploratory study. *Family Business Review*, 22: 109–124.

Cadieux, L. (2007). Succession in small and medium-sized family businesses: toward a typology of predecessor roles during and after instatement of the successor. *Family Business Review*, 20: 95–109.

Chirico, F. (2008). The creation, sharing and transfer of knowledge in family business. *Journal of Small Business and Entrepreneurship*, 21: 413–434.

Chua, J.H., Chrisman, J.J., and Sharma, P. (1999). Defining the family business by behavior. *Entrepreneurship Theory and Practice*, 23: 19–39.

Cruz, C. and Nordqvist, M. (2012). Entrepreneurial orientation in family firms: a generational perspective. *Small Business Economics*, 38: 33–49.

Dawson, A., Irving, G., Sharma, P., Chirico, F., and Markus, J. (2014). Behavioural outcomes of next-generation family members' commitment to their firm. *European Journal of Work and Organizational Psychology*, 23: 570–581.

Day, D.V. (2001). Leadership development: a review in context. *Leadership Quarterly*, 11: 581–613.

De Massis, A., Chua, J.H., and Chrisman, J.J. (2008). Factors preventing intra-family succession. *Family Business Review*, 21: 183–199.

Economist intelligence unit (2008). Succession planning. Idea section in the *Economist*, August 11. Retrieved from: http://www.economist.com/node/11880088 (accessed January 8, 2015).

García-Álvarez, E., López-Sintas, J., and Saldaña Gonzalvo, P. (2002). Socialization patterns of successors in first- to second-generation family businesses. *Family Business Review*, 15: 189–203.

Gersick, K.E., Lansberg, I., Desjardins, M., and Dunn, B. (1999). Stages and transitions: managing change in the family business. *Family Business Review*, 12: 287–297.

Gioia, D.A. and Pitre E. (1990). Multiparadigm perspectives on theory building. *Academy of Management Review*, 15: 584–602.

Gupta, V., MacMillan, I.C., and Surie, G. (2004). Entrepreneurial leadership: developing and measuring a cross-cultural construct. *Journal of Business Venturing*, 19: 241–260.

Haag, K. (2012). Rethinking Family Business Succession – from a Problem to Solve to an Ongoing Process. PhD thesis published by Jönköping International Business School, Jönköping.

Habbershon, T., Nordqvist, M., and Zellweger, T. (2010). Transgenerational entrepreneurship. In M. Nordqvist and T. Zellweger (eds), *Transgenerational Entrepreneurship: Exploring Growth and Performance of Family Firms across Generations* (1–38), Cheltenham, UK and Northampton, MA, USA: Edward Elgar Publishing.

Hall, A. and Nordqvist, M. (2008). Professional management in family businesses: extending the current understanding. *Family Business Review*, 11: 51–69.

Handler, W.C. (1990). Succession in family firms: a mutual role adjustment between entrepreneur and next-generation family members. *Entrepreneurship Theory and Practice*, 15: 37–51.

Handler, W.C. (1992). The succession experience of the next generation. *Family Business Review*, 5: 283–307.

Handler, W.C. (1994). Succession in family business: a review of the research. *Family Business Review*, 7: 133–157.

Hogg, M., Terry, D., and White, K. (1995). A tale of two theories: a critical comparison of identity theory with social identity theory. *Social Psychology Quarterly*, 58: 255–269.

Jaskiewicz, P., Combs, J.G., and Rau, S.B. (2015). Entrepreneurial legacy: toward a theory of how some family firms nurture transgenerational entrepreneurship. *Journal of Business Venturing*, 30: 29–49.

Kansikas, J., Laakkonen, A., Sarpo, V., and Kontinen, T. (2012). Entrepreneurial leadership and familiness as resources for strategic entrepreneurship. *International Journal of Entrepreneurial Behaviour and Research*, 18: 141–158.

Kaplan, A. (1999). From passive to active about solar electricity: innovation decision process and photovoltaic interest generation. *Technovation*, 19: 467–481.

Lambrecht, J. (2005). Multigenerational transition in family businesses: a New Explanatory Model. *Family Business Review*, 18: 267–282.

Lansberg, I. (2007). The tests of a prince. *Harvard Business Review*, 85: 92–101.

Le Breton-Miller, I., Miller, D., and Steier, L.P. (2004). Toward an integrative model of effective FOB succession. *Entrepreneurship Theory and Practice*, 28: 305–328.

Lumpkin, G.T. and Dess, G.G. (1996). Clarifying the entrepreneurial orientation construct and linking it to performance. *Academy of Management Review*, 21: 135–172.

Miles, M.B. and Huberman, M. (1994). *Qualitative Data Analysis: An Expanded Sourcebook* (2nd edn). Thousand Oaks, CA: Sage Publications.

Miller, D., Steier, L., and Le Breton-Miller, I. (2003). Lost in time: intergenerational succession, change, and failure in family business. *Journal of Business Venturing*, 18: 513–531.

Miller, D., Le Breton-Miller, I., Lester, R.H., and Canella Jr., A.A. (2007). Are family superior performers? *Journal of Corporate Finance*, 13: 829–858.

Murray, B. (2003). The succession transition process: a longitudinal perspective. *Family Business Review*, 16: 17–33.

Nicholson, N. (1984). A theory of work role transitions. *Administrative Science Quarterly*, 29: 172–192.

Salvato, C. and Corbetta, G. (2013). Transitional leadership of advisor as a facilitator of successors' leadership construction. *Family Business Review*, 26(3): 235–255.

Salvato, C., Minichilli, A., and Piccarreta, R. (2012). 'Faster route to the CEO suite: nepotism or managerial proficiency?' *Family Business Review*, 25: 206–224.

Sardeshmukh, S.R. and Corbett, A.C. (2011). The duality of internal and external development of successors: opportunity recognition in family firms. *Family Business Review*, 24: 111–125.

Schumpeter, J. (1934). *The Theory of Economic Development*. New Brunswick, NJ: Transaction.

Stevenson, H. (1983). A perspective on entrepreneurship. Harvard Business School Working Paper 9, pp. 384–131.

Turner Foster, A. (1995). Developing leadership in the successor generation. *Family Business Review*, 8: 201–209.

Ward, J.L. (2004). *Perpetuating the Family Business: 50 Lessons Learned from Long-Lasting Successful Families in Business*. New York, NY: Palgrave Macmillan.

3. The next generation: pathways for preparing and involving new owners in Colombian family businesses

Gustavo González Couture and Luis Díaz Matajira

MINI CASE STUDY: A YOUNG LEADER PREPARING FOR . . . WHAT?

Carlos Miguel had just finished writing a report on a shared value initiative undertaken by Mulitplex Río Cauca, a family owned company from Cali (Colombia's third largest city). Mulitplex Río Cauca is part of Cine Colombia, founded in Medellin in 1927, and the country's premier film exhibitor and distributor, generating over US $150m in revenue and employing 1,600 workers.

While writing his report, Carlos could not help noticing the similarities between Mulitplex Río Cauca and the companies owned by his own family. The most recently founded of these firms was a battery-making factory that his grandfather started in the 1950s in Cali, having learnt the trade as a teenager in Argentina. Today, the factory has 600 workers, while another family company that retails auto parts across the country employs twice that number. The companies are managed by the second generation (Carlos' mother, and her three siblings). In terms of revenue, they are in the same multi-million dollar bracket as Cine Colombia.

Carlos thought about his grandfather. He remembered that when he was a teenager, he would accompany him to visit the different divisions and operational sections of the factory while his grandfather patiently explained how things worked. The founder was very proud to have pioneered battery recycling. As well as increasing sales so that within a few years he had the largest market share of all brands, including imported batteries, he established recycling posts to buy used batteries at reasonable prices. He would recycle all the components, including lead, in order to manufacture new products. Moreover, he did this long before governments, consultants and academics became aware of environmental issues.

Carlos Miguel remembered how everyone in the family felt proud that Colombia was one of few countries in Latin America that could boast that it did not dump its used batteries. He understood why Johnsons Control Incorporated (JCI) had been so interested in working with the family's companies, and even in forming an alliance. The family was interested in this too, as JCI was the leading firm in the development of new battery technology.

Carlos Miguel kept thinking about the fact that the new Multiplex Río Cauca theater was right in the middle of the district of Aguablanca, the poorest and most violent part of Cali. Cine Colombia was attempting to offer an interactive medium that would circulate educational and cultural content while at the same time offering alternative leisure activities for young people, and a safe environment for families.

After handing in his report to his boss at the NGO where he worked as a junior consultant, Carlos Miguel left his office in the financial center of Bogotá, and cycled to his loft apartment. On the way, he had to dodge crowded buses, motorcycles that appeared out of nowhere, BMWs and well-kept taxis. Young executives and middle-aged office workers navigated the crowded sidewalks, weaving in and out of the narrow spaces available between hucksters and sidewalk-sellers displaying their wares: fast food, flea market gadgets, magazines, fruit, or whatever else they could sell to earn a living.

Such contrasts revealed the truth of Colombia's inequitable distribution of income and the very harsh conditions in which more than half the population lives. 'How can families make a living selling this stuff?' Carlos Miguel would ask himself. He was well aware of the country's socio-economic situation. He was sensitive to human suffering, in spite of having been born into a well-to-do entrepreneurial family from Cali. His grandparents, parents, uncles and aunts were not just fair employers but also had a caring attitude toward their employees' families. In addition, they contributed to several philanthropic initiatives.

Carlos Miguel then asked himself what he had done with his life. Born into a privileged setting, he attended an exclusive high school in Cali and then studied in an elite university in Bogotá. He traveled overseas to Belgium on an exchange internship at a multinational where he learned about environmentally friendly corporate activities. These experiences influenced his professional interests profoundly.

He was the oldest of the third generation and represented his cousins in the family council or assembly. Nothing was said about his joining the family business (FB), but he knew that his uncle Luis Ernesto – President of the Board – backed him and believed him fit to take over some responsibilities within it. He dreamt of building on proven green technologies and hoped to develop shared value initiatives.

When he arrived home an email was waiting for him from his mother, CEO of the FB. It left him puzzled and shocked. He had been trained up to become a leader of the company, and expected this to happen; however, the email said: 'Son, we have sold the battery factory to JCI and have agreed to work with them for some time. . . . We will keep our auto parts stores. . . . The family still has control of its other businesses and of the family holding company.'

Carlos Miguel now began wondering what he could or should do under these changed circumstances. Because of his work experience in other companies, and because he wanted to play an active role in the FB, he was clear that it was important that he should act as a responsible owner. But how best could he exercise this responsibility: by being an active manager, or by participating in the board? Or should he look to other horizons and be prepared simply to participate intelligently when called to attend the annual family assembly?

INTRODUCTION

The involvement of family members in a company is the key to identifying and defining FBs and in explaining why they constitute a special setting for management research (Shanker and Astrachan, 1996; Astrachan, Klein, and Smyrnios, 2002). Moreover, while some researchers highlight how family involvement may be a source of conflict among family members and within companies (Eddleston and Kellermanns, 2007; Kidwell, Kellermanns, and Eddleston, 2012; Sorenson, 1999), others show how family involvement and influence contribute to wealth generation over time (Habbershon, Williams, and MacMillan, 2003; Habbershon and Williams, 1999; Miller and Le Breton-Miller, 2006).

There is plenty of research in the FB literature about family involvement in general, and especially on leadership transition. However, the ways in which members of the next generation are prepared for leadership is still poorly understood (Long et al., 2014). Most authors appear to refer principally to the type of leadership exercised by family members in senior management positions; in other words, to intra-family management leadership (ML). A key question behind processes such as these is the family's reasons for such involvement. An outstanding motive for involving new generations in successful entrepreneurial families in Colombia is to achieve ML and, thereby, to pass on the baton and maintain or strengthen family control over the business. Families do not appear to prioritize preparing those members of the next generation who will in the future be shareholders but will not actually work in the FB, in order to help them exercise responsible ownership (RO). That is: to prepare them for their role as family members who have a stake in the family's wealth but who are not directly involved in the FB's daily operations.

Based on five cases that illustrate the process of successor development and next generation involvement, this chapter seeks to answer the following question: What pathways do Colombian multigenerational entrepreneurial firms adopt in order to prepare members of the next generation for RO? We argue that the concept of entrepreneurial learning (EL) is helpful for understanding these different pathways; moreover, EL is essential to the development of responsible owners.

EL, understood as the process of acquiring the skills and knowledge necessary to initiate, manage and develop a venture (Corbett, 2005; Politis, 2005) has recently been proposed as a mediating variable between entrepreneurial orientation and firm performance and between 'familiness' and firm performance (Cheng, Ho, and Au, 2013). If this is so, EL becomes a pivotal notion in examining the process by which the involvement of the next generation in the business affairs of entrepreneurial families is ensured.

EL may be approached from opposite directions: either by focusing on individuals or on the social settings in which they participate during the course of their lives. The EL methods proposed by Cheng et al. (2013) may be considered to occupy the middle ground between these poles. They also provide a helpful categorization by referring to *Communities of Practice* (CoPs), which play a creative role and encourage intergenerational learning processes.

In the first approach, the unit of analysis is the individual, who accumulates a 'stock of experiences' and on whom the entrepreneur then relies to run the business (Minniti and Bygrave, 2001; Reuber and Fischer, 1999). The second approach, on the other hand, involves a socially situated learning perspective, provided by the CoP. A particular set of relations between people and social activities, occuring in the world over time, constitutes an intrinsic condition for the existence of knowledge. In our analysis, we use this second perspective as our framework. It allows a better understanding of succession, as a process that is not confined to passing the management baton on to intra-family candidates, but that allows any member of the owning family to influence decisions via other family governance bodies.

For Hamilton (2013), FBs are ideal organizations for understanding the development of entrepreneurs, as their members are, during their whole lifetimes, 'embedded in participation in practice in multiple, overlapping work – and family based communities of practice' (Hamilton, 2013: 120). The CoPs that are relevant to this chapter are, in order of importance: the family; the FB (if children and teenagers have played a role within it); other organizations where family members have worked; and the educational CoP where formal education takes place (schools, vocational training establishments, college, etc.).

SOCIALLY SITUATED PERSPECTIVES ON ENTREPRENEURIAL LEARNING: COMMUNITIES OF PRACTICE FOR RESPONSIBLE OWNERSHIP

CoPs are social settings that enable learning to take place in circumstances where knowledge is conceived of as a social phenomenon. The assumptions established for this social theory of learning by a leading proponent of the approach (Wenger, 1998) are the following:

- We are social beings and as such learning takes place mainly in social settings.
- Knowledge is a matter of competence with respect to valued enterprises (e.g. composing music, fixing machines, growing up as boys or girls).
- Knowing is a matter of participating in the pursuit of such enterprises; in other words, active engagement in the world.
- Meaning – our ability to experience the world and our engagement with it as meaningful – is what learning should ultimately produce (and is also, we would add, along with competence, one of the purposes of knowing).

These assumptions permit us to view learning as the result of social participation. It is not just the result of daily experiences and of encounters with others but of 'a more encompassing process of being active participants in the *practices* of social communities and constructing *identities* in relation to these communities. Participating in a playground clique or in a work team is both a kind of action and a form of belonging. Such participation shapes not only what we do, but also what we are and how we interpret what we do' (Wenger, 1998: 4).

'Community' here refers to 'a way of talking about the social configurations in which our enterprises are defined as worth pursuing and our participation is recognized as competence.' 'Identity,' on the other hand, is 'a way of talking about how learning changes who we are and creates personal histories of becoming in the context of our communities' (Wenger, 1998: 5).

Hamilton (2013), then, uses the socially situated perspective of EL in order to understand how knowledgeable identities – or roles – may be conceived of as entrepreneurial identities-in–practice. These identities change over time. For example, in the past an incumbent founding entrepreneur might have been labeled a 'risk-taker' before becoming an established manager, then 'the owner,' and finally, once retired, a peripheral participant – probably as a board member – known for his or her 'wisdom.'

By juxtaposing generational narratives Hamilton (2013) sheds light on the succession process in FBs. Intergenerational encounters such as these bring together different histories of practice through which the future is negotiated and developed (Hamilton, 2013).

In a first characterization of CoPs and their role in EL processes in FBs, Hamilton (2011) considers the different types that are important for family members: (1) bringing practice to bear when establishing a business; (2) childhood and business, that is: potential management candidates and their relationship with the business; and (3) introducing new practices as a result of the overlapping communities of family and business. This first key concept of Hamilton's is further refined (2013) as the author considers, first, those CoPs where the candidates for ML are prepared: the family, but also what they learn from their experiences in the FB as children, in businesses away from the family, as adults away from the family, through educational CoPs, and finally, in CoPs that permit cycles of reproduction and transformation of the FB.

Consequently, EL, as part of entrepreneurial preparedness, 'has been reconceptualised as a socially situated, cyclical intergenerational phenomenon' with ownership responsibilities (Hamilton, 2013: 148).

We consider the notion of RO to be an encompassing concept that alerts incumbent leaders and members of FBs to the fact that succession is not merely a process of intra-family leadership, but can be exercised through other governance roles. It may even include the need to participate knowledgeably, wisely, and in the best interests of the family, in family assemblies and in other bodies and groups. In brief, it is the concern of all owning family members to act first in the general interest of the family and only second in pursuit of their individual goals. This should be learnable and teachable.

Little research has been carried out into RO despite the existence of the Family Business Network and the fact that the International Family Enterprise Research Academy dedicated its 2005 World Academic Research Forum to the subject. Lambrecht and Uhlaner (2005) presented a literature review and analysis of the state of the art to the forum. They distinguished RO from corporate governance and corporate social responsibility, arguing that as a consequence of RO, family members set up and monitor 'the parameters within which their business is to be run, including among others, the fields of activity to be allowed, and ethical rules to be applied' (Lambrecht and Uhlaner, 2005: 5).

They also identified ways to enhance RO, including the articulation of shared values, the socialization of subsequent generations, the acquisition of competences and skills, strategic planning of the family and of the business, informal gatherings and the establishment of formal governance structures, many of which might be EL practices. As such, the proposal we advance in this chapter, to develop proactive shareholder participation and ML as part of RO, is congruent with the definition of RO provided by Lambrecht and Uhlaner as 'an active and long-term commitment to the family, the business and the community, and balancing these commitments with each other' (Lambrecht and Uhlaner, 2005: 10).

The contributions of Lambrecht and Uhlaner add content to our assertion that in order to increase EL and RO among family members it is important to observe CoPs and entrepreneurial identities-in–practice. This holds in the case of perceived responsibilities and rights (Lambrecht and Uhlaner, 2005). Thus, family members have a responsibility: (a) to develop attributes such as protectiveness, caring, nurturing, willingness to make sacrifices and investing one's full energy and time in the FB and the right, (b) to possess shares that have financial value, to exercise influence and to have access to information about the FB. These are the elements that make up the entrepreneurial identity of family members.

Thus, when it comes to accomplishing an adequate succession process, the challenge for incumbents and concerned FB owners is to enhance a sense of RO in family members. We claim that a well-trodden path is that of developing CoPs that will in turn foster entrepreneurial identities-in–practice, which are essential means to achieving RO.

The five cases examined in this chapter illustrate this interplay between CoPs and entrepreneurial identities-in–practice in order to show not only the importance of viewing ML succession as socially situated, but also the need to think of succession as a process involving more than the mere availability of suitable ML candidates. Rather, we argue, ways need to be found to prepare family members who will in the future be shareholders so that they will exercise RO. As the FB evolves over time, from controlling-founder to sibling partnership, diverse pathways may emerge that represent different dimensions of RO. Thus, initially, the main goal for new generation involvement might be focused on RO in the guise of ML, while during a progression from sibling partnership to a cousin consortium, RO may involve positive shareholder participation, with senior management being open to non-family members (see Figure 3.1).

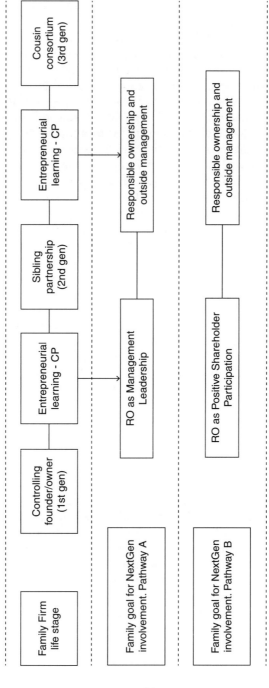

Figure 3.1   Next generation involvement goals through time

Table 3.1 Summary of Colombian STEP cases

Family	Primary Industry	Size	Interviews	Generations	Year of first company foundation
Montoya	Entertainment, Insurance and Car Dealerships	Medium	8	3	1969
Mejía	Car Batteries	Large	11	3	1957
Pacheco	Banking and Construction	Large	11	3	1955
López	Food Industry	Large	17	5	1929
Sáenz	Financial Services	Medium	5	3	1952

PATHWAYS FOR INVOLVEMENT IN FIVE COLOMBIAN CASES OF FAMILY BUSINESSES

Methods

For the purposes of this chapter, we follow an exploratory case study methodology (Eisenhardt, 1989; Eisenhardt and Bourgeois, 1988; Sieger et al., 2011). This is a qualitative approach based on Yin's (2014) multiple-case design, which is appropriate for exploring issues where knowledge is in its infancy. The analysis is based on an examination of the process of family involvement and new generation development of five Colombian cases written up for the STEP Project by the Universidad de los Andes' STEP team between 2007 and 2013. Table 3.1 provides a brief characterization of the companies selected for analysis in the chapter.

Fifty-two people were interviewed during the preparation of the five cases. All interviews were recorded and transcribed. For the purposes of this particular chapter, after the literature review, two researchers read and reviewed all the cases, using an interpretive research approach (Nordqvist, Hall, and Melin, 2009) in order to identify patterns in the process of family involvement and EL.

Analysis

Based on the CoPs mentioned above and with EL conceptualized as being part of a socially situated and cyclical intergenerational phenomenon of entrepreneurial preparedness, we argue that RO is essential to the sustainability of the FB (Hamilton, 2003: 148). Our cases illustrate the interplay between CoPs and entrepreneurial identities-in–practice, in order to show the importance of RO in the succession process where ML is one among many possible processes of succession through which members of the next generation of the family might be involved (see Appendix). This section illustrates the three kinds of CoP mentioned above.

CoP 1: bringing practice to bear when establishing a business

Don Francisco Montoya worked as a junior operator for a record manufacturer in the days of vinyl. He learned that the core of the business consisted in the distribution of records from several manufacturers and brands. In his early twenties he worked his way up the company, ultimately becoming responsible for distributing to the largest retailers. Eventually, Don Francisco himself became a retailer, coming to own the largest chain of record stores in the country.

When he was recently married he briefly flirted with cattle dealing but he failed at the enterprise; it was his young wife who made him see that his entrepreneurial identity-in–practice was that of 'record distributor.' He promptly followed her advice. After developing his business, he had the opportunity to invest in another company, which enabled him to invite his sons to join the FB according to their own interests and in response to their desire to work with their father. Don Francisco recalls:

> When I bought Continautos, the car dealership, Carlos Alberto had finished his degree, and he liked cars. He told me he wanted to be there, so he started to work there and he is still there now. Maybe it was coincidence or luck. As there was already a manager, I suggested that Carlos could begin as a sales manager. That's the route he took, and he is now general manager. Something similar happened with my other sons and my other businesses. (Francisco Montoya, interview)

So we can be sure that at the time, Carlos Alberto's entrepreneurial identity-in–practice was that of 'car-lover.' This explains why he was able to establish not only one of the most competitive auto dealerships in the country, but also one of the best maintenance services on offer.

Ernesto Mejía learnt all about auto battery maintenance and manufacture as an apprentice while his family was living in exile in Argentina. Upon their return to Colombia, when he was in his twenties, he started looking for work and found two openings that interested him: one in the area of battery repair, and another in a bicycle business, which offered better pay. He decided on the first job, envisaging a brighter future for the battery industry than for bicycles, and joined the firm *Distribuidora de Baterías*, now *Coéxito S.A.S.*, which was then owned by its founder. The family sees this decision as a key moment, as it was a difficult choice that determined the path Ernesto and his family would subsequently follow. As his daughter María Fernanda recalls:

That first decision was crucial, because [Monark Bicycles] was an important business, a leading company at the time. They offered him better pay, but he saw that it wasn't the future; he saw better prospects for the battery sector. (María Fernanda, interview)

Later on, Mejía bought the battery servicing store that eventually provided him with the capital and networking required to become, after several years, Colombia's largest battery manufacturer and distributor. In practice, several CoPs and entrepreneurial identities-in–practice contributed to these developments: Ernesto's experience as an apprentice in the battery shop in Argentina; as an employee in the battery shop in Cali, whose owner sold him the business; and as a partner in an automotive parts retailer and chain of stores of which he eventually became sole owner. These CoPs provided him in turn with several entrepreneurial identities: 'battery manufacturer,' 'distributor,' 'retailer,' and 'recycling expert.'

Carlos Pacheco was a junior Certified Public Accountant at the second largest insurance company in the country. He invented a sweepstake scheme that he then improved upon when he founded his own company. Account holders would commit to making fixed monthly payments for an agreed period (80 months), at the end of which the company would return the final amount saved without any accumulated interest. The gain for the customer was to participate in a monthly draw for which the prize was collecting the whole agreed final sum, regardless of how much had been saved up to the time of the draw. The scheme provided Don Carlos with a predictable capital amount that he invested wisely, allowing him to diversify into other financial services. His son Eduardo describes Don Carlos as an 'insurer':

My father learned about capitalization in [Seguros] Bolívar where he was an employee. Then, the insurance business emerged and my father decided to create a capitalization firm with a handfull of partners: the Sociedad Colombiana de Capitalización, later Seguros Patria, the insurance company. Colpatria grew from the merger of these two. In 1969, he began to venture into banking. After buying the Banco de la Costa my dad came and said, 'it is different to be a banker than to be an insurer. As an insurer, you have to ask for money, as a banker people ask you for money.' (Eduardo, interview)

The realities of record distribution and retailing determined Montoya's first CoP, as had the exercise of auto battery manufacturing and maintenance that of Mejía and sophisticated financial services Pacheco's. Furthermore, these CoPs provided entrepreneurial identities-in–practice that inspired the self-confidence and self-efficacy required to start their own businesses.

CoP 2: family members gain experience of the FB as children

The second type of CoP – relevant to members of the next generation – is the one in which family members gain experience of the FB as children; this usually entails the overlapping of family and business communities. The Montoya siblings, while teenagers and still at school, would have to open the family stores on weekend mornings, attend to customers, and close up shop late at night, which they did while their classmates were out practicing sports or partying. Don Francisco remembers this, as he still does the same with his grandchildren:

> On Saturdays or Sundays, I talk with my grandchildren like I used to do with my children, I tell them 'let's play at working.' And we all come here to the office or to the stores. I'm teaching them how to work. And many times they say to me: 'we want to work with you.' (Don Francisco, interview)

The Mejía siblings started much younger, accompanying their parents to the office, stores and even the factory. They would help tidy up, move light boxes from one place to another, and do odd chores just so that they could be close to their parents. They remember that during their vacations, their father would drive to cities where some retailers had not yet paid their invoices, but that they would immediately settle up when they saw the children. María Fernanda remembers:

> When we were little, we always had the chance to be close to the company. Our vacations always involved road trips with stops to visit customers and collect payments while we passed through. We were fortunate to see a Colombia that children today don't see. These vacations were a little frantic, as out of a fortnight there were only four or five quiet days. We drove around the country, got to know cities and towns, ate the traditional food in each place, and finally, we relaxed for a few days, for example, in Cartagena. (María Fernanda, interview)

The Pacheco siblings did not know much about their father's firms when they were young. Their priority was to do very well academically, practice sophisticated sports that would provide them with social skills, go to graduate school, and work overseas in multinational banks. All these CoPs no doubt contributed to the creation of several identities-in–practice. But there is one event that changed the life of the family: Don Carlos's abduction by FARC guerrillas. Despite not having to pay a ransom, given that the army freed him, the episode did radically change the family's lifestyle. Somehow, it brought the siblings closer, but only inasmuch as they were forced to go into exile to gain work experience abroad. In Eduardo's words:

We never talked about the company at home. I believe my father passed away without ever knowing how important he was. We never identified him with Colpatria: we were Pachecos. Today, of course, 'Pacheco' is associated with Colpatria because of my father, but the companies weren't part of our identity. My father was an unostentatious man. But things changed in our family after his kidnapping. We were initially brought up without any security measures. Unfortunately, the third generation of Pachecos has been raised amongst bodyguards, bullet-proof cars and guns. Terrorism in Colombia has several unpleasant faces; the grandchildren of a man who worked hard and contributed significantly to the country's economy, now have a distorted view of society. (Eduardo, interview)

Don Francisco Montoya was also kidnapped. However, in this case, in spite of their father's instruction not to pay any ransom, mother and siblings did fork out, an amount equivalent to the companies' working capital. To the (pleasant) surprise of Don Francisco, upon his return he saw that during the year of his absence his children, despite their youth and relative inexperience, had been able to pull things together and manage the different parts of the business. He remembers that episode and the reasons he did not leave the country:

It was like dying and coming back to life. With all the time in the world to meditate on what I had done with my life I concluded that with the help of Ligia, my wife, we had formed a family and established some important companies that provided employment to thousands of families. . . . [A]fter my release [I saw that] my family had taken better care of all the firms and businesses than I could have. I felt then that I had to keep up these activities. Also, it was like being born again. I resumed work then, full speed ahead. They told me I could live in Miami or London, but what was I going to do there? I had a job and companies in Colombia and I was never going to leave the country. (Don Francisco, interview)

In the Sáenz family too, the second generation was forced to become involved in the FB after the founder, Don Antonio, was abducted. Carolina recalls:

In 1979, my dad was kidnapped. He escaped, and went to live in America for about two months and then returned and that is the time when Claudia joined the company. She had already graduated from college and was starting to work outside the family business, and my dad called her and said, 'I need you to come and work for the company, because we need you.' (Carolina, interview)

An uncertain and insecure environment forged unusual CoPs and contributed to the creation of entrepreneurial identities-in–practice that influenced all family members. The experiences of kidnap that affected the Montoya, Pacheco and Sáenz families illustrate these processes and the way in which childhood and involvement in FBs change. One can hardly imagine what it must be like for a young adult to have to negotiate her or his parent's freedom with terrorists. FB literature in the North does not describe such situations. The fact is that through such occurences family ties between brothers and even cousins are strengthened in ways that no other event accomplishes.

CoP 3: introduction of new practice(s)

The third CoP denotes the introduction of new practice(s) between the overlapping communities of family and business. It is important to note that these boundaries may be blurred because of other CoPs that might have been established within the different business units that make up the FBs.

This third kind of CoP is intermingled with the second key concept introduced by Hamilton, that is: 'legitimate peripheral participation,' whereby 'the social dynamic of a CoP, its power relations and conditions of legitimacy define the possibilities for learning through participation. In terms of FB, conditions of legitimacy could refer to the immediate context of the family; that is, who can join in the activity of the business, the nature of the participation, how and when it occurs and under what conditions' (Hamilton, 2011, p. 16).

When they were young the Pacheco siblings never worked in, nor did they know much about, their father's companies. They underwent their exacting academic training, associated with upper class groups, gradu-ated from MBAs overseas and worked in international banks, before even thinking of working in the financial concerns their father headed. Prior to joining the FB they engaged in the peripheral participation that legitimized the different entrepreneurial identities-in–practice whose fruits would eventually benefit the company. Thus, in the case of Claudia:

> I have never worked here. I graduated from the Universidad de los Andes, then I worked at a financial firm; I did an MA in Boston and worked six years at Fuji Bank in New York. I returned to Colombia and worked for a year. When my first child was born I decided never again to work full time. My interest with Colpatria began when I attended board meetings with my dad. When he retired, I kept coming but I've never been on the payroll of the organization. My career as a banker lasted six years and for the last 20 years, I have run my own travel agency. (Claudia, interview)

With seasoned non-family vice-presidents overseeing them, the young Pacheco adults started their management careers at the bottom. The two oldest siblings worked in the companies for 20 years before being considered apt successors. Nearing his retirement, Don Carlos had the four siblings decide on who would succeed him. The brother who was not voted for left the FB to become a very successful entrepreneur – Don Carlos had intuited his calling – and only after proving himself to his brothers and sister did he return as a responsible owner to participate in several company boards. His sister followed the same path. Claudia recalls the succession process:

> He organized his retirement himself; no one told him to leave. One day he said he would retire and we never knew for how long he had been thinking about it. I think the big change was that each of [my elder brothers](Mario and Eduardo) became presidents of different activities and my dad oversaw them. I believe they started well. No longer counting on my dad's leadership within the organization was obviously a big change, but he had already set things up for a smooth transition. My father left nothing to chance, everything was well calculated. (Claudia, interview)

Candidate successors who have worked in other businesses, contribute their acquired entrepreneurial identities-in–practice. The Pacheco successor CEO understood the new demands of the financial markets and swiftly opened up the possibilities for a multinational bank (GE Capital) to enter into partnership with Colpatria. This illustrates how legitimate peripheral participation is indispensable for the transformation of practices, but that their reproduction is essential too. The partnering with GE Capital involved only one of the business units: the bank, which was the most vulnerable to financial market disruption. The other two units, construction and equity investments, were kept under family control.

Some of Francisco Montoya's companies were acquired accidentally: the auto dealership was purchased when his partner passed away and the surviving family sold out their interest; the same happened with the insurance company. Don Francisco would, wisely, test his children by having them work their way up in different companies, according to their competencies. The auto dealership ended up being headed by the sibling who loved car racing:

> Even though I studied publicity, my passion was racing cars and I raced some good races. My father would jokingly complain that those cars were a lousy business: very expensive and you could never sell them. . . . Every time I can, I attend international auto shows. Frankfurt and Paris are my usual stops. . . . It has been my passion for cars and love for the good life that probably explains my high level of risk. . . . I have learnt from my father to assume high levels of risk. I came into this business at a wonderful time, from selling 150 cars per month, we have climbed to 600. (Carlos Alberto Montoya)

The record retailing chain was headed by the oldest sibling, who had accompanied his father overseas to establish business with multinationals;

another sibling participated in the board of the insurance company; finally, the youngest, though a lawyer, proved herself as the financial director of the holding company.

The López family, whose business had three founding brothers, finally chose the eldest of fourteen cousins to become CEO, with two other cousins performing other VP functions in the family's agribusiness activities: in coffee exportation, oil palm cultivation, processing and distribution. They arrived at this arrangement following a process of trial and error. Initially, most of the cousins – and even in-laws – had been allowed to work in the companies, but as business grew, increasingly professional and specialized management was required, so family members agreed to a healthier business and family relationship where family involvement in the FB would be via participating on the boards of the several companies and the holding company. This case illustrates the importance of successors learning by participation – through ML or by participating in boards – as a legitimizing process. Family members given the opportunity to work in the FB are not always up to the mark and need to opt out. In Aníbal's words:

> My experience of being the son of a businessman who owned several businesses together with my uncles gave the wrong signal that if I flunked at school I could always ask my father for a job with him. It worried me to think of the next generation, that included my son and daughter, being loafers who would eventually come asking for jobs to which they thought they were entitled. . . . That is what I like about the Anglo Saxon spirit: educate your children so they can fend for themselves. It is the spirit I would like to instill in the family's genetic code, in order to override the Spanish attitude of the easy life, comfort, etc. . . . I know there are some members of the third generation who feel they have a birthright to work in what was 'their [inheritance] from their grandfathers.' Somehow, they resent the fact of no longer having the 'right to work.' It is understandable that they feel I am an unpleasant and authoritarian uncle who has changed the rules. (Aníbal López, interview)

The last of Hamilton's key concepts, 'cycles of reproduction and transformation of practices,' contributes to understanding how the social assets of trust, cohesion and shared value are created and passed on from one generation to the next.

> One generation participates in and develops the business and is joined by others who eventually supplant the first generation. There is continuity and, at the same time, discontinuity in that process. The cycles of reproduction and transformation ensure the survival of the FB as it seeks to reconstitute itself as a community of practice in the next generation. The complex, and often troubled, process of succession can be understood in terms of reproducing the FB as it

moves from the hands of one generation to the next. At the same time, however, it must be transformed as it moves from one social, historical, technological, cultural context to another. (Hamilton, 2011, p. 18)

While an intra-generational CoP involving incumbents and candidates for ML is observed in all our cases, what doesn't seem to be formalized is the much needed CoP that would help establish entrepreneurial identities-in–practice among family members who do not participate in the daily operation of the firms. This would help them to become responsible owners despite the fact they are not directly involved.

While the López, Pacheco, Mejía and Sáenz families have experienced decisive, formal, moments involving the planned retirement of the founders, the Montoyas are yet to reach that stage. The Sáenz family was the only one that did not accomplish second-generation intra-family ML.

Of all the cases examined, the López family was the only one that was concerned about RO, probably because of their negative experience when work was offered to all second generation family members, including in-laws. This is what led them to revaluate the mindset according to which family members felt they had the 'right to work.'

> A defining moment came when all the cousins of my generation agreed to develop a succession protocol that would take effect upon the founding brothers' passing. The three had powerful personalities, so they were able to settle all their conflicts while they were alive and even establish a protocol. A representative from each line of descent helped draft the first version. We began to understand that rather than ensuring a 'right to work' for our children it was better to have a clear commitment to a legacy that embraced things other than just the family businesses. We saw how important it was to educate our children so they could fend for themselves outside the family firms, and that our example as hard working professionals was what was important. While working in the family firms, I was setting an example to my daughters, nephews and nieces, of commitment to a legacy. This is the only way, I think, that we can educate the third generation family shareholders to be responsible shareholders. Reaching an agreement on the protocol while the three founding brothers were still alive was one of the important accomplishments of the second generation. (Martín López, interview)

FINAL INSIGHTS

In the cases examined here, we started by observing the pathways of preparation and involvement for members of the next generation and noted a general trend in most of the families examined whereby the goal for second generation family member involvement was that of accomplishing intra-family ML. By contrast, the goal for the third generation was that they should not feel they had 'the right to work' in the FB.

As our observations advanced, and as we examined the relevant succession literature, we noticed that our families weren't concerned with preparing family members for what emerged as an important role: that of exercising RO.

We found then that concepts such as EL, CoPs, entrepreneurial identities-in–practice and even psychological ownership were of assistance in understanding succession better as an ongoing process not as a single event.

We consider that successful ML occurs when the wealth of the family has increased and an adequate relationship exists among the subsystems of the family unit, the business entity and individual family members. These conditions ensure a dominant coalition and a shared vision. In other words, the family leader has accomplished a metasystem leadership model.

But over and above ML of this kind, we consider RO to be successful when, as well as producing results in itself, individual family members participate in family group decisions that: enhance financial growth; contribute to facing and resolving business – and family related conflicts; and guarantee overall family harmony. In other words, RO is successful when individual members have a metasystem mindset that puts the general interest of the family above the individual's. However, it seems that the notion of RO requires further development and research. The present chapter therefore represents a call to return to the motivations behind the 2005 FBN-IFERA meeting, which was intended to encourage just such research.

This emphasis on metasystem needs, embodied in competent FB leaders and responsible family owners, represent the minimum skills that, as our Colombian cases illustrate, are required for successful FB succession to take place. Such competences may not be particular to FBs, but they do indicate potential differentiators with respect to publicly owned corporations, in which 'patient capital' attitudes, fair HR policies, and cultural sensitivity to the context – to mention just a few – are not usually present. It is also important to note that the growing partitioning of the property of family owned corporations has fostered a lack of engagement on the part of shareholders, explaining the flaws in corporate governance that are linked to such irresponsible ownership.

We observed that the educational CoPs in which members of the second generation were educated were usually FB oriented, probably due to the expectation that ML would take place. The formal education of third generation was, by contrast, freer.

The only case in which the siblings were trained up for board positions and RO from the start was that of of the Sáenz family, as Don Antonio wisely understood – the Sáenz siblings all being women – that cultural prejudices in the financial industry of the time would otherwise jeopardize the chances of his daughters gaining any management prominence.

The cases examined here show that FBs and entrepreneurial families face hardships and particularly uncertain environments. Leading an FB and exercising RO under uncertain conditions require mindsets and character strengths exemplified by high self-efficacy, such as that exercised by the siblings of founding members. Furthermore, it is not clear whether Educational CoPs and even work communities outside FBs offer the training that is required in order to exercise RO, so vital to the ongoing success of the FB. Educational CoPs are presently unaware of such needs.

When the expectations held by a member of the next generation of playing a protagonistic management role appear to vanish, RO may ensure a durable interest in contributing to family wealth and legacy. This is why Carlos Miguel's story is a case in point and one that should be given careful consideration by incumbents and family members interested in financial growth and legacy preservation. Carlos Miguel, as the 'owner's grandson,' did odd jobs while accompanying his grandfather to the factory. As a student, he had his first job as a teaching assistant, where he learned the value of money. This was a CoP in which he learnt an entrepreneurial identity-in–practice as an 'assistant to a full professor' – a role that requires considerable initiative. While in Europe, he worked as an apprentice in a multinational, performing a variety of roles. As a junior consultant at Ernst & Young and in a number of other corporations, he had dealings with the middle management of different companies. All these CoPs contributed to his acquiring several entrepreneurial identities-in–practice. If asked to work in the FB, he would bring these identities with him in order to negotiate with the incumbents the appropriate CoP, now and in the future.

But if he is not invited to join, how can the family and the FB make the most of his rich experience, enabling him to contribute to growing wealth and legacy? This is why the notion of RO requires further development.

Formal business education focuses on developing management skills, not on the roles of family member shareholders. This educational CoP is just one of many CoPs that a successor candidate experiences on the way to learning how fulfill either of these roles. The entrepreneurial identity-in–practice that individuals develop through their participation in the CoPs mentioned in this chapter helps establish their entrepreneurial preparedness. We believe this insight offers a novel and promising approach to understanding succession.

REFERENCES

Astrachan, J.H., Klein, S.B., and Smyrnios, K.X. (2002). The F-PEC scale of family influence: a proposal for solving the family business definition problem. *Family Business Review*, 15(1): 45–58.

Cheng, J.C., Ho, F.H., and Au, K. (2013). Transgenerational entrepreneurship and entrepreneurial learning: a case study of Associated Engineers Ltd in Hong Kong. In Sharma, P., Sieger, P., Nason, R.S., and Ramachandran, K. (eds), *Exploring Transgenerational Entrepreneurship: The Role of Resources and Capabilities* (Chapter 4). Cheltenham, UK and Northampton, MA, USA: Edward Elgar Publishing.

Corbett, A.C. (2005). Experiential learning within the process of opportunity identification and exploitation. *Entrepreneurship Theory and Practice*, 29(4): 473–491.

Eddleston, K.A. and Kellermanns, F.W. (2007). Destructive and productive family relationships: a stewardship theory perspective. *Journal of Business Venturing*, 22(4): 545–565.

Eisenhardt, K.M. (1989). Making fast strategic decisions in high-velocity environments. *Academy of Management Journal*, 32(3): 543–576.

Eisenhardt, K.M. and Bourgeois, L.J. (1988). Politics of strategic decision making in high-velocity environments: toward a midrange theory. *Academy of Management Journal*, 31(4): 737–770.

Habbershon, T.G. and Williams, M.L. (1999). A resource-based framework for assessing the strategic advantages of family firms. *Family Business Review*, 12(1): 1–25.

Habbershon, T.G., Williams, M., and MacMillan, I.C. (2003). A unified systems perspective of family firm performance. *Journal of Business Venturing*, 18(4): 451–465.

Hamilton, E. (2011). Entrepreneurial learning in family business: a situated learning perspective. *Journal of Small Business and Enterprise Development*, 18(1): 8–26.

Hamilton, E. (2013). *Entrepreneurship Across Generations: Narrative, Gender and Learning in Family Business*. Cheltenham, UK and Northampton, MA, USA: Edward Elgar Publishing.

Kidwell, R.E., Kellermanns, F.W., and Eddleston, K.A. (2012). Harmony, justice, confusion, and conflict in family firms: implications for ethical climate and the 'Fredo effect'. *Journal of Business Ethics*, 106(4): 503–517.

Lambrecht, J. and Uhlaner, L. (2005). *Responsible Ownership of the Family Business: State-of-the-art*. Paper presented at the FBN-IFERA World Academic Forum, Brussels, Belgium. CD-Rom.

Long, R.G., Chrisman, J.J., Melin, L., Nordqvist, M., and Sharma, P. (2014). *Management Succession in Family Business*. Thousand Oaks, CA: Sage Publications.

Miller, D. and Le Breton-Miller, I. (2006). Family governance and firm performance: agency, stewardship, and capabilities. *Family Business Review*, 19(1): 73–87.

Minniti, M. and Bygrave, W. (2001). A dynamic model of entrepreneurial learning. *Entrepreneurship Theory and Practice*, 25(3): 5–16.

Nordqvist, M., Hall, A., and Melin, L. (2009). Qualitative research on family businesses: the relevance and usefulness of the interpretive approach. *Journal of Management and Organization*, 15(3): 294.

Politis, D. (2005). The process of entrepreneurial learning: a conceptual framework. *Entrepreneurship Theory and Practice*, 29(4): 399–424.

Reuber, A. R. and Fischer, E. (1999). Understanding the consequences of founders' experience. *Journal of Small Business Management*, 37(2): 30–45.

Shanker, M.C. and Astrachan, J.H. (1996). Myths and realities: family businesses' contribution to the US economy – A framework for assessing family business statistics. *Family Business Review*, 9(2): 107–123.

Sieger, P., Zellweger, T., Nason, R.S., and Clinton, E. (2011). Portfolio entrepreneurship in family firms: a resource-based perspective. *Strategic Entrepreneurship Journal*, 5(4): 327–351.

Sorenson, R.L. (1999). Conflict management strategies used by successful family businesses. *Family Business Review*, 12(4): 325–339.

Wenger, E. (1998). *Communities of Practice: Learning, Meaning, and Identity*, Cambridge: Cambridge University Press.

Yin, R.K. (2014). *Case Study Research: Design and Methods*, Thousand Oaks, CA: Sage publications.

APPENDIX

Table 3A.1 Pathways for next generation involvement: examples using Hamilton's categories

Categories*	Pacheco	Montoya	Mejía
Main goal	M L*	M L	M L
First to second generation narratives and stages for preparedness			
Founder bringing practice to bear	After buying the Bank my dad came and said, 'It is different to be a banker than to be an insurer. As an insurer, you have to ask for money, as a banker people ask you for money.'	I had to start working at a young age. I got a job in a record factory. I learnt all the steps, from packing, recording, dealing with musicians and finally I came to understand the whole industry.	Ernesto Mejía Amaya studied electronics and managed to find work as an assistant in a battery company.
Entry second generation	I graduated from college in '74. My brother Mario started working in Colpatria in '76, and that was the first time a Pacheco had come to work in Colpatria. I came later in '81.	When I acquired the car dealership, Carlos Alberto had just finished his degree. And he liked cars . . . so he started to work there. He is still there now.	When I was little, I loved coming here and playing. The assignments I did at university, and even my thesis, were about the recycling plant – about the company.
Succession – exit	It was not hard. The day he said he was going to leave, he just left. He	My kids are in charge. My role today is to check everything. I do not have to come at 8:00,	The handover process occurred when Ernesto Mejía Amaya decided to pass on the keys.

Second and third generation narratives and stages of preparedness

Main goal	R O**	ML/R O	M L
	stayed on the boards for as long as he wanted. We always respected him and what he did until he died.	but I'm building a permanent relationship with them.	He traveled to Argentina to visit the different places where he spent his childhood, and handed over the company keys to the family's second generation.
Childhood and early work in the FB	We have an annual meeting with all members of the family, and those who are interested ask about what's going on in the firm.	On Saturdays or Sundays, I talk with my grandchildren, as I used to do with my children; I tell them 'let's play at working.' And we all come here to the office or to the stores. I'm teaching them how to work. And many times they say to me: 'we want to work with you.'	My father was always concerned that we should study, and we were able to become involved in the company from an early age. In our vacations, each of us had tasks to perform. For example, I answered the telephone and helped with the kardex.
New practice: Adult work experience outside FB	Another thing is that my dad never made a business out of Colpatria, but now we, his children, have to learn to do business on our own.	After I finished at university, I studied Business Administration. I lived a year and a half in New York and there I saw and learnt about the development of mega stores.	The girls were the only ones who worked outside the company. I worked at Arthur Andersen for three years, which was also my father's idea.
New practice: Formal training/education Free to study and follow any career	In the family there is a culture of study, work, dedication, to do something good.	I always thought about education [when my children were growing up]. That was my obsession, because I did	Most of us have two degrees – the one our father wanted for us, and the one we wanted. All of us have complemented

Table 3A.1 (continued)

Categories*	Pacheco	Montoya	Mejía
Main goal	R O**	ML/R O	M L
	This family has always honored those who do well and have degrees.	not study. Then I was always worried about their education. Nowadays you need a degree.	our education in the subjects that interest us. My younger sister, however, didn't follow my father's instructions and studied the course she wanted.
New practice: Joining the FB	Well, our vision began to change the day my grandfather decided that the third generation would not work in the company. We have attended some seminars on our own part, but I feel that, at least, we should have been trained to be good members of the board.	Maria Paula has the task of going out with them [members of new generations] many times to show them the offices, and I say: 'This is what we do here.'	Diego worked closely with Ricardo Ortiz, one of the first engineers who managed the plant and the commercial department. Luis Ernesto worked with other people, especially Edgar Oróstegui, who was a relative of my father and managed the finance department.

Categories*

	López	Sáenz
Main goal	M L	R O
Founder bringing practice to bear	My uncle León, who was single at the time, first entered the coffee business by buying coffee, milling it and then selling to large exporters. Afonso joined him and my father Luis kept his steady job in order to back his brother's ventures. During the '40s they had several partnerships with other coffee brokers and even ventured into the hardware business. The three then agreed to focus on exporting coffee.	In the early 1950s Antonio Sáenz had access to a database that provided information to travel agencies about its clients and their ability to pay. He realized that this database was an important source of information and that it could constitute the initial phase of a business opportunity.
Entry of second generation	One of the most outstanding family policies is that concerning the non-employment of family members in the companies. It came about due to the unfortunate experience that resulted from all second generation cousins and their in-laws having a 'right to work' in any of the family's companies.	In '79, my dad was kidnapped. He was freed and went to live in the US for about two months and then returned. That was when Claudia joined the company. She had already graduated from college.
Succession – exit	When the founding brothers had reached their eighties and succession rules had to be settled while they were still alive, a consultant in family companies advised the family about succession issues. Then	He started the search for a general manager from outside the family years earlier. One of his concerns was that if someone in the family took charge of the operations it could later become a source of conflict. Later, after

First to second generation narratives and stages for preparedness

73

Categories*	López	Sáenz
Main goal	M L — the first two generations agreed to a protocol whereby, from then on, third generation members would not have a 'right to work.'	R O — some try outs, he realized that John Jairo should be the General Manager, and his daughters agreed.
Main goal	R O	R O
Childhood and early work in FB	The three families felt it was a must to teach our values from childhood. They always respected each family's way of educating their children . . . but everyone instilled values and principles in their siblings from early childhood. But most of all they educated by example.	When I was around 12 years old and we went to the office with him, and experienced the feeling that you get in a big office and several departments.
New practice: Adult work experience outside FB		My daughter graduated from the Universidad de los Andes, in Industrial Engineering, and she is currently working on a company strategy. The basic idea is to work five years there and then somehow find a link here.
New practice: Formal training/education Free to study and follow any career	Mariana studied business administration; she has an MBA and is very business-minded, while my daughters are art majors and not like most of their cousins. While I had little choice but to	

Second and third generation narratives and stages of preparedness

74

| | work in the family business, since it was my father's wish that I did so, I have tried to be very cautious with my daughters about the FBs, to the point where they appear to be emotionally detached on the subject when compared with some of their cousins. | |
| New practice: Joining the FB | While working in the FB, I was setting an example to my daughters, nephews and nieces, about commitment to a legacy. This is the only way, I think, that we can educate the third generation family shareholders to be responsible. Reaching an agreement on the protocol while the three founding brothers were still alive is the greatest accomplishment of the second generation. | We consider that the best way to professionalize the company is by hiring an external manager and the new generation joining, say, the same level as us, [involved in] strategic developments and in defining and controlling things, but not in daily operations. |

Note: * Management Leadership; ** Responsible Ownership.

Source: Based upon Hamilton (2013).

4. Challenges of collective leadership
Kavil Ramachandran and Navneet Bhatnagar

MINI CASE STUDY: PREPARING THE NEXT GENERATION AT KPRT FOR SUCCESSION

In 2014, K.P. Ramesh, founder-chairman of the KPRT group[1] seriously started thinking about his successor which would be effected in 2020 when he would turn 70. As always, he wanted to start the homework early on, and wanted to devise a succession plan that would maintain continuity of business and family legacy. Though he had three equally capable next generation members, the dilemma was to whom among them to handover the leadership mantle. Among the equals, he could not anoint one individual to be 'more equal' than the others. An alternative that crossed his mind was to evolve some form of collective leadership mechanism. But how? Will it work? Ramesh struggled to find answers to such questions.

Hyderabad based KPRT group was a large player in India's infrastructure sector, with interests in power, road and airport businesses. Ramesh's entrepreneurial journey had been long and interesting. During the 1980s, Ramesh and his three brothers continued the trading business that they had inherited from their father, but later added two spinning mills and a steel rolling mill to their business. Unlike his brothers, Ramesh dreamt big, and amicably separated with them in 1988. Since then, the group had seen tremendous growth.

Family Involvement

The KPRT business family consisted of founder K.P. Ramesh (65), his sons Ravi (38) and Kumar (37) and son-in-law, Shiv Bodapati (SB) (49) (see Figure 4.1). Ravi, Kumar and SB had all taken active roles in KPRT's operations over the years and moved to lead different businesses as the group grew rapidly. Ravi headed corporate shared services and international business. He coordinated various group projects. SB headed the group's road, construction and real estate business, while Kumar became the head of airport and aviation sector operations of the group.

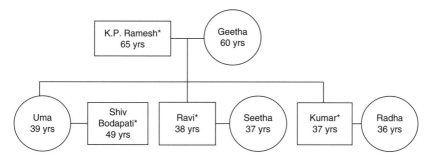

Note: * Family members involved in business.

Source: Internal reports of the KPRT group.

Figure 4.1 KPRT family tree and family's involvement in business

Working Towards a Smooth Succession and Collective Leadership

Ramesh believed that KPRT's leadership should remain among the family members after he stepped down in 2020. Women in the family were not directly involved in the business but were deeply involved in philanthropic activities through the group's corporate social responsibility arm. In 2004, Ramesh restructured the business, and gave greater strategic responsibilities to the three male members. This led to the evolution of collective strategic decision-making in the group. In 2006, the group was restructured further. An apex strategic decision-making council was formed consisting of the four family members and two non-family executives. Roles and responsibilities of all key family members were clearly defined and they were assigned tasks based on their strengths. This ensured that there were no dysfunctional conflicts. Differences, if any, were better anticipated and quickly resolved through frank discussions. In 2008, they collectively decided to rotate the key roles played by family members every three years so that all the three next-generation family members could gain experience in all business areas. In the first round of such rotation, Ramesh asked the three of them to decide among themselves their respective roles, and was happy that without any external facilitation, they decided the new roles based on an evaluation of each other's strengths and weaknesses. The second round of rotation was done the same way in 2012. They made most of the business decisions by consensus and voting was very rare. This did not lead to sub-optimal decisions as they objectively evaluated each decision situation. Besides, having worked together on various business projects, all three of them were close to each other and had mutual respect for each other's capabilities. For instance, SB was appreciative of Kumar's ingenuity, 'Kumar is an out-of-box thinker, the thought leader amongst all of us,' he commented.

All the three next generation members had proven their business management capabilities. 'All three of them understand each other very well and have for long, enjoyed equal status in both the business and the family,' explained Ramesh. In such a scenario it was proving difficult for him to pick one over the other as his successor. Ramesh was apprehensive that doing so might lead to an imbalance in their stature and may become a potential source of friction and conflict in the family. Besides, SB was his son-in-law. Appointing him to be the successor would have meant skipping the direct blood-line for succession. He was not sure whether this would be perceived with concern by anybody. On the other hand, the prospect of Ravi or Kumar superseding SB – the senior-most among the three, might disturb SB and Ramesh's daughter Uma. Therefore, Ramesh was in a dilemma.

Though the family constitution laid clear succession guidelines, Ramesh pondered whether these required to be revisited. As all the three next-generation members were equally capable and complemented each other well, Ramesh pondered whether a collective leadership model was perhaps the best way to take the business forward. Ramesh had decided to finalize the succession plan within the next 2–3 years and utilize the remaining period to mentor the next generation for leadership roles. Deciding on how to execute the succession plan and ensuring a smooth transition to a collective leadership mechanism, was his major challenge.

INTRODUCTION

Leadership succession has always been a major topic of research in family business (Brockhaus, 2004). After reviewing several studies, Astrachan et al. (2002) concluded that most family business leaders wish to retain control of their business within the family. Sharma, Chrisman, and Chua (2003) observed that succession is a planned process that is triggered by the presence of a trusted successor who is open to take on the leadership role. A major dilemma faced by many business families is the selection of one individual to lead the business when the choice is among a group of equally competent next generation members. Often issues such as dilemmas of merit versus age and social compulsions affect smooth succession. It is in this context that the idea of collective leadership (Pozza, 2010) becomes relevant for succession, where a group of family members can collectively lead the business by adopting a joint decision-making mechanism. Based on case research, this chapter presents a conceptual framework for collective leadership which a family business can explore as a viable option for leadership succession.

KPRT'S BUSINESS JOURNEY AND SUCCESSION PLANNING

During his entrepreneurial journey, Ramesh acquired in small lots a controlling stake in a Hyderabad based small private sector bank. He had to take over its chairmanship when the bank faced a leadership crisis in 1993. Managing the bank gave Ramesh valuable exposure to the world of finance and broadened his business outlook. He also learnt how lack of good governance leads to family feuds and business breakup. His involvement with the bank helped Ramesh find promising diversification opportunities. During this period, he experimented with several entrepreneurial ideas. In the early 2000s, Ramesh recognized the big opportunity presented by India's growing infrastructure sector. Soon, he ventured into construction of highways and airports.

In 2004, Ramesh restructured the group and shifted family executives from operations to strategy. The group's operations in power, roads and airports were brought under KPRT Infrastructure Ltd, which Ramesh took public in 2006. The same year, Ramesh exited the bank he was managing, when a German bank came forward to take it over.

The group consistently registered impressive growth over the years in revenue, profits and assets as shown in Table 4.1.

In another round of restructuring in 2006, the next generation members decided among themselves their roles and the board formally defined their terms of engagement. They gradually evolved a mechanism for collective functioning, with the active support of the family business board. The

Table 4.1   KPRT infrastructure – financial performance

(in INR Billions)	FY 2009	FY 2010	FY 2011	FY 2012	FY 2013	CAGR (%)
Gross Revenue	4.47	5.12	6.46	8.47	99.73	22%
EBITDA	1.06	1.36	1.55	1.65	24.77	23%
Total Assets	22.29	31.79	41.33	56.22	63.81	30%

Notes:
CAGR – compounded annual growth rate.
Average exchange rate from 2009 to 2013: 1 USD = INR 55.

Source: Annual Financial Reports of the company.

group had earned a reputation for high governance standards from early on. Simultaneously, the family created a comprehensive family constitution in 2007 that defined long-term sustainable governance structure, roles, responsibilities, norms and policies covering most aspects of the family business including succession. Retirement age for family executives was fixed at 70 years. As per the constitution guidelines, Ravi, Kumar and SB would select a successor unanimously from among themselves. If they did not reach a consensus, then a family appointed board consisting of two independent directors and a 'deadlock' facilitator would decide on succession after interviewing all the three. This process was to take place three years before Ramesh retired. Once decided, the successor would work as deputy chairman to be mentored by Ramesh. This was to ensure smooth leadership transition.

However, as the situation evolved, Ramesh realized that all three of them had unique capabilities and complemented each other and that might make it difficult for the three to choose one among them as 'the' successor over the others. He thought that none of the three would be comfortable working under the leadership of an 'equal.' It was then that he thought whether constitutional provisions on succession need to be amended to provide for the option of collective leadership. He noted, 'We already have governance structures like the family business board and the family council that support joint decision-making.' He recognized that they had developed a unique decision-making process (Table 4.2). The presence of such a mechanism was instrumental to fostering collective leadership. The moderate cohesion among next generation members and their ability to anticipate and resolve conflict also boded well for collective leadership to work as a sustainable leadership model for KPRT group. Evolving from collective decision-making to collective leadership made most sense, but the challenge was how best to manage this transition.

An alternative approach was to designate the three as the group's CEO, COO and CFO, for fixed terms on rotational basis. Yet another option was

---

BOX 4.1   MAJOR DECISIONS AT KPRT THAT EXHIBITED COLLECTIVE DECISION-MAKING

Agreement to work together.
Development of family constitution.
Formation of family council and family business board.
Agreement to rotate leadership positions among themselves.
Agreement to find a leader among the next generation members.

Source: Authors' interactions with family members.

Table 4.2   *Joint decision-making at KPRT*

Extent of Involvement in Decision Process^	Share Information	Advise	Decide	Implement
Logistics, Purchase and Materials	FBB	Rm, Rv	SB, K	SB, K
Business Strategy	FBB	Rm	SB, Rv, K	SB, Rv, K
Finance and Debt Management	FBB	Rm	SB, Rv, K	Rv
Sales and Marketing	FBB	SB	Rv, K	K
Government Interface and Liaison	FBB	Rm, SB	Rv, K	SB, K
Family Wealth Management	FBB	Rm, SB	SB, Rv, K	Rv, K
Process of Making Crucial Decision at KPRT in near term				
Decision	Share Information	Advise	Decide	Implement
Which businesses to continue/ exit?	FBB	Rm	SB, Rv, K	K
Which geographies to enter/exit?	FBB	Rm	SB, Rv, K	Rv
Debt Restructuring	FBB		SB, Rv, K	Rv
How to evolve Ownership Control?	FBB	Rm	SB, Rv, K	SB, Rv

Notes:
Rm – Ramesh, Rv – Ravi, K – Kumar and FBB – Family Business Board (includes all four family members).
^For instance, the decision on Logistics, Purchase and Materials would be taken by SB and K and implemented by them. They would be advised by Rm and Rv, while the information on the decision would be made available to FBB.

to constitute an apex business board comprising all three, as the topmost decision-making body which could make decisions based on consensus or majority, with or without external advisors. If the three next generation members continued to work as a team, it would have been easier for Ramesh to retire. This would have saved the family from any potential conflict on succession issue and the negative fallout of such a conflict on the business. Ramesh had concerns as well. What if the collective approach did not work? What would happen to the chain of command? Which governance structure should be adopted to ensure that the three remained together forever? How should he prepare the next generation members to adopt a collective leadership model to lead the group in future? Collective leadership could make or break the prospects of KPRT group and its family legacy. Ramesh was aware that he had only about six years to make this transition a smooth ride for KPRT group. He had developed a timeline for implementing the transition (see Figure 4.2).

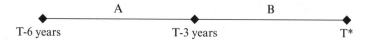

T-6 years   T-3 years   T*

Decisions planned in Phase A

- Finalize succession plan through consultative process.
- Refine and further strengthen family and business decision-making mechanism.
- Calibrate family and business systems and processes to make them adaptable or conducive to the new mode of leadership.

Decisions planned in Phase B

- Groom and mentor the successor(s) for leadership roles.
- Transition of network relationships and strategic decision-making.
- Promoting successor(s) as the new leadership as founder steps back into an advisory role.

Figure 4.2   Transition timeline developed by Ramesh

COLLECTIVE LEADERSHIP

Collective capabilities of a team are known to be much more than those of individuals working on their own. Consequently, organizations increasingly rely on work teams as businesses operate in complex, unpredictable and dynamic environments that demand diverse knowledge and skill sets (Hiller et al., 2006). This is particularly so at middle management levels, leaving top leadership mostly driven by all-powerful individuals.

Research in this area is also limited (Contractor et al., 2012). However, a close look at the studies conducted on top management teams highlights their potential for research. For instance, top management teams are known to influence organizational structure and strategy (Hambrick and Mason, 1984), organizational outcomes (Finkelstein and Hambrick, 1990) and organizational inertia (Hambrick, Geletkanycz, and Fredrickson, 1993). Denis, Lamothe, and Langley (2001) find that complementarity among members of the leadership group allows them to cover all activity domains and operate in a concerted manner. The greatest advantage of collective leadership is that it improves organizational effectiveness. In fact, evidence suggests that a team with shared leadership, having a clear sense of direction and purpose is more effective than the one that is led by a single leader (Carson, Tesluk, and Marrone, 2007).

Long-tenure top management teams that allow higher discretion to managers have been found to have a positive effect on an organization's strategic performance outcomes (Finkelstein and Hambrick, 1990). Managerial discretion or delegation can only be facilitated when the firm has adequate systems and processes that promote professional conduct and effective governance. Yet another critical factor that is a prerequisite for collective leadership is harmonious relationship among leadership team members.

COLLECTIVE LEADERSHIP IN FAMILY BUSINESS CONTEXT

A family firm's decision-making process normally undergoes major changes as both the family and business expands. Initially the controlling owner exercises complete control over all business decisions. Subsequently, when the firm transitions to a sibling partnership or a cousin consortium, a joint decision-making mechanism is evolved. This calls for a distinct set of skills and abilities that the successors need to have. Shared ownership and management demand accountability in acknowledging each other's needs, perspectives and preferences. Maintaining an effective balance of power among the siblings/cousins then emerges as the biggest challenge. It becomes crucial to carry everyone along.

Homogeneous top management teams are known to make strategic decisions more quickly and are positively associated with firm profitability in stable environments when compared with heterogeneous teams (Hambrick and Mason, 1984). Because of their shared goals and values, siblings and cousins have a high likelihood of forming a more homogenous group, which augurs well for collective leadership in a family business context. The familial cohesion is likely to be the binding force that keeps the family decision-makers together, fostering collective leadership. Family members also have a collective responsibility towards protecting the family wealth which also is an important factor bonding them well. In essence, family firms that set up mechanisms for consultations and joint decision-making early on facilitate emergence of collective leadership.

VARIANTS OF COLLECTIVE LEADERSHIP

Collective leadership can take multiple forms because every family business is unique in itself and can adopt a leadership style that best suits its requirements. It may initially emerge as a conflict avoidance mechanism but can later become an integral part of leadership governance. The degree of formalization and application of systems and processes of such mechanisms may differ across family businesses. For instance, KPRT had a much formalized structure for joint decision-making with well-defined roles and processes for the board and family council while many other family businesses may have quite informal mechanisms for joint decision-making. Based on the manner in which it evolves and gets operationalized, collective leadership can be classified into the following two broad categories:

1. Consultative Leadership

The basic premise of this style of leadership is to involve others in the decision-making process. It employs the skills, experiences and ideas of others to improve team/organizational performance. When this leadership style is followed in a family business, the top leader(s) consults all family members before making any major business decision. This also minimizes the possibility of major conflicts that may erupt in a top-down decision-making situation. The consultation process may differ in the degree of formalization. Nonetheless, all family members active in business feel empowered and involved in the decision-making process.

2. Contextual/Situational or Dynamic Leadership

These family businesses are led by a collective leadership that is cognizant of the situational needs and evolves a dynamic model of leadership. While there will be a figurehead chairperson (which may be rotational), the decision-making group evolves itself in a way that makes it more effective in a given situation. This change may include a variation in decision-making hierarchy, exchange of leadership roles among its members or change in decision-making mechanism per se. Complementary roles played by various members of the collective leadership group are critical to achieving organizational objectives (Denis, Lamothe, and Langley, 2001). Shared leadership with dynamic delegation capabilities is found to be effective in dealing with contingencies (Klein et al., 2006) and is also effective in conflict resolution. In the case of KPRT group, this variant of collective leadership was clearly evident when the leadership team constantly evolved as it responded to different business situations.

CHALLENGES TO SUSTAINING COLLECTIVE LEADERSHIP

Success of collective leadership cannot be taken for granted. Sustaining collective leadership requires active encouragement of lateral peer influence and constant demonstration of trust and confidence among leadership team members (Pearce, 2004). For collective leadership to work, on the one hand, the successors need to have persuasiveness, empathy, ability to listen, compassion and patience. On the other, they need to be focused, decisive and objective in order to be really effective as leaders. All individuals possibly cannot have all these qualities combined, and therefore there is a need to institute a systematic and objective mechanism for decision-making. Creation of a family constitution helps in defining a code of conduct and norms of managing the business and family. It could then facilitate the establishment of family and business governance structures such as a family council and a family business board. What is required for sustaining collective leadership is to cultivate it by strengthening familial bonds.

METHODOLOGY

We employed case method of research to examine the phenomenon of collective leadership in family firms. Case method has been advocated as an effective method for business research (Gibbert et al., 2008; Yin, 1994; Eisenhardt, 1989), especially for developing a fundamental understanding of a management phenomenon. Based on the interviews with the four family executives in KPRT, we observed and categorized their business decisions according to the structural domains. We then identified the process followed and extent of involvement of individual members in decision-making. We noticed the following as a pattern:

1. In certain instances, one person took the decision and kept the others informed;
2. In certain other instances, one or more persons took the decision, but took advice of some others; and
3. In certain other instances, all the members were involved in taking decisions.

It was observed that in many instances, a family member played multiple roles across this decision-making process. In order to arrive at a conceptual framework for collective leadership, we keenly observed KPRT group's family and business governance structures and mechanisms. We examined as to how their collective leadership evolved and what sort of structure, systems and processes the group had for collective leadership, and decision-making. We also studied their shared vision and values that shaped the group's family and business togetherness.

The KPRT case was deemed appropriate to be the focal case to study the phenomenon of collective leadership because all the next generation male members of the owner family were actively involved in managing the business, were equally good in terms of their capabilities, and had proven leadership quality and business acumen. Besides, it had most of the conditions present that could facilitate collective leadership such as equal importance given to all next generation members, strong family governance mechanisms and close ties among next generation members of the owner family.

FINDINGS AND DISCUSSION

We noticed several instances of the practice of collective leadership in KPRT group when Ramesh, the founder was still active. The observations made in the KPRT case study on leadership interactions, decision patterns and structural mechanisms were used to develop a conceptual framework of collective leadership, which we term as the 4C Model of Collective Leadership. Though the findings presented in this chapter are primarily based on the KPRT case, similar observations were made of collective leadership practices followed by two more Indian family businesses, namely Aurobindo (Ramachandran and Bhatnagar, 2014) and Murugappa (Ward and Zsolnay, 2004). The similarities and dissimilarities among their leadership and family business managements were compared. It was found that all the three family businesses were driven largely by effective collective leadership of family members.

A distinguishing factor at KPRT group was the active, mindful role played by the founder, K.P. Ramesh, who provided opportunities for next generation members not only to develop as individuals but also as a team by understanding the strengths and limitations of themselves and others. The founder chairman of the KPRT group took proactive steps in building and cementing family togetherness. This was done at both the family and business levels.

Founders/first generation entrepreneurs are known to influence top management teams and the ways in which organizations function and evolve (Finkelstein, 1992; Smith et al., 1994; Shamir and Howell, 1999; Nelson, 2003). We observe that collective leadership emerges as a viable leadership option where the founders/first generation leaders play an active role in fostering team management. In the case of another Indian family business, Aurobindo Pharma Ltd., two close friends co-founded and grew the company from a small manufacturing operation to a global organization with presence in over 50 countries. They adopted the model of collective leadership and divided their leadership roles based on their individual strengths – thus giving individual turfs to each one of them. In both the businesses, KPRT and Aurobindo, founders had played a pivotal role in promoting collective leadership. An important point to note is that leadership decision-making was spread across multiple dimensions including top management, family council and the board. K.P. Ramesh had a vision from early on for the group to emerge strong on corporate governance parameters. He took proactive measures to create institutionalized governance mechanisms that ensured objective, systematic and joint decision-making. Thus, we observe that collective leadership fosters well where the founder has proactively promoted governance structures to facilitate collective decision-making.

Hence, we posit that:

Proposition 1:   Collective leadership fosters well in family businesses that have an active founder/co-founder who *creates* mechanisms for and promotes collective functioning/decision-making from early on and are supported by governance structures that enable joint decision-making.

Another important factor at KPRT group that contributed to the evolution of joint decision-making and collective leadership was that the family members were close to each other yet enjoyed their own individual spaces. For instance, 'All the three next generation members have excelled in their own areas but have been close to each other both as individuals and also in managing the business. This makes the option of collective leadership a promising one for our business,' commented Ramesh on family cohesion. Family science researchers have long established the many positive influences of family cohesion on family continuity and happiness (Cumsille and Epstein, 1994; Barber and Buehler, 1996; Richmond and Stocker, 2006; Leidy, Guerra, and Toro, 2010; Olson, 2000). They suggest that family cohesion has four levels – disengaged (very low cohesion), separated (low to moderate cohesion), connected (moderate to high) and enmeshed (very high). Moderate level of cohesion (i.e. connected and separated) results in a more balanced and functional family system. This is so because it allows the family members to remain both separated (with personal time, relationships, activities and interests) and connected (together with other family members, having joint decision-making, shared activities and interests, shared relationships, emotional closeness and loyalty). KPRT group had this ideal 'moderate cohesion' in the family and business. Personal space of each family member was valued and not encroached. Each family member had his own work domain with personal decision-making space, while at the same time they were bonded together both within the family and business.

Thus, moderate cohesion is a positive factor in fostering collective leadership. We observed similar phenomena in the other two Indian family businesses too. Yet another example is that of the highly diversified Murugappa group. The five generation old Murugappa group lays a lot of emphasis on inculcating values, tradition and family cohesion, leading to the practice of collective leadership in the business. The group evolved mechanisms that allowed different members to lead as the situations warranted thus giving them individual decision-making space. Such experiences, including 'contextual leadership,' facilitated the establishment of collective leadership in the group (*Source:* Authors' personal discussions with members of Murugappa family). Thus, moderate cohesion among family members facilitates collective leadership.

Therefore, we posit that:

Proposition 2:   Collective leadership fosters in family businesses that have a moderate degree of *cohesion* among family members/co-founders.

In the family business context, collective leadership is quite relevant, especially in matters of succession as evident in the KPRT case. Business families often groom their next generation members to take on leadership roles in future with complementary capabilities. Just as the KPRT case illustrates, often siblings or cousins work together and prove themselves to be equally worthy of succeeding the existing family business leader. In such cases it is often very difficult to pick one member over the other as 'the' leader. Forcing such a choice may lead to discontent, dysfunctional conflict or even separation, eventualities that Ramesh wanted to avoid in the KPRT group. It is therefore prudent for family businesses to groom the next generation members for shared decision-making and execution of leadership tasks.

Formation of collective leadership is quite a challenge for family firms due to many reasons. For instance, children of a successful and decisive entrepreneur often lack the skills of shared decision-making and self-less collaboration (Ward, 1997) required for good collective leadership. Multigenerational family firms may be prone to conflict and resource depletion, as more family members (cousins, in-laws or other relatives) join with varied perspectives and goals (Miller and Le Breton-Miller, 2006). Consensus building becomes very difficult in such a scenario, especially when next generation members do not share a common vision for the family business. In such situations, self-interest of family members may give rise to agency problems, thus posing a serious threat to collective leadership.

Family business researchers have noted the detrimental effects of conflict on both the family and business (Gordon and Nicholson, 2008; Lee and Rogoff, 1996). These may range from sibling rivalries, marital discord to ownership and succession issues (Kellermanns and Eddleston, 2004). Differences in levels of aspirations, perspectives and orientation, and styles of functioning lead to divergence among family members. This affects possibilities of practising collective leadership. Later generation members may not have the same level of passion for the business. Also, inter-factor influence of some of these lead to ego clashes too, particularly where multiple family members are equally capable (in terms of experience and qualifications) in managing the business. Therefore, it is important to identify the 'fault lines' and anticipate areas of potential conflicts. Clear, objective, open and swift communication helps in minimizing conflicts. In case, even after taking all precautions, conflict occurs then it is best to confront the issue from the front. Swift resolution of any conflict is always advisable (Kellermanns and Schlippe, 2011) to minimize its negative fallout.

There has been a constant process of creating centripetal forces in the KPRT family as the individuals, family and business underwent changes over a period of time. Such facilitation helps even out possibilities of emergence of power centres and creates an atmosphere of trust and togetherness which are fundamental to collective leadership. In the case of KPRT, SB, Ravi and Kumar had all been proven to be skilful business managers, none of them would have liked to be perceived as any lesser than the other. The KPRT group's reshuffle of their portfolios in 2008 was primarily done to arrive at the right personality–job fit for the next generation members. This was done by the three next generation members without outside intervention. They constantly restructured the top leadership team to effectively meet the needs of any particular situation by harnessing the strengths of each family member. For instance, Ravi took charge when it came to matters of finance and Kumar led innovative thinking in the group and took leadership of the top management team when the situation so demanded, while SB took leadership of the power business, which was his strength. All three of them had demonstrated willingness to move out of their 'comfort zones' and take up new responsibilities. Collective decision-making and transparent information sharing ensured that each member knew both the strategic and tactical directions of the business. The Family Business Board and the Family Council became effective forums that prevented conflicts through prior anticipation and/or became platforms for early resolution.

Hence, we posit that:

Proposition 3:   Collective leadership fosters well in family businesses that anticipate areas of potential *conflict* among family members and evolve effective mechanisms to prevent/resolve them.

Collective leadership also has a cultural dimension. Some particular communities such as the 'Marwari' and 'Sindhi' communities in India (Lamb, 1955; Menning, 1997) have been following collectivist culture for centuries. Joint living, collective decision-making, shared business and family wealth etc. are naturally accepted by members of such communities. In the KPRT case as well, the Ramesh family belonged to a collectivist community in southern India that has strong internal bonding. Though collectivism is ingrained in the 'DNA' of such collectivist communities, younger generations seem to be increasingly affected by growing individualism. Therefore, developing collective leadership seems to be becoming a challenge even for such collectivist societies. Though in the KPRT case there were no strong individualistic tendencies among the next generation members, it was essential to keep reinforcing the family togetherness which Ramesh tried to achieve through strong family governance. Thus we observe that it is important to cultivate and regularly work towards strengthening the bonds among leadership team members.

Hence we posit that:

Proposition 4:   Collective leadership is effective only if the family business constructively *cultivates* and continuously works towards strengthening interpersonal bonds among members of the leadership team.

CONCEPTUAL FRAMEWORK FOR COLLECTIVE LEADERSHIP

Observations from the cases studied point to specific building blocks that facilitate collective leadership in family businesses. At the fundamental level, this requires inculcation of family values across family members. A shared vision was another commonality among the three businesses. Values and vision shape the way both the family and the business conduct themselves and influence leadership. Opportunity to create and enjoy material wealth also played a significant role. Collective leadership also requires appropriate governance structures and systems. All the three

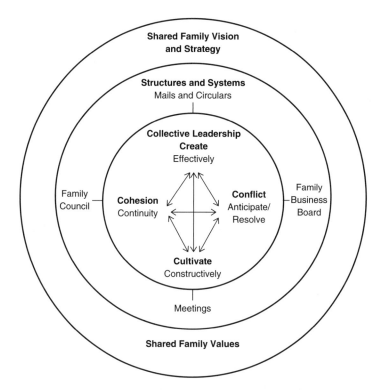

Figure 4.3   Conceptual framework for collective leadership in a family business

businesses we studied had set up a governance structure each for the family and the business. These structures with appropriate systems and processes need to be regularly refined for them to remain relevant and effective in strengthening collective leadership. Based on our observations in the KPRT case, we propose a 4C framework for collective leadership (see Figure 4.3).

The four interactive forces that influence and shape collective leadership are:

1. *Create* effectively – the enabling mechanisms for collective leadership proactively created by the founder/first generation entrepreneur.
2. *Cohesion* continuity – regularly working to strengthen bonds of togetherness while providing individual space to the family members.
3. *Conflict*: anticipate and resolve – constantly guarding the fault lines and working towards swift resolution.

4. *Cultivate* constructively – proactively working towards strengthening interpersonal bonds.

These forces constantly shape the collective leadership and are supported by a circle of structure and systems, comprising the family council and family business board. Regular and open channels of communication effected through meetings, mails and circulars help in keeping everyone informed. All of these systems and mechanisms need to be regularly refined and calibrated to fit the dynamic requirements of the family business.

The circle of structures and systems is enveloped by the circle bearing shared family vision, strategy and values. The vision and strategy undergoes periodic refinement in today's frequently evolving environment. These strategic shifts influence the functioning of collective leadership. The most enduring element of the framework is the shared family values, which influence everything a family business does. Family values are resolute and shared across generations. These core values influence all other aspects of the framework. The collective leadership framework (as shown in Figure 4.3) enables due representation of both the family and the business in the collective leadership. The framework deliberately refrains from prescribing any specific form that the collective leadership may acquire. This is done because every family business and the circumstances in which it operates are unique in some way. Therefore, it is fit for the members of the managing family to decide as to what form the collective leadership should take. Among the alternatives that they may choose are:

1. Equal status and clearly spelt out decision-making rights to all members in the top leadership (for example, each one may be a director with equal rights and rewards).
2. Shared top executive positions that are rotated among the collective leadership after a fixed term (for instance, members may be designated as CEO, CFO and COO for a fixed term, after which they rotate positions in an agreed manner).
3. Shared leadership responsibility based on best competence/personality-role fit (for instance, a member with competence and proven expertise in managing finance may lead that area, while a member who is market savvy or a deft communicator may lead marketing).

CONCLUSION

'Collectivism' and team based leadership is an alternative leadership model that has not attracted adequate attention of researchers. Family businesses, by nature, form one of the best contexts for collective leadership to flourish. The above discussion provides some of the basic dimensions to be considered to study collective leadership. Though collective leadership is based on cohesion, the family firm must ensure that there is role clarity among all family business leaders. It is beneficial for the family firms to formulate a clear power structure and define both the collective and individual domains.

Collective leadership becomes a viable mode for succession where selecting one member or the other is extremely difficult, given very similar capabilities and strengths. Family firms must explore the option of process-based collective leadership in which the decision-making power is jointly exercised by the leadership group.

Implications

Family firms with several capable members belonging to the next generation may explore and adopt the collective model of leadership suggested here. This is even more relevant to those businesses where the next generation members score very close to each other in terms of their capabilities, education and training, business acumen and proven track record of effective performance. In such a close match of capabilities, anointing one person as the successor may lead to dysfunctional conflict and can mar the succession process. On the other hand, collective leadership based on objective governance mechanisms can be very effective and deliver the benefit of complementary skill sets of all the next generation members. Family firms can prepare their next generations for collective leadership by:

1. Inculcating shared values such as flexibility, transparency and caring and business vision among family members.
2. Setting up a family business board as the apex business decision-making body of the family.
3. Strict adherence to governance principles.
4. Providing a facilitating environment supported by family seniors or external advisors.
5. Regular refinement of the structural mechanisms to keep pace with the changing internal and external environments.

It is important not to lose the collective spirit of family while imbibing the arguments for separating ownership and management in business. Visionary family firms prepare their next generation members for collective leadership to ensure long-term survival and stability of their business.

We suggest that this can be achieved by working simultaneously on multiple fronts as shown in Figure 4.3. The spirit of 'familiness' prevailing in the family is the most crucial determinant of the destiny of a family business. This spirit should encourage family business leaders to explore collective leadership as a route to sustain their business across generations. That would strengthen 'togetherness' and ensure continuity of purpose and entrepreneurship.

However, further research exploration in this direction will provide deeper insight. The interest of family firms will be served well if they actively work towards developing collective leadership as a sustainable succession option.

NOTE

1. The business location, names of the 'KPRT' family business group and that of the individuals mentioned in the case have been disguised for confidentiality reasons.

REFERENCES

Astrachan, J.H., Allen, I.E., and Spinelli, S. (2002). Mass mutual/Raymond Institute *American Family Business Survey*. Springfield, MA: Mass Mutual Financial Group.

Barber, B.K. and Buehler, C. (1996). Family cohesion and enmeshment: different constructs, different effects. *Journal of Marriage and the Family*, 433–441.

Brockhaus, R.H. (2004). Family business succession: suggestions for future research. *Family Business Review*, 17(2): 165–177.

Carson, J.B., Tesluk, P.E., and Marrone, J.A. (2007). Shared leadership in teams: an investigation of antecedent conditions and performance. *Academy of Management Journal*, 50(5): 1217–1234.

Contractor, N.S., DeChurch, L.A., Carson, J., Carter, D.R., and Keegan, B. (2012). The topology of collective leadership. *The Leadership Quarterly*, 23(6): 994–1011.

Cumsille, P.E. and Epstein, N. (1994). Family cohesion, family adaptability, social support, and adolescent depressive symptoms in outpatient clinic families. *Journal of Family Psychology*, 8(2): 202–214.

Denis, J.L., Lamothe, L., and Langley, A. (2001). The dynamics of collective leadership and strategic change in pluralistic organizations. *Academy of Management Journal*, 44(4): 809–837.

Eisenhardt, K.M. (1989). Building theories from case study research. *Academy of Management Review*, 14(4): 532–550.

Finkelstein, S. (1992). Power in top management teams: dimensions, measurement, and validation. *Academy of Management Journal*, 35(3): 505–538.

Finkelstein, S. and Hambrick, D.C. (1990). Top-management team tenure and organizational outcomes: the moderating role of managerial discretion. *Administrative Science Quarterly*, 35: 484–503.

Gibbert, M., Ruigrok, W., and Wicki, B. (2008). What passes as a rigorous case study? *Strategic Management Journal*, 29(13): 1465–1474.

Gordon, G. and Nicholson, N. (2008). *Family Wars. Classic Conflicts in Family Business and How to Deal With Them*. London/Philadelphia: Kogan Page.

Hambrick, D.C. and Mason, P.A. (1984). Upper echelons: the organization as a reflection of its top managers. *Academy of Management Review*, 9(2): 193–206.

Hambrick, D.C., Geletkanycz, M.A., and Fredrickson, J.W. (1993). Top executive commitment to the status quo: some tests of its determinants. *Strategic Management Journal*, 14(6): 401–418.

Hiller, N.J., Day, D.V., and Vance, R.J. (2006). Collective enactment of leadership roles and team effectiveness: a field study. *The Leadership Quarterly*, 17(4): 387–397.

Kellermanns, F.W. and Eddleston, K. (2004). Feuding families: when conflict does a family firm good. *Entrepreneurship Theory and Practice*, 28(3): 209–228.

Kellermanns, F.W. and Schlippe, A.v. (2011). Beziehungskonflikte in Familienunternehmen und ihre Bedeutung für die Unternehmensführung (slightly modified and updated). In A. Koeberele-Schmid (ed.), *Governance in Familienunternehmen* (2nd edn) (429–442). Berlin: Erich Schmidt Verlag.

Klein, K.J., Ziegert, J.C., Knight, A.P., and Xiao, Y. (2006). Dynamic delegation: shared, hierarchical, and deindividualized leadership in extreme action teams. *Administrative Science Quarterly*, 51(4): 590–621.

Lamb, H.B. (1955). The Indian business communities and the evolution of an industrialist class. *Pacific Affairs*, 101–116.

Lee, M.-S. and Rogoff, E.G. (1996). Research note: Comparison of small businesses with family participation versus small businesses without family participation: an investigation of differences in goals, attitudes, and family/business conflict. *Family Business Review*, 9(4): 423–437.

Leidy, M.S., Guerra, N.G., and Toro, R.I. (2010). Positive parenting, family cohesion, and child social competence among immigrant Latino families. *Journal of Family Psychology*, 24(3): 252–260.

Menning, G. (1997). Ethnic enterprise in the decentralised textile industry of Surat, India. *Journal of Entrepreneurship*, 6(2): 141–164.

Miller, D. and Le Breton-Miller, I. (2006). Family governance and firm performance: agency, stewardship, and capabilities. *Family Business Review*, 19(1): 73–87.

Nelson, T. (2003). The persistence of founder influence: management, ownership, and performance effects at initial public offering. *Strategic Management Journal*, 24(8): 707–724.

Olson, D.H. (2000). Circumplex model of marital and family systems. *Journal of Family Therapy*, 22: 144–167.

Pearce, C.L. (2004). The future of leadership: combining vertical and shared leadership to transform knowledge work. *The Academy of Management Executive*, 18(1): 47–57.

Pozza, E.J. (2010). *Family Business* (3rd edn). London: Cengage Learning.

Ramachandran, K. and Bhatnagar, N. (2014). Professionalization efforts at Aurobindo Pharma, in Sharma, P., Yusof, M., Parada, M.J., DeWitt, R-L., and Auletta, N. (eds), *Global STEP Booklet, Volume II; Sustaining Entrepreneurial Family Businesses: Developing the Core, Expanding the Boundaries* (Chapter 6, 45–50), retrieved on May 13, 2015 from http://digitalknowledge.babson.edu/cgi/viewcontent.cgi?article=1012&context=sumrep.

Richmond, M.K. and Stocker, C.M. (2006). Associations between family cohesion and adolescent siblings' externalizing behavior. *Journal of Family Psychology*, 20(4): 663–669.
Shamir, B. and Howell, J.M. (1999). Organizational and contextual influences on the emergence and effectiveness of charismatic leadership. *The Leadership Quarterly*, 10(2): 257–283.
Sharma, P., Chrisman, J.J., and Chua, J.H. (2003). Succession planning as planned behavior: some empirical results. *Family Business Review*, 16(1): 1–15.
Smith, K.G., Smith, K.A., Olian, J.D., Sims Jr, H.P., O'Bannon, D.P., and Scully, J.A. (1994). Top management team demography and process: the role of social integration and communication. *Administrative Science Quarterly*, 412–438.
Ward, J.L. (1997). Growing the family business: special challenges and best practices. *Family Business Review*, 10(4): 323–337.
Ward, J.L. and Zsolnay, C.A. (2004). *The Murugappa Group: Centuries Old Business Heritage and Tradition*. Evanston, IL: Kellogg School of Management, Northwestern University.
Yin, R.K. (1994). *Case Study Research: Design and Methods*. London: Sage Publications.

PART II

Familial values and professionalization

5. Transgenerational professionalization of family firms: the role of next generation leaders

Mara Brumana, Lucio Cassia, Alfredo De Massis, Allan Discua Cruz and Tommaso Minola*

> We would have never taken this risk and grown this venture across generations without going through a professionalization path.
> (Marcello Persico, 2nd generation family member, talking about the acquisition of a new venture in Spain)

MINI CASE STUDY: PERSICO SpA

Persico SpA was established in 1976 in Nembro (Bergamo, Italy) by Pierino Persico, a brilliant craftsman who enjoyed creating models for diverse artefacts. The company was originally founded as a wooden model workshop and in a few years became an established and reputable business that grew significantly by focusing on the manufacturing of moulds (hollow containers used to give shape to molten or hot liquid materials as they cool and harden). Over the years, Persico SpA became a well-diversified business with several business divisions. The first two were Persico Automotive, which progressively specialized in the manufacturing of moulds for interior parts and sound–heat insulation for vehicles, and Persico Rotomoulding, dedicated to the production of rotational aluminium moulds. Persico SpA developed strong expertise in these fields, gradually becoming the leading European manufacturer in both markets.

To promote the firm's growth in different industries, sectors and products, Pierino carefully selected professional family and non-family managers, granting them autonomy in managing and developing the different business units. In 1984, the company launched Persico Rotomoulding after obtaining a license for a rotational moulding system. The Engineering department was created in 2002 for the development of a patented rotational moulding machine with a completely automated cycle. A fourth division, Persico Marine, was created in 2004 to develop nautical projects from design up to prototype manufacturing.

By the year 1998, Persico SpA had turned into a second generation family firm. The first generation is represented by the founder Pierino and the second generation by his two daughters, Claudia and Alessandra, and his son, Marcello. In recent decades, the two generations have jointly led the firm. While Pierino is chairman, the second generation members are managing directors of the three divisions: Automotive, Rotomoulding and Marine. The second generation recognizes Pierino as the 'most entrepreneurial' figure in the firm, always associated with superior creativity, inner passion and commitment. He is also known for his enthusiasm for new ideas, supporting new initiatives, his belief in innovation and his ability to foresee potential opportunities.

Pierino in turn acknowledges that in the modern era new challenges tend to make the second generation's representatives the new family entrepreneurs. His views are insightful for the company and those leading it:

> [W]hat has worked well so far is not assumed, despite all our efforts, to ensure our future tomorrow. . . . Today we have reached such a level of sophistication that it is now really up to my children . . . when we talk about internationalization, employment of skilled top managers, entry in new markets, acquisitions, partnerships . . . I feel I am leaving such a challenge in their hands, and on the other, such great responsibilities. . . . They are the decision-makers of the development, now it is all theirs . . . today the craftsman's mindset is no longer sufficient to make the business entrepreneurial and survive; greater attention to external and international markets is needed.

Pierino recognizes the prowess and abilities of the second generation in facing business challenges and seeking new opportunities. Pierino is aware of the complexity of pursuing entrepreneurial opportunities in the current economic context and affirms that the professional skills of the second generation leaders are particularly relevant in facing such challenges.

The second generation members pursue international business opportunities and alliances, which in 2011 led to the potential acquisition of Future Fibres, a firm in Spain looking for a partner to build carbon masts. This initiative would allow Persico's marine division to strengthen its value chain with new activities such as planning and design while providing a link to boat racing teams worldwide, which had tremendous commercial potential. Future Fibres was open to acquisition by Persico. However, this path involved risks related to a substantial financial investment and the evident need for operational and cultural integration with Future Fibres. The key challenges were preserving Persico's and Future

Fibre's identities in their local contexts while also meeting the family objectives.

Contrary to mainstream managerial logic, which emphasizes engaging external advisors, the Persico family decided to exploit internally available professional skills, specifically those that Marcello had acquired while working at the Boston Consulting Group, one of the 'Big Four' consultancies in the world. Aided by Persico's application of specialized management tools – performance and financial evaluations, strategic planning tools and structured governance mechanisms – Marcello launched the corporate venture with a high degree of autonomy from his father. Persico thus acquired 25 per cent of Future Fibres. In subsequent years and through a series of capital investments, Persico came to acquire control of 75 per cent (a threshold reached in 2013) of Future Fibres.

DISCUSSION QUESTIONS

1. Which skills and entrepreneurial attitudes significantly distinguish the two generations involved in Persico and how do these relate to professionalization?
2. What factors influence the family firm's choice to professionalize by using internal versus external resources?

INTRODUCTION

This chapter deals with 'transgenerational professionalization' or the professionalization of the family firm that occurs in parallel with transferring leadership from one generation to the next. Attention to transgenerational professionalization is important since renewing business policies and improving professionalization are particularly relevant when significant disruptions – such as an intra-family succession – occur in family firms (Dekker et al., 2013).

While research provides relevant insights into family firm professionalization, a transgenerational perspective on professionalization and its effects on the entrepreneurial attitudes of next generation leaders is still lacking. We believe this study will conceptually and empirically add to the understanding of professionalization in family firms, particularly in a theoretical transgenerational entrepreneurship framework.

Drawing on a longitudinal case study conducted within the Successful Transgenerational Entrepreneurship Practices (STEP) project, this chapter contributes to the current debate on family firm professionalization and highlights the specific role played by next generation leaders. Particularly, we investigate the specific drivers that can sustain or constrain the transgenerational professionalization of a family firm and its effects on the entrepreneurial attitudes of next generation leaders. The evidence is drawn from Persico SpA, an Italian family firm established in 1976 specializing in mould manufacturing. It has developed a well-diversified portfolio of four divisions and become leader in different markets at the European level. The divisions are led by professional family members and non-family managers. The overall corporate structure allows each division to be run independently with a sustained entrepreneurial orientation.

Our findings confirm the most recent perspectives and go beyond the limits of binary approaches to family firm professionalization (Dekker et al., 2015). Evidence from Persico illustrates that transgenerational learning, organizational structures based on the family structure, internal growth, environmental challenges and the entrepreneurial orientation of the founding generation are conducive to transgenerational professionalization. Conversely, an overlap of ownership and management and emotional involvement can hinder family firm transgenerational professionalization. The evidence allows us to consider the impact of transgenerational professionalization on the entrepreneurial attitudes of next generation leaders.

Overall, this exploratory study puts forward propositions on the enabling and constraining factors that influence the transgenerational professionalization of family firms. Particularly, it explores the role of next generation family leaders in accomplishing firm professionalization in the generational transition and fostering entrepreneurial orientation.

The chapter is structured as follows. First, we introduce the Italian family business context and extant literature on professionalization and transgenerational professionalization in family firms. Thereafter, we describe the methodology and case study analyzed: Persico SpA. Finally, we develop an emerging framework and a related set of propositions highlighting factors that play a key role in the professionalization of family firms in a generational transition. We also explore the link between transgenerational professionalization and transgenerational entrepreneurship. The limitations of the study and future research directions are also provided.

THEORETICAL BACKGROUND

Family Businesses in Italy

Family firms dominate the Italian economic landscape and have a significant impact on society. Ninety-two per cent of all Italian firms, including 42 of the 100 largest firms in the country, and 58 per cent of those with annual earnings of over 50 million euro, are family businesses (CERIF, 2008; Osservatorio AUB, 2011). Italian family firms account for 52 per cent of national employment and contribute 70 per cent of the total industrial GDP (CERIF, 2008). Thus, family firms have a strong influence in the creation of employment, social and economic wealth (Habbershon and Pistrui, 2002; Shanker and Astrachan, 1996). Between 2003 and 2011, as compared with non-family firms, Italian family firms have performed exceptionally well. These firms have reported experienced increased employment, and above average returns on equity and investment (Osservatorio AUB, 2009, 2010, 2011).

In Italy, family business succession in the family sphere is socially expected and often intended. Yet current studies show that only 50 per cent of Italian family businesses survive the transition from the first to the second generation, and only 15 per cent pass from the second to the third generation (CNEL, 2006). At the end of 2008, the statistics on Italian family firms reporting earnings of over 50 million euro show that 30.9 per cent are led by the founding or first generation member, 50.7 per cent by the second generation, 14.6 per cent by the third and only 3.8 per cent by the fourth or subsequent generation (Osservatorio AUB, 2009). Interestingly, although succession is intended, low growth and profitability mark Italian family firms when the business is transferred from one generation to the next.

Currently, the succession panorama in Italian family enterprises is challenging. According to a recent report, 80 per cent of 80,000 Italian entrepreneurs consider the succession decision as one of the most problematic issues facing existing firms (Osservatorio AUB, 2009). As succession is a process at the heart of any family business (De Massis et al., 2014a; Howorth et al., 2010) and a way of keeping the family involved in the business (Yu, 2013) it draws the attention of researchers and consultants alike. In such a critical yet fragile process for family firms (De Massis, Chua and Chrisman, 2008), identifying the factors that may facilitate their survival over time and the development of next generation leaders is paramount. Recent studies caution that the lack of succession planning, closely linked to the absence of timely professionalization, could explain the demise of family businesses (Chittoor and Das, 2007). Thus, researchers and practitioners need to consider the key processes that support the professionalization of firms during generational transitions (Gimeno and Parada, 2013).

Professionalization and Transgenerational Entrepreneurship in Family Businesses

In mainstream business literature, firm professionalization refers to the firm's evolution through its organizational life cycle and consists of the introduction of complex management and organizational systems such as formal planning, regular scheduled meetings, defined responsibilities, performance appraisal systems, formal training, management development, formal governance bodies and control systems (Flamholtz, 1986; Flamholtz and Randle, 2007).

Prior studies highlight that family firms can significantly benefit from professionalization as it can prepare family and non-family employees for upcoming challenges. Human resource practices, training and development, recruitment packages, morale maintenance, performance appraisals and competitive compensation (e.g. cash incentives at different levels of the organization) have proven favourable to family firm performance (Carlson et al., 2006). Focusing on the role of training in firms, Kotey and Folker (2007) argue that management training can benefit the survival and performance of small and medium enterprises (English, 2001) and that education is a key factor of firm growth (MacRae, 1991). Thus, training and education are essential components of professionalization, particularly when family firms grow and reach outside their local borders (Wright and Nasierowski, 1994).

Extant literature also converges on common assumptions on professionalization in family firms. A lack of entrepreneurial and professional behaviours is often associated with family firms (Habbershon and Pistrui, 2002). Indeed, most family businesses have the following characteristics: small size (Gumpert and Boyd, 1984), stagnation (Daily and Dollinger, 1992), nepotism (Vinton, 1998) and conflict (Prince, 1990). Furthermore, Kotey and Folker (2007) underline that family firms are inclined to informal management styles and may only adopt more formal practices when facing growth (Reid and Adams, 2001; Leon-Guerrero, McCann and Haley, 1998). Additionally, in family firm literature, professionalization most often entails hiring external non-family managers and the majority of empirical studies focus on this particular aspect (Chua et al., 2003; Dekker et al., 2015). For instance, Colombo et al. (2014) studied a matched sample of 144 Italian high-tech firms and found that family firms are more reluctant to hire non-family employees in correspondence with an increase in sales compared with their non-family ownership counterparts. In addition, they found that in comparison with firms led by same generation teams of siblings, cousins or husbands/wives, those led by parental teams with multiple generations are less likely to hire employees in correspondence with an increase in sales. This signals the importance of adopting an 'intergenerational' perspective when studying family firm professionalization. Professional management is largely equated with the entry of external, non-family managers, whereas family members are generally considered as non-professional and thus prone to being replaced or ignored in positions that can enhance firm performance and growth. Overall, the influence of the family on a business is traditionally perceived as complicating the firm's professionalization, and this complexity is likely to increase when a transgenerational perspective is adopted due to the temporal evolution of the family and the business systems (De Massis et al., 2014c).

We believe that one reason for the misperceptions surrounding professionalization and family firms is that current research views this form of business organization as too traditional and neglects the transgenerational perspective on the professionalization of family firms and its effects on the entrepreneurial attitudes of next generation leaders. Hall and Nordqvist (2008) highlight, for example, that prior studies equate professionalization with bureaucracy, occurring mostly outside the family firm realm, and mainly related to the attainment of formal education and training. Recent studies paint a more balanced picture. Stewart and Hitt (2012) show that there are different modes of professionalization that can be affected by several dimensions that may overlap in the family and business spheres. Thus, as family firms pursue multiple and diverse goals (Kotlar and De Massis, 2013; Westhead and Howorth, 2007), diverse forms of professionalization emerge (Stewart and Hitt, 2012). These recent studies highlight that further research is needed on how professionalization may affect family businesses. While an increasing body of knowledge has been developed in the family business domain, limited attention has been paid to professionalization in the perspective of transgenerational entrepreneurship (Gimeno and Parada, 2013).

This chapter investigates *transgenerational professionalization*, defined as the professionalization of the family firm that occurs in parallel with the process of transferring leadership from one generation to the next. Professionalization and the renewal of family firm policies go hand in hand, particularly when a significant disruption such as intra-family succession occurs (Dekker et al., 2013). In this study, we acknowledge that professionalization in family firms is a dynamic process (Hall and Nordqvist, 2008) and a multidimensional concept (Dekker et al., 2013; Stewart and Hitt, 2012) that may further explain the heterogeneity of family firms. We argue that transgenerational entrepreneurship, namely, the ability to achieve continuity, growth and wealth by passing on mindsets and capabilities for value creation across different generations (Nordqvist and Zellweger, 2010) is a relevant working framework to approach the study of professionalization. To advance knowledge, we consider the studies of Gimeno and Parada (2013), Fletcher (2002), Stewart and Hitt (2012) and Hall and Nordqvist (2008) to conceptualize professionalization in a transgenerational entrepreneurship perspective.

THE PERSICO CASE

The Firm

Persico SpA is a second generation family firm located in Bergamo, Italy. The firm was established in 1976 by Pierino Persico and is active in the manufacturing of moulds. Over the years, it has developed a well-diversified business and become European leader in specific markets. Persico SpA comprises four business units: Automotive, Rotomoulding, Engineering and Marine. The Automotive division supplies equipment for the production of interior parts and sound–heat insulation to the automotive industry. The Rotomoulding division is world leader in the supply of equipment for rotational moulding serving the automotive, furniture, agricultural, ecology, packaging, gardening and other industries. The Engineering department develops complex automated production lines and was established to provide a customer service function. The Marine division focuses on boat (pleasure yachts, hulls for racing boats) design and engineering, model construction and pre-series production as well as co-design support. The current organizational structure of each division is autonomous while ensuring interaction and knowledge exchange. As shown in Figure 5.1, specific units assist the main divisions while the operational, technical and marketing offices are located at the individual division level.

The history of Persico is characterized by outstanding entrepreneurial impetus: an extraordinary ability to innovate supported by R&D investments (4–5 per cent of total sales), proactiveness and risk taking, which evolved following the involvement of second generation members. Accordingly, the firm has launched an increasing number of entrepreneurial initiatives over the last five years. To name a few: entry into the marine industry, innovation through the development of new products, increased presence in Europe and the United States. These initiatives show the second generation's commitment to nurturing and continuing the firm's entrepreneurial orientation. At the same time, the second generation intentionally promotes the progressive managerialization and professionalization of Persico to meet emergent needs.

Company revenues doubled from 2000 to 2008, and the company

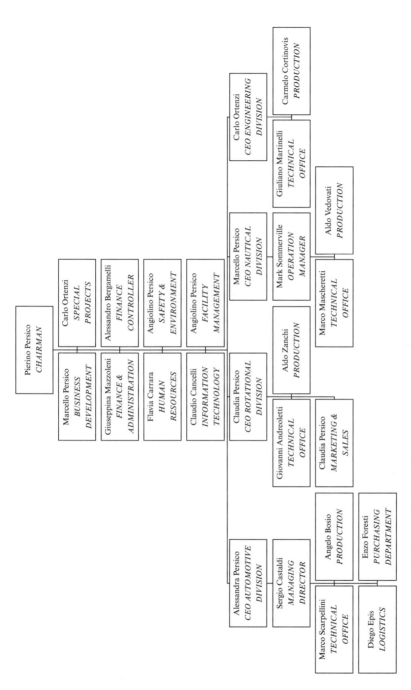

Figure 5.1   Persico SpA organization chart

thrived despite the recent global economic turmoil. In 2010, Persico registered total revenues of 51.3 million euro[1] and employed 190 staff. Financial
and economic indicators show around 6 per cent ROE and 4 per cent ROA,
reporting an increase in 2010. The stable dividend distribution, the focus
on increasing equity and the reduction of long-term debt are testimony
of Persico's willingness to invest in the long-term rather than to pursue
short-term financial returns.

The Family and the Business

Persico SpA is currently led by the second generation. Figure 5.2 shows
the Persico family tree showing only the members who have or have had an
active role in the firm.

The company has always been tightly owned and controlled by the
Persico family. Pierino is the main shareholder, owning 35 per cent of
equity and retains the usufruct[2] of 18 per cent of shares (equally distributed among his three children). His wife is the second largest shareholder
with 20 per cent of shares. The remaining company shares are all equally
distributed among the second generation, each owning 9 per cent of
capital (plus 6 per cent each in usufruct to their father). Pierino Persico is
chairman of the board, and his children are the managing directors of the
three divisions (Rotomoulding, Automotive and Marine).

The first generation of the family in the firm is represented by

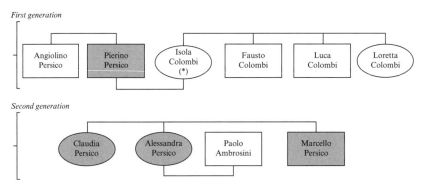

Notes:
Rectangles represent males and ellipses females; the members interviewed for this study are
highlighted.
* Isola Colombi, wife of Pierino Persico, is a shareholder of the company but is not
involved in the business.

Figure 5.2   Persico family members active in the business

Pierino Persico: a charismatic leader who is still active in the business and is well-known in the local community. His two daughters, Claudia and Alessandra, and his son, Marcello, represent the second generation. Claudia is managing director of the Rotomoulding division; she has a degree in marketing and communications from IULM University in Milan. She joined Persico SpA in 1998 after a briefly working in a partner company in the United States. Alessandra (two years younger than Claudia) is managing director of the Automotive division. She has a bachelor degree in engineering with a focus on logistics and production from the Politecnico di Milano. She joined the firm in 2001 in a temporary role but her involvement increased after an order from the United States was not successfully fulfilled. She was determined not to let this happen again and attained the position of managing director. Marcello (six years younger than Alessandra) is managing director of the Marine division and also director of the Business Development unit. He has a degree in business management from Bocconi University (graduated in 2005) and joined the company after two years with the Boston Consulting Group. A 'shared leadership' approach among the second generation family members, with each of the three siblings individually leading three main divisions, is one of the most particular attributes of Persico SpA. Other relatives work (or have worked) in the company with minor roles. The Engineering Department is a cross-divisional support unit managed by Carlo Ortenzi (non-family member), a professional who joined the company in 2004.

Method

The case study has been developed according to the STEP Project methodology, namely, through a series of personal in-depth interviews with 'strategically relevant actors' and the analysis of secondary data such as financial reports, company patent awards and newspaper reports. Secondary sources were used to verify the interview data and ensure objectivity in the data collection process. The use of multiple data sources enabled the triangulation of evidences (Yin, 2003). The interviews focused on the transgenerational potential of the new generations, the professionalization of the firm and its main drivers, challenges, strengths and weaknesses. The case has been analyzed longitudinally. The interviews were conducted between 2010 and 2012[3] and included the firm's most influential top managers. The aim was to reach all the active family members representing the two generations and non-family managers to gather multiple points of view. The interviewee profiles are reported in Table 5.1. Each interview lasted on average 2.5 hours and was then recorded and transcribed.

Table 5.1   Profile of the Persico SpA interviewees

Name	Family/ Non-family	Current position in the firm (as of February 2011)	Joined Persico in
Pierino Persico	Family	Chairman of the Board	1976
Claudia Persico	Family	Managing Director of the Rotomoulding division	1998
Alessandra Persico	Family	Managing Director of Automotive division	2001
Marcello Persico	Family	Managing Director of the Marine division	2008
Alessandro Bergamelli	Non-family	Controller	1999
Lorenzo Bergamo	Non-family	R&D Manager	2001
Flavia Carrara	Non-family	Human Resources Manager	2007
Giusi Mazzoleni	Non-family	Finance and Administration Manager	2000

Evidence of Transgenerational Professionalization

The professionalization of Persico SpA is strictly related to the succession as repeatedly highlighted during the interviews. In particular, Claudia and Marcello, when asked to point out the second generation's main contribution, immediately and spontaneously mentioned the words 'managerialization' and 'professionalization'. A transition from the 'entrepreneurial domain' to the 'managerial domain' took place across the two generations: the small and 'familiar' laboratory became a large and well-structured firm with a turnover of 50 million euro and almost 200 employees. The second generation members argued that this transition was the result of the second generation's efforts. The interviewees recognized very different individual traits and capabilities in the members of the two generations. Pierino is a creative and 'revolutionary' individual often referred to as 'entrepreneurial'. His offspring are perceived as more 'methodical and rational', often described as 'more managerial'.

The concrete activities and initiatives show that the professionalization of Persico SpA was transgenerational, that is, it occurred during the transfer of leadership from the first to the second generation. The second generation members first supported the creation of a Balanced Scorecard system, starting with the Automotive division. This meant the definition of performance indicators and measures linked to reward mechanisms (see Craig and Moores, 2005). Thereafter, quantitative incentive measures were tied to benefits in the Rotomoulding division. The reward system was based on measurable, structured and detailed drivers for almost all the workforce with a current trend of increasing benefits on total compensation. The introduction of these initial tools supported individual staff initiatives and commitment and thus proactiveness in the firm.

Additional initiatives in the Automotive division included a vendor rating system and a structured quality control system that helps identify faulty products. The latest initiative is a product life cycle management system implemented in the last three years. These initiatives implied significant investments in equipment (software and hardware) and has advanced the process of managing product-related design, production and maintenance information. In the Marine division, formal order administration methods were introduced to improve the tracking of orders and to enable detailed analyses and reports of production costs and time. In the Rotomoulding division, a new method of production planning was introduced to forecast and cater for floating demand. All these tools and mechanisms required the accurate definition of business and operational processes and have increased efficiency due to the better allocation of tasks and responsibilities.

Further company-wide initiatives include the creation of a centralized purchasing department with positive effects on cost efficiency. The strategic and business planning system (see Jones, 1982; Ward, 1988) led to the introduction of diverse and formal business practices: annual forecasts are now drawn up (e.g. forecasts on annual research and development costs), which help set goals and targets for managers in the divisions which are monitored and adjusted on a monthly basis. The change and improvement in recruiting processes is another illustrative example of the firm's professionalization. The second generation members promote the formal recruitment systems to foster the firm's innovativeness, proactiveness and competitive aggressiveness. Moreover, the approach to risk has evolved. This is evidenced by the adoption of business plans in support of an acquisition in the United States. The business plans have benefited from sophisticated analyses and strategic decisions on 'greenfield' investments versus acquisitions (Kogut and Singh, 1988), on the selection of target firms, as well as due diligence assessments, research on target customers, potential market analyses, cash flow forecasts and complex financial scenarios.

All these managerial tools, mechanisms and projects can be defined as transgenerational since they were introduced and developed by the second generation members or at least promoted by them when development was delegated to non-family managers (see Table 5.2).

The evidence presented shows the second generation members' efforts and achievements in the professionalization of Persico SpA.

Table 5.2   Professionalization tools, role of the 2nd generation and organizational impact

Transgenerational professionalization tools	Role of second generation	Organizational impact
Use of budget (annual forecasts and business plans)	P	Supporting the internationalization process
Formalized goals and objectives and firm performance evaluation system (e.g. Balanced Scorecard)	P	Supporting proactiveness in the firm
Incentive payment system	P	Supporting proactiveness in the firm
Non-family managers	I&D	Supporting innovation and the internalization process
Order administration system	P	Increased efficiency
Centralized purchasing department and production planning	I&D	Increased efficiency
Formal recruitment system	I&D	Supporting innovation, proactiveness and competitive aggressiveness in the firm
Formal training	I&D	Supporting the internationalization process

Note: I&D = Introducing and Developing; P = Promoting.

Further potential improvements and actions emerged during the interview discussions. For example, training is not structurally planned. Instead, it responds to immediate 'on demand' and situational needs (McConaughy, 2000; Kotey and Folker, 2007). However, actions are being taken in relation to such issues. For example, to support the internationalization process, Alessandra organized a German language course for the Engineering division. Claudia encouraged and supported the participation of top managers of the Rotomoulding division in an executive course on entrepreneurship and innovation for the internationalization of small and medium enterprises (see Table 5.2).

The second generation acknowledges that there is still plenty to be done. As Marcello Persico noted when talking about the firm, 'The more it grows, the more it becomes managerial. . . . Yet other more complex initiatives could boost some managerial aspects even more, and there is still a lot to do, but we are changing the organization practices and habits step by step'. For instance, the formalization and communication of a long-term strategy appears to be lacking. Furthermore, according to the interviewees, some aspects of budgeting, planning and monitoring the profitability of innovations need to be improved. Non-family interviewees emphasized that it is sometimes critical to find the best balance between immediate costs and expected benefits in introducing some drivers or measurements. They acknowledge that the second generation members are not only responding to the increasing demand for professionalization but have acquired the appropriate competencies to meet these demands.

TRANSGENERATIONAL PROFESSIONALIZATION OF THE FAMILY FIRM: AN EMERGING FRAMEWORK

This section describes the emergent propositions based on the Persico SpA case. Specific factors emerged in the analysis that play a pivotal role in the professionalization of family firms in generational succession. Figure 5.3 summarizes our main findings graphically presenting the propositions that emerged from our case study.

Transgenerational Learning

An antecedent of family firm transgenerational professionalization is transgenerational learning, which concerns the shifting of education and knowledge towards domains such as economics and management in the transition from the first to the second generation. Particularly, the second generation's leadership and authority in the firm has benefited from formal education as well as learning within the family business through the inter-action with the founding generation. Whereas the father holds the highest level of tacit and technical knowledge acquired 'with decades of experience in the field' as expressed by Claudia, the three siblings have a specialized background in engineering, management and economics through pursuing formal and specialized education. Claudia, Alessandra and Marcello have degrees in marketing and communication, production and logistics engineering, and business management respectively. The formal education paths were supported by Pierino who is aware that the changing organizational conditions and the increasing challenges in the environment require new capabilities and competencies. Pierino sees the second generation as 'methodical, rational, with more trust in figures, data, market analysis, business plans, forecasts'. Although Pierino underlines the need for professionalization, as Claudia stated he is 'More creative, inventive, he trusts instinct,

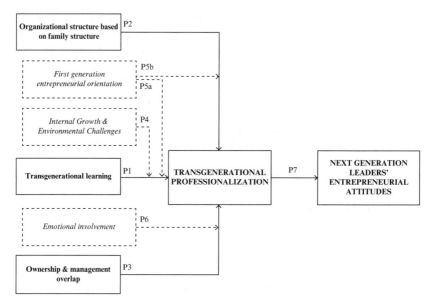

Note: Solid lines show the main antecedents and dotted lines show the moderators.

Figure 5.3   A transgenerational perspective on the professionalization of the family firm and its effect on the entrepreneurial attitudes of next generation leaders

intuition, inspiration, perception, impulse and tends to reject qualified and professional management principles'. The siblings' exposure to and interaction with Pierino's entrepreneurial behaviour and their high level of education have translated into transgenerational professionalization. In other words, the second generation, due to its education and family background, owns and exploits managerial capabilities (and explicitly 'the method') that have become necessary for the firm. This leads us to the first proposition:

Proposition 1: Transgenerational learning (both university education and family exposure) positively affects the transgenerational professionalization of family firms.

Organizational Structure Based on Family Structure

The organizational structure of the firm, with three of the four divisions led by members of the second generation, played a pivotal role in the development of next generation leaders. In his interview, Marcello, a second generation member highlighted that if Persico SpA had only one main business demanding their involvement in similar activities, even with different roles 'there probably would have been significant differences and the approach to the company would have been much less stimulating'. Being leaders of a single division suggests a certain level of equality among members of the second generation and mirrors the family structure. Such structure motivates next generation leaders to feel responsible and apply and test their professional skills. Another second generation member, Alessandra expressed during the interview, that while they all belong to the same family business this organizational structure favours their personal capabilities as each is 'managing his/her own different business'. As a consequence, the professionalization of each business unit is enhanced and tailored to the specific division's needs. For example, Table 5.2 suggests that the reward systems and production planning tools have been implemented to address each division's specific context and the second generation's management style.

Moreover, the type of organizational structure in Persico SpA, with a clear separation between business lines, responsibilities and domains, has facilitated the development of interpersonal relations, fostered fruitful discussions and minimized conflicts. Such a structure would thus foster family altruism (Eddleston et al., 2008). We suggest that not only can generational succession promote organizational change but that the link is mutual: the organizational structure can influence the success of the new generation's entry and the professionalization of the firm. This leads us to propose:

Proposition 2:   An organizational structure based on family structure positively affects the transgenerational professionalization of family firms.

Ownership and Management Overlap

The strong ownership and management overlap that characterizes most family firms appears to strengthen the alignment of goals (Daily and Dollinger, 1992), reducing agency costs (Aronoff and Ward, 1995; Karra et al., 2006), favouring decision-making processes and the pursuit of entrepreneurial initiatives. Yet such overlap also appears to obstruct the professionalization path since it intrinsically entails a lesser demand for external reporting and transparency (Carney, 2005). Conversely, in non-family firms, the top management is accountable to external owners on expected outcomes, adopt more advanced professional methods such as industrial plans, budgets, forecasts, and adhere to long term strategies. As highlighted by some interviewees, Persico SpA has formal board of director meetings and complies with governance guidelines but there are no external shareholders on the board and consultations among family members mainly take place informally. This approach weakens the demand for professional initiatives. As a non-family manager pointed out, the 'perfect overlap' between ownership and management is likely to be the reason for the absence of a structured and institutionalized long-term strategic plan in Persico SpA. This leads us to infer that the ownership and management overlap that is typical of family firms may hinder or delay the professionalization of family firms.

A further characteristic of family firms that highlights the ownership and management overlap is the centralization of leadership in the hands of family members. This can minimize the contributions of non-family managers in terms of professionalization. According to non-family interviewees, the level of centralization in the decision-making process in the firm is very high. Although many of the interviewees pointed out the Persico family's tendency to delegate technical matters to non-family managers, when decisions have long-term implications, the family members seem to own the process. However, the objectivity of non-family managers could provide some benefits for the professionalization of the firm. Family leadership is likely to centralize business issues and stifle delegation. Hence, the family domain can constrain the contribution of non-family managers in terms of professionalization.

Proposition 3:   A strong ownership and management overlap negatively affects the transgenerational professionalization of family firms.

Internal Growth and Environmental Challenges

Internal firm growth and external industry challenges have driven the firm towards increasing professionalization. During the interviews, family members often pointed out the relevance of internal firm growth and the external context in the professionalization process. Indeed, an increase in professionalization could be considered a logical response to growth in the life cycle of the firm and to increased competition in the environment. 'The real issue' Pierino claims 'is that we are living in a context that is becoming more and more difficult, and the technologies we use are more and more complex' and also 'it is since primary school that I cannot find peace; I mean that every day brings new challenges'. Concerning the growth of the organization, all family members including Pierino acknowledge the evolving professional and managerial business needs, 'I really understand we need engineers and managers to add value; we necessarily have to leverage them to compete . . . we need to grow with strong management, there's no way out'. Regarding the environmental variables, the clearest evidence of the reaction to the surrounding challenges is the new approach to risk taken by the second generation leaders. The siblings explain that new projects are scouted, systematically analyzed and assessed by adopting modern risk management practices; in essence, in a more professional way than in the past. Claudia stated, 'We begin to perceive a new rational approach when deciding how to invest'. Internal growth and environmental challenges thus interact with the relationship between transgenerational learning and the transgenerational professionalization of the family firm. This leads us to the following moderating proposition.

Proposition 4:   The positive effect of transgenerational learning on the transgenerational professionalization of family firms is enhanced in the presence of internal firm growth and external industry challenges.

First Generation Entrepreneurial Orientation

Entrepreneurial Orientation (EO), a construct central to the scholarly conversation on corporate entrepreneurship (Hoskisson et al., 2011), refers to strategy-making processes and styles of firms that pursue entrepreneurial opportunities. The dimensions of EO are autonomy, innovativeness, risk taking, proactiveness and competitive aggressiveness (Lumpkin and Dess, 1996). In Persico SpA, autonomy played a key role in the generational transition and the firm's professionalization process. Particularly, the high level of autonomy granted to the second generation reinforced the effect of transgenerational learning and the organizational structure on the firm's professionalization.

'No one can do everything, be everywhere, and know everything' says Pierino Persico while the non-family interviewees stated, 'Pierino has progressively left a high degree of autonomy to his children'. He openly recognizes the decisive importance of his children in the recent development of the firm. For instance, he highlighted the independence of Marcello in developing the Marine division, which would have been closed years ago without his leadership. In particular, the new generation owns the 'managerial talent' included in the pool of human capital resources suggested in mainstream studies (Barney, 1991). Top management values and philosophies are the main determinants of competitive strategic choices (Andrews, 1980) and as the new generation has greater managerial capabilities, the freedom to act becomes essential. Moreover, a high level of autonomy granted to second generation leaders is well suited to an organizational structure that is based on the family structure as it further reduces intra-family conflicts and hence fosters family altruism (Eddleston et al., 2008). In sum, the higher the autonomy granted to the members of the new generation, the faster and smoother their approach to professionalizing the firm. In other words, the first generation entrepreneurial orientation moderates the relationships between transgenerational learning and organizational structure, and the transgenerational professionalization of the family firm, thus leading to the following propositions:

Proposition 5a: The positive effect of transgenerational learning on the transgenerational professionalization of family firms is enhanced when the first generation has a higher entrepreneurial orientation.

Proposition 5b: The positive effect of the organizational structure on the transgenerational professionalization of family firms is enhanced when the first generation has a high entrepreneurial orientation.

Emotional Involvement

The influence of the family on the business has been said to yield positive effects. The personal involvement of family members has traditionally been a strength of family firms, reinforcing their commitment to it. However, the same attribute can turn into a risk factor for firm professionalization. Prior studies suggest that family ties may influence different scenarios for the training of family members in business (De Paola and Scoppa, 2003). The overlapping roles of working family members (relatives, owners, managers) can reinforce family and company loyalty and speed up the decision-making processes but can also mix family and business issues and therefore impede business objectivity (Tagiuri and Davis, 1996). Relatives who work together share a sense of common identity, which can shape a shared mission yet stifle individual freedom and creativity. A long, common and shared set of experiences allows family members to know each other's strengths and weaknesses: mutual awareness and common experiences can be used for constructive (mutual support, quicker communication) or destructive purposes (e.g. to undermine the authority of others). Emotional involvement can promote trust and loyalty yet can also prompt hostility and complicate work interactions.

In Persico SpA, emotional involvement acts as a constraining factor of professionalization, enhancing the negative effect of the ownership and management overlap. 'The stronger family involvement is in the business, the lower the level of delegation granted to non-family leaders', stated a top non-family manager. Empirical evidence suggests that the emotional involvement and personal conviction of family members may affect business operations and human resource management. For example, maintaining non-profitable business lines for personal or family reasons rather than business logic. In one particular incident, the family's concerns for an employee led them to continue his employment despite the conflicting opinion of non-family managers. The lack of external shareholders can contribute to tension between family and business issues (Tagiuri and Davis, 1996). Thus, emotional involvement may impede a 'family-as-investor' mindset (Habbershon and Pistrui, 2002), which institutionalizes a distinctive function of the owner/shareholder, moving from a 'personalized' to a 'performance' perspective that manages and measures performance against the owners' risk/return profile. Emotional involvement thus moderates the relationship between the ownership and management overlap and the transgenerational professionalization of the family firm. This leads us to propose the following:

Proposition 6:   The negative effect of the ownership and management overlap on the transgenerational professionalization of family firms is enhanced in case of high levels of emotional involvement.

Transgenerational Professionalization and the Entrepreneurial Attitudes of Next Generation Family Firm Leaders

Family firms that underperform are often characterized by a lack of formal control systems, limited accountability and transparency that translates into a more informal, instinctive and less planned approach when engaging in diverse projects. On the other hand, increasing formalization and external monitoring could lead to wiser risk-taking behaviour and better financial outcomes (Naldi et al., 2007). Zahra (2005) underlines the need for family firms to develop the 'regenerative capability' that allows them to survive in a changing environment by renewing (and, we add, professionalizing) their business.

In Persico SpA, transgenerational professionalization had an effect on the attitudes of the second generation leaders. This was evident in the new approach to risk-taking such as focusing on new ventures and acquisitions, which contributed to business diversification.

While Pierino is still considered by both family and non-family members as 'the entrepreneur', his entrepreneurial spirit is perceived as having transcended to his children 'in their DNA'. The firm's entrepreneurial attitude has been sustained by the second generation and the approach to risk evolved from intuitive to rational and methodical. This approach has fostered confidence in new opportunities and particularly in international operations. In other words, entrepreneurial attitudes and behaviours have been driven and supported by firm professionalization. From 2000 to 2010, domestic revenues for Persico SPA decreased from two to one third of the company's total turnover. The second generation members engaged in the search for international business opportunities. As a result, Persico SpA has recently acquired a business in the US (Autoplas Systems, Detroit) and one in Spain (Future Fibres, Valencia). The evidence suggests that this advancement falls into a stage-based internationalization category (Johanson and Vahlne, 1977) relying on managerial tools previously introduced in the firm. At the same time, the equity investments in Spain and the US are evidence of new entrepreneurial efforts triggered and carried forward by the second generation leaders. This approach is evidence of the innovative and risk-taking attitude of the next generation leaders.

Proposition 7: Transgenerational professionalization enhances the entrepreneurial attitudes of next generation leaders of family firms.

LIMITATIONS AND FUTURE RESEARCH

The findings of this study are encouraging although its development has not been without challenges and limitations. First, the research relied on a single case study. Although the case study method has been acknowledged as a suitable and powerful method for in-depth and contextualized investigations of family business-related topics, this approach also suffers from serious limitations, especially related to the external validity of results (De Massis and Kotlar, 2014). Second, the study was conducted in one specific context (Italy) and we are thus cautious in suggesting that the findings of this study allow inferences in other cultural contexts. Yet recent studies in alternative contexts where family businesses have thrived from professionalization of family members across generations (Roscoe, Discua Cruz and Howorth, 2013) would suggest that the findings of this study may have wider applicability. Current portrayals of long established STEP family businesses (De Massis et al., 2014b) highlight that transgenerational professionalization may have far-reaching implications in the family business domain and hence warrants further attention.

A relevant question arises from this study: is transgenerational professionalization more prevalent in some contexts than others? Previous studies by Colli, Fernandez and Rose (2003) suggest that some contexts may traditionally nurture the professionalization of succeeding family members to a greater extent. Thus, transgenerational professionalization may be linked to a wider cultural dynamic (Gupta and Levenburg, 2010). Consequently, the findings of our study should be tested in different contexts to corroborate or invalidate their robustness. Additional research is required to obtain a broader picture of transgenerational professionalization in family firms.

CONCLUSIONS

While existing studies provide relevant insights on professionalization in family firms, what is still lacking is a dynamic and cross-generational perspective on professionalization in family firms. Drawing on a longitudinal case study conducted within the STEP project, this research sheds light on transgenerational professionalization. We offer some emergent propositions on the enabling and constraining factors that influence the professionalization of family firms in a generational succession. Moreover, we explore the nexus between transgenerational professionalization and transgenerational entrepreneurship by looking at how the professionalization process influences the entrepreneurial attitudes of next generation leaders.

NOTES

*   Authors of this chapter are listed alphabetically.
1.   USD 68.5 million (exchange rate on 31 December 2010).
2.   Usufruct refers to a legal right accorded to a person or party that confers the temporary right to use and derive income or benefit from someone else's property, provided its substance is neither impaired nor altered.
3.   The 2012 interviews were conducted after the publication of the Persico STEP case.

REFERENCES

Andrews, K.R. (1980). *The Concept of Corporate Strategy*. Chicago, IL: Homewood Publishing.
Aronoff, C.E. and Ward, J.L. (1995). Family-owned businesses: a thing of the past or a model for the future? *Family Business Review*, 8(2): 121–130.
Barney, J. (1991). Firm resources and sustained competitive advantage. *Journal of management*, 17(1): 99–120.
Carlson, D.S., Upton, N. and Seaman, S. (2006). The impact of human resource practices and compensation design on performance: an analysis of family-owned SMEs. *Journal of Small Business Management*, 44(4): 531–543.
Carney, M. (2005). Corporate governance and competitive advantage in family-controlled firms. *Entrepreneurship Theory and Practice*, 29(3): 249–265.
CERIF (Centro di Ricerca sulle Imprese di Famiglia) (2008). Le Imprese di

Famiglia: Imprenditori è il Momento di Lasciare il Testimone? Convegno CERIF, 21 November.

Chittoor, R. and Das, R. (2007). Professionalization of management and succession performance. A vital linkage. *Family Business Review*, 20(1): 65–79.

Chua, J.H., Chrisman, J.J. and Sharma, P. (2003). Succession and nonsuccession concerns of family firms and agency relationship with nonfamily managers. *Family Business Review*, 16(2): 89–107.

CNEL (2006). Consiglio Nazionale dell'Economia e del Lavoro.

Colli, A., Fernandez, P. and Rose, M. (2003). National determinants of family firm development? Family firms in Britain, Spain and Italy in the nineteenth and twentieth centuries. *Enterprise and Society*, 4(1): 28–64.

Colombo, M.G., De Massis, A., Piva, E., Rossi-Lamastra, C. and Wright, M. (2014). Sales and employment changes in entrepreneurial ventures with family ownership: empirical evidence from high-tech industries. *Journal of Small Business Management*, 52(2): 226–245.

Craig, J. and Moores, K. (2005). Balanced scorecards to drive the strategic planning of family firms. *Family Business Review*, 18(2): 105–122.

Daily, C.M. and Dollinger, M.J. (1992). An empirical examination of ownership structure in family and professionally managed firms. *Family Business Review*, 5(2): 117–136.

De Massis, A. and Kotlar, J. (2014). The case study method in family business research: guidelines for qualitative scholarship. *Journal of Family Business Strategy*, 5(1): 15–29.

De Massis, A., Chua, J. and Chrisman, J. (2008). Factors preventing intra-family succession. *Family Business Review*, 21(2): 183–199.

De Massis, A., Chirico, F., Kotlar J. and Naldi L. (2014c). The temporal evolution of proactiveness in family firms: the horizontal S-curve hypothesis. *Family Business Review*, 27(1): 35–50.

De Massis, A., Kotlar, J., Chua, J.H. and Chrisman, J.J. (2014a). Ability and willingness as sufficiency conditions for family-oriented particularistic behavior: implications for theory and empirical studies. *Journal of Small Business Management*, 52(2): 344–364.

De Massis, A., Discua Cruz, A., Jackson, J., Kotlar, J. and Mazzelli, A. (2014b). Beales hotels: embracing change while minding their own business for more than 200 years. In Sharma, P., Yusof, M., Parada, M.J., DeWitt, R. and Auletta, N. (eds), *The Global STEP Booklet, Volume II – Sustaining Entrepreneurial Family Businesses: Developing the Core, Expanding the Boundaries* (81–86). Babson Park, MA: Babson College Centre for Entrepreneurship.

De Paola, M. and Scoppa, V. (2003). Family ties and training provision in an insider–outsider framework. *The Journal of Socio-Economics*, 32(2): 197–217.

Dekker, J., Lybaert, N., Steijvers, T. and Depaire, B. (2015). The effect of family business professionalization as a multidimensional construct on firm performance. *Journal of Small Business Management*, 53(2): 516–538.

Dekker, J.C., Lybaert, N., Steijvers, T., Depaire, B. and Mercken, R. (2013). Family firm types based on the professionalization construct: exploratory research. *Family Business Review*, 26(1): 81–99.

Eddleston, K.A., Kellermanns, F.W. and Sarathy, R. (2008). Resource configuration in family firms: linking resources, strategic planning and technological opportunities to performance. *Journal of Management Studies*, 45(1): 26–50.

English, J. (2001). *How to Organise and Operate a Small Business* (8th edn), Sydney: Allen & Unwin.

Flamholtz, E. (1986). *How to Make the Transition from an Entrepreneurship to a Professionally Managed Firm*. San Francisco, CA: Jossey-Bass.

Flamholtz, E. and Randle, Y. (2007). *Growing Pains: Transitioning From an Entrepreneurship to a Professionally Managed Firm*. San Francisco, CA: Jossey-Bass.

Fletcher, D. (2002). A network perspective of cultural organising and 'professional management' in the small family business. *Journal of Small Business and Enterprise Development*, 9(4): 400–415.

Gimeno, A. and Parada, M.J. (2013). Professionalization of the family business: decision-making domains. In Sharma, P., Sieger, P., Nason, R.S., Gonzalez, A.C. and Ramachandran, K. (eds), *Exploring Transgenerational Entrepreneurship: The Role of Resources and Capabilities* (42–61). Cheltenham, UK and Northampton, MA, USA: Edward Elgar Publishing.

Gumpert, D.E. and Boyd, D.P. (1984). The loneliness of the small-business owner. *Harvard Business Review*, 62(6): 18.

Gupta, V. and Levenburg, N. (2010). A thematic analysis of cultural variations in family businesses: the CASE project. *Family Business Review*, 23(2): 155–169.

Habbershon, T.G. and Pistrui, J. (2002). Enterprising families domain: family-influenced ownership groups in pursuit of transgenerational wealth. *Family Business Review*, 15(3): 223–237.

Hall, A. and Nordqvist, M. (2008). Professional management in family businesses: toward an extended understanding. *Family Business Review*, 21(1): 51–69.

Hoskisson, R.E., Covin, J., Volberda, H.W. and Johnson, R.A. (2011). Revitalizing entrepreneurship: the search for new research opportunities. *Journal of Management Studies*, 48(6): 1141–1168.

Howorth, C., Rose, M., Hamilton, E. and Westhead, P. (2010). Family firm diversity and development: an introduction. *International Small Business Journal*, 28(5): 437–451.

Johanson, J. and Vahlne, J.-E. (1977). The internationalization process of the firm: a model of knowledge development and increasing foreign market commitments. *Journal of International Business Studies*, 8(1): 23–32.

Jones, W.D. (1982). Characteristics of planning in small firms. *Journal of Small Business Management*, 20(3): 15–19.

Karra, N., Tracey, P. and Phillips, N. (2006). Altruism and agency in the family firm: exploring the role of family, kinship, and ethnicity. *Entrepreneurship Theory and Practice*, 30(6): 861–877.

Kogut, B. and Singh, H. (1988). The effect of national culture on the choice of entry mode. *Journal of International Business Studies*, 19(3): 411–432.

Kotey, B. and Folker, C. (2007). Employee training in SMEs: effect of size and firm type – family and nonfamily. *Journal of Small Business Management*, 45(2): 214–238.

Kotlar, J. and De Massis, A. (2013). Goal setting in family firms: goal diversity, social interactions, and collective commitment to family-centered goals. *Entrepreneurship Theory and Practice*, 37(6): 1263–1288.

Leon-Guerrero, A.Y., McCann III, J.E. and Haley Jr, J.D. (1998). A study of practice utilization in family businesses. *Family Business Review*, 11(2): 107–120.

Lumpkin, G.T. and Dess, G.G. (1996). Clarifying the entrepreneurial orientation construct and linking it to performance. *Academy of Management Review*, 21(1): 135–172.

MacRae, D. (1991). Characteristics of high and low growth small and medium-sized businesses. Paper presented at the 21st European Small Business Seminar, Barcelona.

McConaughy, D.L. (2000). Family CEOs vs. nonfamily CEOs in the family-controlled firm: an examination of the level and sensitivity of pay to performance. *Family Business Review*, 13(2): 121–131.

Naldi, L., Nordqvist, M., Sjöberg, K. and Wiklund, J. (2007). Entrepreneurial orientation, risk taking, and performance in family firms. *Family Business Review*, 20(1): 33–47.

Nordqvist, M. and Zellweger, T. (eds) (2010). *Transgenerational Entrepreneurship: Exploring Growth and Performance in Family Firms across Generations*. Cheltenham, UK and Northampton, MA, USA: Edward Elgar Publishing.

Osservatorio AIdAF-Unicredit-Bocconi (AUB) (2009). Sulle aziende familiari italiane di medie e grandi dimensioni.

Osservatorio AIdAF-Unicredit-Bocconi (AUB) (2010). Sulle aziende familiari italiane di medie e grandi dimensioni.

Osservatorio AIdAF-Unicredit-Bocconi (AUB) (2011). Sulle aziende familiari italiane di medie e grandi dimensioni.

Prince, R.A. (1990). Family business mediation: a conflict resolution model. *Family Business Review*, 3(3): 209–223.

Reid, R.S. and Adams, J.S. (2001). Human resource management – a survey of practices within family and non-family firms. *Journal of European Industrial Training*, 25(6): 310–320.

Roscoe, P., Discua Cruz, A. and Howorth, C. (2013). How does an old firm learn new tricks? A material account of entrepreneurial opportunity. *Business History*, 55(1): 53–72.

Shanker, M.C. and Astrachan, J.H. (1996). Myths and realities: family businesses' contribution to the US economy – a framework for assessing family business statistics. *Family Business Review*, 9(2): 107–123.

Stewart, A. and Hitt, M.A. (2012). Why can't a family business be more like a non-family business? Modes of professionalization in family firms. *Family Business Review*, 25(1): 58–86.

Tagiuri, R. and Davis, J. (1996). Bivalent attributes of the family firm. *Family Business Review*, 9(2): 199–208.

Vinton, K.L. (1998). Nepotism: an interdisciplinary model. *Family Business Review*, 11(4): 297–303.

Ward, J.L. (1988). The special role of strategic planning for family businesses. *Family Business Review*, 1(2): 105–117.

Westhead, P. and Howorth, C. (2007). 'Types' of private family firms: an exploratory conceptual and empirical analysis. *Entrepreneurship and Regional Development*, 19(5): 405–431.

Wright, P.C. and Nasierowski, W. (1994). The expatriate family firm and cross-cultural management training: a conceptual framework. *Human Resource Development Quarterly*, 5(2): 153.

Yin, R.K. (2003). *Case Study Research, Design and Methods* (3rd edn). Thousand Oaks, CA: Sage Publications.

Yu, A. (2013). Understanding the landscape of family business. In Sorenson, R.L., Yu, A., Brigham, K.H. and Lumpkin, G.T. (eds), *The Landscape Of Family Business* (9–36). Cheltenham, UK and Northampton, MA, USA: Edward Elgar Publishing.

Zahra, S.A. (2005). Entrepreneurial risk taking in family firms. *Family Business Review*, 18(1): 23–40.

6. The re-establishment of family values as a driver of transgenerational potential

Ilse A. Matser, Frank H. Bos, Margré Heetebrij-van Dalfsen and J.P. Coen Rigtering

MINI CASE STUDY

'This is not what I had in mind when we decided to go on a winter-sports vacation with our daughters and sons-in-law!' As her entire family was having dinner together in the finest Italian restaurant to be found in the French ski resort of Arc 1950, Bianca Ommens was visibly disappointed when her husband's phone rang for the fiftieth time that day. Jan Ommens apologized, saying that he had no choice but to take the call – it was crucial. Moments thereafter, Maarten's phone began to ring and he left the table with the same excuse. This was the proverbial straw that broke the camel's back: the phones had been ringing all day – regardless of whether the family was skiing, taking the lifts or eating a meal.

Bianca had never before felt so disappointed. She had always been well aware of the consequences of having an entrepreneur for a husband. However, since her sons-in-law, Maarten and Keesjan, had entered the company a year ago, the family dynamics seemed to have changed radically.

Jan Ommens is the CEO of Diemen-Contour,[1] a family owned company active in the mobiltech industry which produces textile products for non-aesthetic purposes. More specifically, it is a specialized car-mat producer with a global client base that includes such automotive companies as Audi and Peugeot. The firm is a leader in its industry.

Jan Ommens grew up in a small town in the northern part of the Netherlands. Early in his childhood, he became fascinated with the business world and he was determined to become a successful entrepreneur. After finishing his secondary education, he was offered a rare opportunity to join a wholesaler of carpet-related products. After one year in wholesale, at the age of 17, Jan decided to start his own company together with his older brother, Henk Ommens. The company focused on home furnishings, especially carpets. Seven years later, in 1988, Jan met Johan Van Diemen, the founder of Diemen Matten. Jan was searching for a new opportunity – his business was going strong but it was no longer challenging. As an acquaintance of Jan's father, Johan Van Diemen had confidence in Jan's skills and intentions. He agreed to sell his company to Jan.

In 1991, following an acquisition in the UK, the company's name was changed to Diemen-Contour. To fuel Jan's strategic goal of becoming market leader, the company actively entered new markets. Although Diemen-Contour had started as a production company servicing the local aftersales car-mat market, it slowly moved into new markets, such as the original equipment suppliers (OES) market, which focused on selling car mats to car dealers, and the original equipment manufacturers (OEM) market, which directly supplied mats to automotive manufacturers. Under Jan's leadership, Diemen-Contour grew from around 11 employees in 1988 to 850 employees in 2013. Diemen-Contour had become a global company servicing Europe, the US, South America, Asia and Australia. Its main production plants were located in Poland and Australia.

From the beginning, Jan had a strong vision based on the values he inherited from his father. He felt that Diemen-Contour should be guided and managed according to the family values of integrity, respect and trust. These values informed and guided Jan with respect to his leadership style and the development of the organizational culture. Jan was highly people oriented, and he concentrated on serving and convincing people through personal communication. Moreover, he was emotionally connected to his employees and clients, and he built relationships based on trust and mutual respect. Accessibility and ensuring that people felt comfortable in his presence were important elements of his leadership style.

As the company expanded, the organizational structure changed from being highly informal and centralized toward becoming more formal and decentralized. Consequently, Jan had to delegate some of his tasks and responsibilities with regard to strategy, structure and business control. Based on his assumption that people are trustworthy, Jan granted a significant level of freedom to a number of people in key management positions.

In 1995, the management team (MT) consisted of Jan Ommens and four non-family members. Jan focused on his role as entrepreneur and delegated the daily managerial tasks to the non-family members of the MT, who were empowered to manage the company according to their own principles. They had worked together with Jan since the start in 1988 and they proved to be good leaders in the initial pioneering years. In light of their skills, knowledge and hands-on mentality, Jan trusted these managers with the responsibilities of controlling the company. However, their leadership styles differed significantly from Jan's. In particular, they were more formal and directive. The non-family managers gradually introduced an increasing level of bureaucracy into the company's structure and control systems aimed at managing the company's rapid growth.

This bureaucratization trend was strengthened when the company decided to focus on the OEM market and sought to obtain an ISO/TS certificate, which would ensure that the company met the higher product-quality standards typical of this market segment. In order to meet the ISO/TS requirements, a professional quality management system, including detailed descriptions of practices and protocols, was developed.

As a result of the changes in daily leadership and structure, the company culture also changed. The original culture introduced by Jan, which allowed for high levels of trust and autonomy, was replaced with a bureaucratic system in which avoiding failure was one of the leading principles. Many employees felt that the company had become too rigid. In addition, the communication between Jan and the non-family managers deteriorated as the situation worsened and the managerial day-to-day problems piled up. Jan quickly realized that a major change was needed in order to secure the firm's future. The company was growing rapidly, and he felt that these developments had overwhelmed the MT.

At that point in time, family involvement in the company also became an issue. Maarten Van Dalen, Jan's son-in-law, joined the company in 2007 after finishing his MBA in 2006. He rapidly moved into the function of project manager because of his affinity for managing teams and individuals. Rene Ommens, one of Jan's nephews, joined the company as assistant CFO in 2007. Keesjan De Cruif, Jan's eldest son-in-law, came into the company the same year. He had studied civil engineering and began his career at an engineering agency. When Jan offered him a job in a new daughter company, he decided to take on the challenge. After a few years, Keesjan became the manager of R&D at Diemen-Contour. There was a close connection between Jan and this second generation with regard to the vision for the future and the strategic decisions that had to be made. Jan felt that these youngsters had the capacities and the skills necessary to take the organization to the next level.

Jan realized that he had to make an important decision that would not only affect the company's future but would most likely also affect the family dynamics. He had never thought of Diemen-Contour as a family firm. However, given all of the problems that he and close relatives were facing, handing over the firm to the next generation seemed to be a less viable option. Key factors, such as the company's culture and control systems, did not correspond with his own core values or those of his family.

Jan considered his options: should he sell the business or clear the path for the next generation?

INTRODUCTION

The Diemen-Contour case shows that a family business can be successful in terms of returns on investment and growth but still get stuck in daily operations. The employees were unhappy, management faced a continually increasing number of problems, and the founder and CEO was so frustrated that he considered selling his company. Diemen-Contour's problems were related to the introduction of formalized control mechanisms by the board's external managers. In the context of growing family firms, such efforts are usually referred to as 'professionalization processes' and are believed to be crucial for long-term success. The prevailing notion is that family firms need to be managed more like non-family businesses in order to overcome the weaknesses inherent in their ownership and management structures (Martínez et al., 2007). However, Stewart and Hitt (2012) argue that professionalization is not an inherent strength in itself. Indeed, given the influence that a family can have on the mode of professionalization (Stewart and Hitt, 2012) and the difficulties professional managers face in dealing with idiosyncratic family cultures (Hall and Nordqvist, 2008), we cannot assume that family firms can fully operate as non-family firms or that the advantages stemming from professionalization apply to family firms. In addition, certain circumstances may require more entrepreneurial management styles that are rather informal in nature (Stevenson and Jarillo, 1990) and more responsive to change (Covin and Slevin, 1989).

The ultimate goal of family businesses can be described as transgenerational entrepreneurship – the processes through which a family uses and develops entrepreneurial mindsets and family influenced capabilities to create new streams of entrepreneurial, financial and social value across generations (Habbershon et al., 2010: 141). This value creation can only occur across generations if the owners see merit in handing over the firm to the next generation. In the Diemen-Contour case, the firm was 'flourishing' five years after the internal crisis. At that time, the founder was running the company together with his son-in-law, and the family was making official arrangements for the transfer of ownership to the next generation. However, the firm had gone through significant changes in order to fulfill its true transgenerational potential. The entrepreneur was only willing to transfer the firm to the next generation after the problems stemming from the professionalization efforts were resolved. The key to this positive turnaround was the fact that the family re-established their specific family values and implemented these values as the guiding principles for the company's managerial practices.

While the transgenerational potential of family businesses has been related to firm performance (e.g. Habbershon et al., 2003), few field studies investigate how family values can affect a business or how those values are transmitted to the next generation (Parada and Viladás, 2010). The aim of this study, therefore, is to show how family values can act as guiding principles for management practices in fast-growing family firms. We respond to the call for a better theoretical and empirical understanding of how family values influence the transgenerational potential of family businesses. Consequently, we use the family as the focal point of analysis (Zellweger et al., 2012). The primary research question is the following: How can a focus on family values help the family firm remain competitive and facilitate transgenerational potential?

We chose a case-study approach to answering this research question and zoom in on the micro level. This focus on the micro level contributes to a better understanding of the interrelations between family values, industry requirements and the business system.

This chapter makes two distinct contributions to the literature. First, it enhances our understanding of the link between family values and management practices. Second, it provided insights into how shared family values facilitate the transgenerational potential of family firms.

The next section provides a short overview of the relevant literature, which is followed by a description of the methodology and case characteristics. The findings from the case are then presented. The final sections present the discussion and the conclusions.

THEORETICAL FOUNDATION

Professionalization in Family Businesses

As firms grow, they face new challenges in coordinating and organizing work and activities. Usually, organizational structures become more complex due to the introduction of new departments, and communication becomes more formalized (Greiner, 1972). In addition, the entrepreneur has to delegate tasks and responsibilities in order to cope with the increasing workload and organizational complexity. This delegation process typically introduces new management layers. This type of organizational transformation is often described as professionalization (Gimeno and Parada, 2014). In the context of family businesses, professionalization is often viewed as a necessary process in the firm's life cycle. The basic argument is that by professionalizing management and governance bodies, family firms can overcome their traditional weaknesses and succeed (e.g. Martínez et al., 2007). Along the same lines, the appointment of external (non-family) managers with a business-school education is viewed as a critical factor in the professionalization process in family firms (e.g. Hall and Nordqvist, 2008).

In family firms, professionalization often coincides with succession (Dyer, 1989). Some scholars strongly favor non-family professional managers as successor candidates (Chittoor and Das, 2007), while others argue that it is important to take firm characteristics into account (Hall and Nordqvist, 2008; Lin and Hu, 2007). Lin and Hu (2007) suggest that the success of a new CEO depends on the combination of the firm's operating features and its governance mechanisms. For example, if a firm hires a professional manager because it needs special talents but the controlling family introduces tight controls on the non-family CEO, the firm's performance will be hampered.

Several other issues fuel discussions of the effectiveness of professional management in family firms. In their literature review, Stewart and Hitt (2012) find strong support for professionalization in family firms, in general. However, they also acknowledge that some successful family firms fail to professionalize. Hall and Nordqvist (2008) put forth that, in family firms, the attention paid to the cultural context is key for establishing successful professional management practices. These authors state that 'professional management in family businesses means an in-depth enough understanding of the owner family's dominant goals and meanings of being in business (i.e. cultural competence) to be able to make effective use of relevant education and experience (i.e. formal competence)' (Hall and Nordqvist, 2008: 63). This is in line with Stewart and Hitt (2012), who argue that different modes of professionalization in family firms can be identified when the family's vision, and its abilities to envision and to manage a particular mode are taken into consideration.

Stewart and Hitt (2012) highlight the 'entrepreneurially operated family firm' as one successful mode of professionalization. These firms pursue the opportunities found in informal operations and limit the use of formalization and standardization. Their argument is that some family firms are better served by entrepreneurial management than by professional management. They give four arguments to support this claim: (1) informal social ties may enhance internal coordination and knowledge sharing, (2) informal methods stemming from firm-specific practices can outperform more formal professional practices, (3) executives can operate with discretion derived from the focus on the use of entrepreneurial cognitions, which allows for timely strategic decisions and can help the company cope with unexpected changes, and (4) the combination of the family and business domains may create additional opportunities for entrepreneurial endeavors.

Family Values

'Values' can be defined in line with Rokeach (1973: 5), who suggests that they are 'generalized, enduring beliefs about the personal and social desirability of certain modes of conduct (instrumental values) or end-states of existence (terminal values)'. The instrumental values can be further subcategorized into moral values and competence values, and terminal values can be divided into personal values and social values (Rokeach, 1973). Sorenson (2013) incorporates this categorization into the family business context. He reasons that the primary purpose of families is to build and sustain family relationships. Therefore, when families are actively involved in the business, one might expect the family firm to prioritize moral and social values more than non-family firms, as these types of values are focused on long-term relationships and community building. This prioritization of moral values within the family business is confirmed by Koiranen (2002).

Denison et al.'s (2004) study is one of the few to link the family business culture with financial performance. These authors find several significant positive differences between family enterprises and non-family firms. Clear family values serve as a starting point in the creation of a family business culture. Scholars have argued that such clear values (e.g. commitment, hard work, legacy transmission and a long-term orientation) not only support a family business's success and sustainability, but also serve as a means of governing the business without introducing formal governance institutions, such as supervisory or advisory boards (Parada et al., 2010). More specifically, Steier (2001) and Sundaramurthy (2008) emphasize the strategic advantages enjoyed by family firms when trust stemming from family relationships allows them to reduce the transaction costs related to formal governance mechanisms.

Sorenson (2013) describes how families' social connections may influence the business values. A family firm's founder has an opportunity to build the organizational culture around his or her own values and beliefs. Some founders may promote family values in the firm, especially when they view the business as a family business and hope that other family members will join the firm (Sorenson, 2013). When multiple family members work in the business, this effect becomes stronger. Moreover, its strength grows when multiple family member owners agree on values and/or actively promote those values in the business (Sorenson, 2013). For example, the importance of religious beliefs within a family can support the formation of shared family values and lead to their overt manifestation in the business (Paterson et al., 2013).

Instead of concentrating on family values that apply for all families, it is appropriate to take a micro view that focuses on the values in a particular family and on the impact of those values on the organizational culture within the family firm. This micro view helps to improve our understanding of how and why specific cultures enable or restrict daily management practices (Hall and Nordqvist, 2008). The cultural patterns identified by Dyer (1988) allow us to distinguish among different family business cultures. The foundations for these cultural patterns are the group's basic assumptions regarding human nature, the nature of relationships, the nature of truth, time, the environment, the nature of human activity and whether preferential treatment should be given to certain individuals (Dyer, 1988).

However, cultural patterns must evolve as leadership is transferred to the next generation and as new conditions emerge in the external environment (Dyer, 1988). For example, firms that face an increasingly turbulent environment need to foster assumptions that create a culture that enables them to quickly respond to changes, to develop new ideas and to improve decision-making (Dyer, 1988). Parada et al. (2010) demonstrate a dynamic approach to these value changes in family firms and suggest that family firm values consist of impermanent values that can change over time as well as a core set of permanent values.

Transgenerational Potential through Family Entrepreneurial Orientation

The idea that the long-term prosperity of the family business system requires positive outcomes in both the business dimension and the family dimension is widely acknowledged (e.g. Ward, 1987; Litz, 2008; Sharma, 2004). Litz (2008) argues that long-term success requires synergy within the subsystems (a net positive effect of transfers within each dimension) and symmetry in the overall balance of transfers between the two subsystems. Indeed, the concept of transgenerational entrepreneurship emphasizes the need for families to create new streams of value across generations, and it recognizes that this value is derived from a combination of entrepreneurial, financial and social outcomes (Habbershon et al., 2010; Nordqvist and Zellweger, 2010). However, whether a (family) firm is transferred from one generation to the next is a matter of choice. In this respect, Gersick et al. (1997) argue that the generation in charge of the firm, especially the controlling owner, has to consider whether the next generation should be involved in the firm. In this regard, it is logical to assess not only the capabilities and willingness of the next generation, but also the potential outcomes for the family. The main question in this regard is whether it is worthwhile to stay involved as a family in the business. Family involvement is a precondition for family firm status, but the financial, entrepreneurial and social outcomes determine whether the firm will be handed over to the next generation.

A key element in improving the entrepreneurial, financial and social outcomes of a family business is the family's entrepreneurial orientation (FEO) (Nordqvist and Zellweger, 2010; Zellweger et al., 2012). FEO denotes the extent to which the overall managerial practices can be viewed as entrepreneurial and reflects the risk taking, innovativeness, proactiveness, competitive aggressiveness and level of autonomy within a family firm (see Lumpkin and Dess, 1996; Zellweger et al., 2012). Such entrepreneurial management practices have been shown to improve firm performance (Rauch et al., 2009), especially in rapidly changing and hostile environments (Covin and Slevin, 1989). At the family level, FEO can be conceptualized as the family's overall orientation towards entrepreneurial management and strategic action (Habbershon et al., 2010). An assessment of entrepreneurial managerial practices at the family level is particularly relevant for transgenerational potential because 'families are willing to foster change and growth of business activities, but they do so for the benefit of the next generation' (Zellweger et al., 2012: 148).

METHODOLOGY AND CASE CHARACTERISTICS

The Diemen-Contour case study aimed to qualitatively explore the factors that contribute to the transgenerational potential of a family firm. In order to collect rich, high-quality primary and secondary data, the following methodological approach was developed and executed. First, a literature review of the core theoretical concepts was conducted. Then, in order to gather the necessary in-depth primary data, interviews were undertaken with key actors who held strategically relevant positions. In addition to the head entrepreneur (Jan Ommens), and his chief operational officer (COO) and successor Maarten Van Dalen (son-in-law), interviews were conducted with the sales manager (non-family), the human resources manager (non-family) and Annelies Ommens (daughter and operational manager in the affiliated company, Dico International).

The interviews lasted around 90 minutes each. The main goal of the interviews was to collect sufficient data about the family and the company to allow for the development of an in-depth case centered on the concept of transgenerational potential. The interview questions were predominantly process oriented, and interviewees were asked to provide examples to clarify abstract answers and situations. The transcripts of the interviews were independently coded by the authors. Based on these independent codings, the final case was built.

Diemen-Contour Case Characteristics

Profile of the firm

Diemen-Contour, a business owned by the Ommens family, is active in the 'mobiltech' industry. It seeks to service the automotive industry with specific, high-tech textiles for automotive applications. More specifically, Diemen-Contour is a specialized car-mat producer with a global client base illustrated by the geographical differentiation of its sales-and-marketing function (Figure 6.1). Clients include automotive companies such as Audi and Peugeot. The firm holds a leading position in the industry.

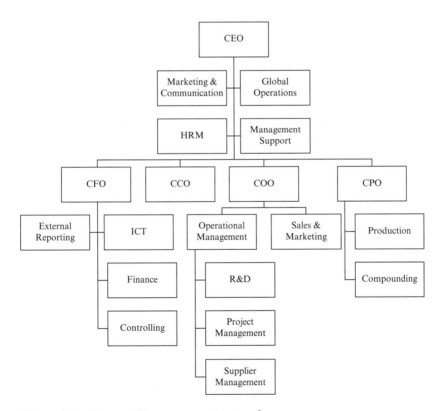

Figure 6.1   Diemen-Contour organization chart

*Table 6.1   Milestones of Diemen-Contour reflecting its development from
a local company into a global company*

Year	Milestone
1991	Diemen Matten takes over Contour Carpets (UK) and the company is renamed Diemen-Contour (DC).
1996	Diemen-Contour moves production to Poland.
2005	Diemen-Contour receives an ISO/TS certificate, which enables the firm to service the OEM market. The ISO/TS requires a significant amount of administration and the introduction of a series of protocols. As a result, Diemen-Contour's overhead increases significantly, leading to the development of a bureaucratic management system.
2008	*Organizational redevelopment* In response to growing problems within the business, the Ommens family decides to redevelop the strategy, structure and culture of Diemen-Contour, and to reunite these elements with the core family values. As a result, the company is revitalized, which supports Jan in his intention to transfer the company to the next generation.
2011	*Family involvement in management increases* Two family members – Maarten Van Dalen (Jan's son-in-law) and Rene Ommens (Jan's cousin) – join Diemen-Contour's management team. Maarten is as COO the second in command.
2012	*Diemen-Contour's new strategy: Global presence* In its efforts to reach the next level, Diemen-Contour presents its global strategy, which is based on four areas: a global presence, innovation and design, sustainability, and operational excellence. Plans are developed for new production facilities in Mexico and China, and Diemen-Contour focuses on servicing the OEM market on a global basis.

Family and the firm's life stages

Diemen-Contour's story started in 1988 with Jan Ommens' takeover of Diemen Matten, which was founded in 1952 by Johan Van Diemen. At the time of the takeover, Diemen Matten had 11 employees and around EUR 460,000 in annual revenue.

In reflecting on the situation at Diemen Matten when he took it over, Jan stated: 'I quickly noticed that, with all due respect to the Van Diemen family, things had to change to maintain continuity'. With this in mind, Jan began to develop plans and initiatives aimed at helping Diemen Matten grow and prosper. In the ensuing years, Diemen Matten/Diemen-Contour developed from a local company into a global company, as outlined in Table 6.1.

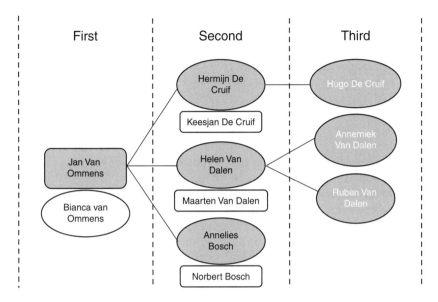

Figure 6.2   The Ommens family tree

Family and family involvement

The Ommens' immediate family tree is depicted in Figure 6.2.

Jan and his wife Bianca have three daughters, all of whom are married. Some of these couples have children, who are still very young at the time of the analysis. With respect to the family's involvement in ownership, Jan is the only owner of Diemen-Contour and he holds 100 percent of the shares. Family involvement in the management includes next to the immediate family also a cousin, as is evident in Table 6.2.

Table 6.2   Family involvement in the management of Diemen-Contour

Person	Age	Role in the family	Role in the company
Jan Ommens	58	Father	Founder and CEO
Maarten Van Dalen	31	Son-in-law	COO
Keesjan De Cruif	36	Son-in-law	Manager R&D
Annelies Bosch-Ommens	28	Daughter	Operations Management
René Ommens	34	Cousin	CFO

CASE FINDINGS

In this section, we present findings from the Diemen-Contour case that relate to our principal research question: How can a focus on family values help a family firm remain competitive and facilitate transgenerational potential?

The Values of the Ommens Family

Jan strongly felt that Diemen-Contour should be guided and managed according to the core family values. In Jan's view, the most important of those values were respect and trust. With respect to the values he learned from his father, Jan highlighted 'integrity, correctness, work ethics . . . and one thing he said to me regularly – enthusiasm.' These values informed and guided Jan on a daily basis with respect to his management style and the development of the intended business culture.

As the above quote illustrates, Jan's values were influenced by the previous generation. In that sense, they can be regarded as family specific. However, the Ommens' family values also had a more generic origin that is related to the family's religious background and the working culture of the community in the northern part of the Netherlands. Typical values related to these elements are trust, working for the good of society, loyalty, and work ethics.

On the basis of these values, Jan developed his own management style. For example, based on the assumption that people are trustworthy, Jan offered high levels of autonomy to a number of people holding key management positions in the company. The sales manager of Diemen-Contour France referred to this, stating: 'Jan has always had strong bonds with people. He manages by trusting people.'

Professionalization of the Family Firm: Family and the Firm Grow Apart

From a family point of view, Jan Ommens was the link between the family and the firm. Through his management style, the family values were incorporated into the business culture. However, as the company grew, Jan was unable to effectively manage the company single-handedly and a larger management team was needed. Consequently, the management style was increasingly influenced by and mediated through other newly appointed members of the management team. In 1995, the management team consisted of Jan and four non-family members. As the firm grew, Jan focused on his role as leading entrepreneur, and he increasingly delegated daily management to other management-team members. Accordingly, these managers were empowered to manage the company according to their own management principles. Even though the managers were familiar with Jan's core values, they appeared to be much more formal and directive than Jan. As a result, company values started to change and deviate from family values. As the HRM manager noted:

> Actually, the road to Jan was not open for everybody anymore. . . . I think the average worker did not notice any family involvement at that time. Rather, they saw daily management by non-family managers. . . . You could not be here at a time when they were not also here, even if you worked at night.

The non-family managers gradually introduced bureaucratic working procedures to manage the growth. This trend was strengthened by the decision to focus on the OEM market and the need to obtain an ISO/TS certificate, which was necessary for ensuring that the company met the high product-quality standards of this market segment. According to one of the interviewees, the main result was that the company became a 'town hall', referring to a more bureaucratic, administrative culture. Instead of the initially intended culture that allowed for sufficient levels of trust and autonomy, the newly introduced bureaucratic management system led to a gradual shift in the company culture, such that avoiding failure became the leading principle. Employees had significantly less autonomy. As one of interviewees summarized: 'What happened? The company became too rigid', referring to a significant decrease in intrapreneurship and strategic flexibility.

Re-aligning the Family Business with Family Values to Ensure Continuity Across Generations

When the problems with respect to the firm's management practices and business culture became so apparent that they started to affect Jan and the family on a personal level, Jan realized something had to be done to secure the firm's continuity. Jan described the stressful situation in the business as follows:

> If I had to go on like that . . . within a couple of years, you would probably need to take a few days off . . . for my funeral. However, I would not let that happen.

At the same point in time, Maarten Van Dalen became involved in the Ommens family because of his relationship with one of Jan's daughters. Maarten had studied business administration and had his own entrepreneurial ambitions. Given this background, Maarten and Jan increasingly discussed the critical situation in the business during family meetings. On several occasions, Jan asked Maarten whether he would be interested in joining the firm. In 2007, Maarten agreed to work for the firm, although not in a management position. Reflecting on this decision, Maarten explained:

> There were these business problems [regarding the firm's management practices and business culture] that we often discussed over a cup of coffee on Sunday mornings. Jan told me that he would appreciate it if I would join Diemen-Contour. At first, I said I was not ready. However, after a series of discussions, I decided to go for it. Why? I saw it as an enormous opportunity to learn a lot in a very short time.

While working for the family business, Maarten experienced the business situation at first hand, which enabled him to more productively discuss it with Jan. Maarten explained his view:

> The company had reached its limits. Jan knew that as well. Management seemed to have the wrong focus. . . . I was part of the company and saw it happen. I talked about it with Jan and asked whether he had a clear picture.

Maarten's entrance into the company began to reconnect the family to the firm. Informal discussions with Maarten and personal observations helped Jan more accurately judge the situation. In Jan and Maarten's view, key elements, such as the company's management, practices and business culture, no longer corresponded with the family's core values. A search for renewal was launched in 2008, and significant changes were realized in an effort to re-align the company's management practices and business culture with the family's core values. Jan teamed up with a non-family interim-manager who understood the Ommens' family values. Reflecting on this phase of renewal, Maarten noted:

> We reorganized radically. Around 70 percent of all of the people in the company changed positions. They were all tested with regard to their talents and skills. The guiding principle in this renewal was a focus on people and autonomy. As a result . . . people start to laugh again. Work hard again. . . . Then what happened? People start to behave entrepreneurially again.

The company structure shifted to accompany this renewed focus on people and autonomy. Central to the new company structure were autonomous teams, which were referred to as 'cells.' These cells related to their own client groups, most of which were country based. As the cells were regarded as profit centers, they had their own profit and loss accounts.

As a result of these internal changes, the company was revitalized and started to grow again. In addition, while Jan had little intention of transferring the company to the next generation during the internal crisis, this became a viable option, as the company's situation seemed to improve significantly. At the same time, family involvement in management expanded. This, in turn, enabled Jan and other family employees to further shape and solidify the internal changes around the core family values.

The internal changes at Diemen-Contour centered on nurturing and employing (employee) excellence and talent, respect, work ethics, integrity and ambition. One interviewee summarized the new perspective as: 'behave normally and realize excellent results.' To ensure that the changes would endure, they were institutionalized in the company's performance-management system and in its HR development program. As the HRM manager stated:

> [The focus is on] taking care of our employees. We have introduced performance management. Yes, we had evaluation sessions in the past, but they were more like: 'Well, is there anything I can do for you? No? Ok. See you next year.' Today, we have a professional performance-management process, most of which was invented and implemented by Maarten. . . . Twice each year our employees have an evaluation session. Goals are formulated. . . . Feedback is shared. We have formulated organizational values that are discussed. Employees appreciate that.

Summary of the Main Finding

Although multiple findings have been presented throughout this case, they all point towards one main finding – the role and importance of family values as guidelines for managerial practices and business culture. Through these practices and culture, family values contribute to the transgenerational potential of the family firm. How family values of the Ommens' family shape managerial practices is illustrated in Figure 6.3.

In summary, Diemen-Contour again returned to its roots in the core family values. As a result, it was renewed and Jan Ommens was able to

Key family values:	
• Trust 'people are good.' • Integrity 'what you say is what you do.' • Respect 'always treat someone in a dignified way.' • Enthusiasm 'live and work with energy.'	• Communication of the values to all stakeholders. • New company structure based on creating small autonomous teams. • Values institutionalized in the company through a management training program, performance management systems, recruitment and policies.

Figure 6.3   Family values as a basis for managerial practices and business culture

work towards transferring the company to the next generation without fear about what the future might bring.

DISCUSSION

This study contributes to family business research in three ways. First, it illustrates why professionalization efforts in family businesses do not always result in positive outcomes. Second, it highlights the importance of family values as a guiding principle for managerial practices and how such values are used to re-invent managerial practices. Third, it provides enhanced insights into how family values are related to the transgenerational potential of family businesses. Together, these contributions address an important gap in the literature, which has thus far been unable to sufficiently explain the transgenerational potential of family businesses (Zellweger et al., 2012).

The apparent links among family influence, business culture and firm performance are established in a quantitative study by Craig et al. (2014). Based on a sample of 250 SMEs in the US, Craig et al. (2014) conclude that there is a positive link between family values and management practices, and that these management practices improve firm performance. Our in-depth analysis of the historical developments in Diemen-Contour not only confirms these findings but also points to the importance of contextual variables that seem to play a crucial role in the process.

Jan's efforts to ensure growth and professionalization by appointing non-family members to key managerial positions serves as a textbook example of professionalization in family firms. This type of move is described by Martínez et al. (2007) as an important way to grow and over-come internal managerial crises. The combination of the autonomy that Jan offered to the non-family managers and the firm's ambition to move into the OEM market, which required a focus on quality and reliability, caused the managers to move away from the family's original vision, and to incorporate strict working procedures and bureaucratic controls. Even though these managers were selected on the basis of their achievements, as well as their familiarity with the company's culture and family values, they were unable to prevent the development of a rigid structure with unwanted side effects for the daily operations and the company culture. In addition, they were unable to stay true to the family values.

The fact that bureaucratic controls are not the only way to live up to the quality demands of the ISO/TS certificate is evidenced by the fact that Diemen-Contour, with the new structure and policies, could still easily meet such standards.

In the post-crisis Diemen-Contour, the level of autonomy granted to employees increased and, in a more general sense, entrepreneurial behavior was encouraged. In addition, the family's involvement in the business was actively promoted in order to ensure appropriate guidance for the development of the organizational culture. This leads us to suggest that major discrepancies among the organizational structure, procedures and family values lead to conflicts that can be resolved through family debates and a re-alignment of the management practices with the family values.

The STEP framework suggests that the transgenerational potential of a family firm is the result of the entrepreneurial, financial and social performance of the firm (Nordqvist and Zellweger, 2010). Our research offers much needed insights into the relative importance of each of these dimensions. The crisis at Diemen-Contour was not about financial performance. Rather, it was, first and foremost, a crisis of social performance, as the problems in the business started to affect the family as a whole. These mainly administrative and operational problems could conceivably be resolved without a fundamental discussion of family values. However, the re-alignment of the family values with managerial practices marked a turning point in Jan's view of whether the firm could be passed on to the next generation. Next to that the re-alignment of the management practices with the family values improved the entrepreneurial performance of the business that led to an extra positive effect on the transgenerational potential of the family firm. Therefore, an understanding of the interrelations between family values and managerial practices is crucial. We theorize that, through the social-performance dimension, family values not only affect managerial practices but also the willingness to pass the firm on to the next generation. This redirects us to Dyer's (1988) seminal work on cultural assumptions and continuity in family firms, and provides an interesting avenue for future research.

The limitations that stem from our methodological approach are those that are commonly associated with single case studies. In this regard, we mainly offer new insights that should be tested in quantitative studies, preferably longitudinal or experimental studies aimed at analyzing the direction of the causal effects. In addition, we were unable to assess the true leadership qualities of the two non-family managers, and we were forced to rely on information from secondary sources regarding events during the managerial crisis. Even though we interviewed multiple non-family members with the aim of overcoming this limitation, we cannot fully eliminate any biased views of these events. We were also unable to evaluate the extent to which family members were able to stay true to the family values under the pressures of obtaining the prestigious ISO/TS certificate and the aggressive growth strategy. Another important limitation is the fact that Diemen-Contour was a first-generation family business. Jan Ommens did not view the company as a family business at first. The family might have perceived a decision to sell the business, rather than pass it on to the next generation, as a legitimate decision. If a family business has already been passed on from generation to generation, this dynamic could be very different.

CONCLUSION

In conclusion, this study shows that family values can act as guiding principles for managerial practices. Such values originate from fundamental beliefs about, for example, human behavior, the truth or society (see Dyer, 1988). They are re-enforced and incorporated into the FEO through debate and through the involvement of family members in the management.

A discrepancy between the family's values and the organizational culture may result in more fundamental questions about the firm and its intergenerational potential, making family values and their impact on the business essential to our understanding of succession processes. In the case of Diemen Contour due to all the business problems and the effect they had on the family, the founder seriously thought about selling the firm instead of handing it over to the next generation.

Professionalization within family firms may create discrepancies, as it may threaten the management style and existing organizational culture. Therefore, family firms that are experiencing an internal crisis and those that have high growth ambitions should carefully consider the types of managerial controls, strategies and procedures in relation to the family's values and the operating environment.

For instance, high quality and ISO/TS certification was necessary to meet industry standards. However, instead of relying on bureaucratic procedures, the business now uses small autonomous groups and family values act as guidelines for managerial practices. As a result, quality levels were maintained but the new way of working has also led to entrepreneurial initiatives and innovation.

Professionalization should preferably be a balanced process in which both the business side and the family values are taken into account.

NOTE

1. The names of the people and of the company have been changed to ensure anonymity.

REFERENCES

Chittoor, R. and Das, R. (2007). Professionalization of management and succession performance. A vital linkage. *Family Business Review*, 20(1): 65–79.

Covin, J.G. and Slevin, D.P. (1989). Strategic management in small firms in hostile and benign environments. *Strategic Management Journal*, 10(1): 75–87.

Craig, J.B., Dibrell, C., and Garrett, R. (2014). Examining relationships among family influence, family culture, flexible planning systems, innovativeness and firm performance. *Journal of Family Business Strategy*, 5(3): 229–238.

Denison, D., Lief, C., and Ward, J.L. (2004). Culture in family-owned enterprises: recognizing and leveraging unique strengths. *Family Business Review*, 17(1): 61–70.

Dyer, W.G. (1988). Culture and continuity in family firms. *Family Business Review*, 1(1): 37–50.

Dyer, W.G. (1989). Integrating professional management into a family owned business. *Family Business Review*, 2(3): 221–235.

Gersick, K.E., Davis, J.A., Hampton, M., and Lansberg, I. (1997). *Generation to Generation: Life Cycles of the Family Business*. Boston, MA: Harvard Business School Press.

Gimeno, A. and Parada, M.J. (2014). Professionalization of the family business: decision making domains. In Sharma, P., Sieger, P., Nason, R.S., Gonzalez, A.C., and Ramachandran, K. (eds), *Exploring Transgenerational Entrepreneurship: The Role of Resources and Capabilities* (42–61). Cheltenham, UK and Northampton, MA, USA: Edward Elgar Publishing.

Greiner, L. (1972). Evolution and revolution as organizations grow. *Harvard Business Review*, 37–46.

Habbershon, T.G., Nordqvist, M., and Zellweger, T. (2010). Transgenerational entrepreneurship. In Nordqvist, M. and Zellweger, T. (eds), *Transgenerational Entrepreneurship: Exploring Growth and Performance in Family Firms Across Generations* (141–160). Cheltenham, UK and Northampton, MA, USA: Edward Elgar Publishing.

Habbershon, T.G., Williams, M., and MacMillan, I.C. (2003). A unified systems perspective of family firm performance. *Journal of Business Venturing*, 17(4): 451–465.

Hall, A. and Nordqvist, M. (2008). Professional management in family businesses: toward an extended understanding. *Family Business Review*, (21): 51–69.

Koiranen, M. (2002). Over 100 years of age but still entrepreneurially active in business: exploring the values and family characteristics of old Finnish family firms. *Family Business Review*, 15(3): 175–187.

Lin, S.H. and Hu, S.Y. (2007). A family member or professional management? The choice of a CEO and its impact on performance. *Corporate Governance: An International Review*, 15(6): 1348–1362.

Litz, R.A. (2008). Two sides of a one-sided phenomenon: conceptualizing the family business and business family as a Möbius strip. *Family Business Review*, 21(3): 217–236.

Lumpkin, G.T. and Dess, G.G. (1996). Clarifying the entrepreneurial orientation construct and linking it to performance. *Academy of Management Review*, 21(1): 135–172.

Martínez, J.I., Stöhr, B.S., and Quiroga, B.F. (2007). Family ownership and firm performance: evidence from public companies in Chile. *Family Business Review*, 20(2): 83–94.

Nordqvist, M. and Zellweger, T.M. (2010). *Transgenerational Entrepreneurship, Exploring Growth and Performance in Family Firms across Generations.* Cheltenham, UK and Northampton, MA, USA: Edward Elgar Publishing.

Parada, M.J. and Viladás, H. (2010). Narratives: a powerful device for values transmission in family businesses. *Journal of Organizational Change Management*, 23(2): 166–172.

Parada, M.J., Nordqvist, M., and Gimeno, A. (2010). Institutionalizing the family business: the role of professional associations in fostering a change of values. *Family Business Review*, (23): 355–372.

Paterson, T.A., Specht, D., and Duchon, D. (2013). Exploring costs and consequences of religious expression in family businesses. *Journal of Management, Spirituality and Religion*, 10(2): 138–158.

Rauch, A., Wiklund, J., Lumpkin, G.T., and Frese, M. (2009). Entrepreneurial orientation and business performance: an assessment of past research and suggestions for the future. *Entrepreneurship Theory and Practice*, 33(3): 761–787.

Rokeach, M. (1973). *The Nature of Human Values* (Vol. 438). New York: Free Press.

Sharma, P. (2004). An overview of the field of family business studies: current status and directions for the future. *Family Business Review*, 17(1): 1–36.

Sorenson, R.L. (2013). How moral and social values become embedded in family firms. *Journal of Management, Spirituality and Religion*, 10(2): 116–137.

Steier, L. (2001). Family firms, plural forms of governance, and the evolving role of trust. *Family Business Review*, 14(4): 353–368.

Stevenson, H.H. and Jarillo, J.C. (1990). A paradigm of entrepreneurship: entrepreneurial management. *Strategic Management Journal*, 11(4): 17–27.

Stewart, A. and Hitt, M.A. (2012). Why can't a family business be more like a non-family business? Modes of professionalization in family firms. *Family Business Review*, 25(1): 58–86.

Sundaramurthy, C. (2008). Sustaining trust within family businesses. *Family Business Review*, 21(1): 89–102.

Ward, J.L. (1987). *Keeping the Family Business Healthy: How to Plan for Continuing Growth, Profitability, and Family Leadership*. London: Macmillan.

Zellweger, T., Nason, R., and Nordqvist, M. (2012). From longevity of firms to transgenerational entrepreneurship of families. *Family Business Review*, 25(2): 136–155.

7. What should be passed on to the successor? The case of a long-standing Japanese family-owned small sake brewery

Katsushi Yamaguchi, Naomi Kozono and Hiro Higashide

MINI CASE STUDY

Tamura Sake Brewery is a small Japanese sake brewery located in Fussa city, a rural area in western Tokyo, Japan. Tamura Sake Brewery has been making sake at the current location since its foundation in 1822. Its traditional Japanese-style building and the land are distinguished from the surroundings. Tamura Sake Brewery has been owned and managed by the Tamura family for sixteen generations.

The current CEO, Hanjuro Tamura, is 55 years old. After graduating from university, he worked for three years at a large producer of alcoholic beverages. Then, at age 25, he joined Tamura Sake Brewery and soon became the senior managing director. After his father (the predecessor) died in 2008, Hanjuro became the sixteenth CEO of the family business. He has been involved in the business for nearly 30 years and is the only family member who is actively involved. His mother and wife do not have specific positions in the company, but they do non-managerial work, such as taking care of the brewers.

Tamura Sake Brewery's main business is sake brewing. Ninety percent of its annual sales come from customers in Tokyo, and the remaining 10 percent comes from other parts of Japan and from exports. Tamura Sake Brewery also owns a franchise business and a real estate agency. It has around 20 employees, including production staff (brewers), marketing staff, and administrative personnel.

Hanjuro perceived that the business condition of the sake-brewing industry 'got worse' in the last decade. Demand for Japanese sake in the country continues to shrink. In 2011, annual sales of sake in Japan were only one third of that in 1970. Along with the shrinking demand, the number of sake breweries is also decreasing. There were 16 sake breweries in Tokyo when Hanjuro entered the family business in the early 1980s; today there are only seven.

People in the local area take pride in Tamura Sake Brewery because it survives in such a tough business environment, and it is highly reputed thanks to its long history. Hanjuro recognizes the attitude of the locals toward Tamura Sake Brewery. He strongly desires that it remain reputed by the community forever. He feels a sense of responsibility to sustain Tamura Sake Brewery as the reliable company that it is.

Because of this, he always thinks about the business from a long-term perspective. He makes everyday decisions based on his anticipation of their consequences 100 years into the future. It is natural for him to think ahead about succession. In fact, he considers that 90 percent of his responsibility is to train the next generation.

Hanjuro has already decided that he will let his eldest son take over the business, following the family's tradition of primogeniture. The eldest son is now 16 years old and attends high school. In about five years, the son will graduate from university and start his business career.

Hanjuro thinks about developing his son as a future leader of the business. His son is not as mentally mature as he expects him to be. He wonders what and how he should teach his eldest son to be his successor: 'Does he need to acquire some specific skills and knowledge first?' 'No. There must be something more important to teach. However, what is it?'

When he thought back to his own learning experience, he recalled the most striking lesson he learned from his father and the chairman of another brewery.

Episode 1

About 40 years ago, the then CEO (Hanjuro's father) decided to let the existing brewers go and hire new brewers. It was a big decision because Tamura Sake Brewery, until that time, had hired brewers from the same region in the central north of Japan for 150 years. After World War II, the economy of that region developed, and more attractive job opportunities became available. Youngsters no longer had to go to Tokyo to earn money as brewers. As a result, the number of new-born brewers was predicted to decrease soon. Thus, following the advice of an officer of a public institution that trained brewers, Tamura Sake Brewery decided to hire sake brewers from a different region starting the next year. It took a few years for brewers to acquire a mastery of the unique method of sake production at Tamura Sake Brewery. Therefore, Tamura Sake Brewery gradually let the existing brewers go as it increased the number of new brewers. After three years, all of the existing brewers were replaced with new ones.

It was obviously a reasonable decision for the company from an economic standpoint. However, it was against the will of Hanjuro's father. He deeply respected the brewers who had served the company for generations, but he had to lay them off for economic reasons. He felt deeply sorry for those whom he had to fire. Hanjuro often saw his father regretting the decision and showing concern for the former brewers.

One day, about a dozen years later, in 1986, when Hanjuro was 28 years old and serving as the senior managing director, Hanjuro's father held a memorial service for deceased former brewers, who had been asked to leave more than a decade ago. Hanjuro's father held the event to meet the former brewers and express his apology. However, no one blamed his father. On the contrary, they welcomed him and expressed their gratitude for the way he treated them.

Hanjuro, too, attended the event, and he felt overwhelmed by the devotion of his father to the former employees. Hanjuro deeply admired his father on this occasion.

Hanjuro reflected, 'My father always told me to respect the brewers. Honestly, I didn't understand why it was so important. However, at that moment, I finally understood what he meant.'

Then he remembered another striking experience.

Episode 2

In 2011, a great earthquake and tsunami devastated northeastern Japan. After the disaster, the chairman of another family-owned brewery nearby visited Hanjuro. The chairman persuaded Hanjuro to donate a huge amount of money to the northeastern region. In those days, Hanjuro was struggling with a large amount of debt that he had incurred to pay his inheritance tax. He was reluctant to donate such huge amount of money. The chairman told Hanjuro:

> We, sake breweries, have come along with the local community. We came along because of the trust relationship with the community. As a result, while the community trusted us, we contributed to the community. Sometimes they helped us. We have lived in this way.
>
> [The disaster] happened to occur in the northeastern Japan. It's part of Japan. In that sense, in the face of this life-or-death matter, we should not mind losing our own wealth because we have owed the community for a long time and have come along with the region. . . . It's worth doing [donating a large amount of

money]. In reality, there must be value for us. Therefore, let's do it. (An account of the chairman of another brewery)

Hanjuro felt overwhelmed by the chairman's theory. He thought he had learned a lot from the chairman's way of thinking. Finally, he accepted the offer to donate money.

He recalled the moment. 'I learned so much. Yes, I learned, really. We have lived with the community. Therefore, we should give back to the community when the community is in crisis. . . . It is definitely our responsibility.'

Now he knew what he should pass on to his son. However, he was not confident enough. He worried about whether he could train his son by himself. When he looked back at the past 30 years since he started his career at Tamura Sake Brewery, he remembered a veteran manager who has served the Tamura family since his grandfather was the CEO. Hanjuro recalled, 'He always guided me in the right direction. He often said to me, "That way is not acceptable in the Tamura family, sir." Thanks to his feedback, I gradually understood what was right and what was wrong at Tamura Sake Brewery. I should ask for his help this time.'

Questions for Discussion

1. What does the incumbent CEO most want to pass on to his successor?
2. Why does he think this is so important?
3. How he can teach his son about this?

INTRODUCTION

The opening mini case study described the struggle of the incumbent CEO of a long-standing Japanese family business, a 192-year-old sake brewery, regarding what values he should pass on to the incoming successor.

Companies in Japan continue much longer than companies in any other country around the world. Goto (2012) estimated that 3,900 Japanese companies have remained in business longer than 200 years, and this figure greatly outnumbers that of 57 other countries/regions. Almost all of these long-standing businesses are estimated to be family-owned (Goto, 2009). Among those Japanese companies, the sake brewing industry has the largest number of companies that have remained in business longer than 200 years, followed by Japanese-style inns, art and crafts dealers and stores, Japanese confectionaries, and restaurants (Goto, 2009).

In contrast, the most significant challenge for family businesses around the world is to remain in business for future generations. According to Cater and Justis (2010), only 30 percent of family businesses continue to the second generation and only 10 to 15 percent survive to the third. The survival rate decreases to only 3 to 5 percent in the fourth generation.

The role of the successor is essential to achieving continuity. Hence, this chapter focuses on the issue of successor development in long-standing family businesses, especially long-standing small- and medium-sized enterprises (SMEs), since most of the centuries-old family businesses in Japan are SMEs (Goto, 2012). Despite the fact that such businesses are common, only a few studies have investigated the development of successors in long-standing family-owned SMEs.

A number of studies have addressed issues regarding successor development in family-owned businesses, either directly or indirectly, and provided important implications for this topic. They covered a wide range of aspects, such as the role of the incumbent (Cadieux, 2007), the benefits of early exposure and entry into the family business (Barach et al., 1988; Cabrera-Suárez, 2005), the role of conversation at the dinner table (Cheng et al., 2013); and the influence of previous work experience either inside or outside the family business (Sardeshmukh and Corbett, 2011; Cabrera-Suárez, 2005). Although most of these studies investigated SMEs, they targeted newer family businesses that were in the first to the third generation.

Only a handful of studies have specifically addressed the issue of developing a successor to a long-standing family firm. Although these studies provided important implications about successor development practices, they (Miller and Le Breton-Miller, 2005; Ward, 2004) focused on large companies rather than SMEs. Other studies included some long-standing family businesses in their samples. However, they (Handler, 1990; Cater and Justis, 2009) included newer businesses as well.

The purpose of this chapter is to address the gap in the research and broadly investigate and identify important issues in the development of successors in long-standing family-owned SMEs in Japan. Based on an interview with an incumbent CEO of a long-standing Japanese family-owned small sake brewery, this chapter investigates the following questions:

1. What does the incumbent CEO want to pass on to his successor?
2. What caused him to think this way? What factors influenced his thinking?
3. How can the incumbent CEO pass on it (answer to the first question) to his successor?

Focusing on a small centuries-old family business in Japan, this chapter contributes to the literature on successor development and the longevity of family businesses.

LITERATURE REVIEW

As discussed in the introduction, although a number of studies have addressed issues regarding successor development in family businesses, most of them targeted relatively newer family businesses: only a few focused specifically on successor development in long-standing family firms.

Among the studies that investigated successor development in newer family businesses, a wide range of topics were covered, providing evidence of various factors that affect the development of successor and succession outcomes. Cabrera-Suárez (2005) studied the succession process in seven Spanish small family businesses and identified characteristics of a successful succession process. These characteristics include early involvement in the family business, working experience in the same industry, assignment of challenging and responsible tasks with the assistance of the predecessor, and mentoring from non-family senior colleagues.

These findings were supported by other studies. For example, in a study of the succession process in US manufacturing firms, meaningful developmental experiences, such as the assignment of challenging tasks or mentoring from senior employees, increased the successors' ability to recognize opportunities (Sardeshmukh and Corbett, 2011). Barach et al. (1988) suggested, based on their study of the second or third generation, that early entry into the family business, through summer and low-level jobs, allowed the successor to gain knowledge about the basic operation and to be reacted to favorably by employees.

Conversation at the dinner table from an early age and outside work experience were identified as important learning experiences in the entrepreneurial learning process of a Hong Kong family firm in the airport engineering service industry (Cheng et al., 2013).

Cadieux (2007) explored the latter phase of the succession process (from the time the successors took managerial positions to the withdrawal of the predecessors) in five small Canadian family firms in the second generation and identified 18 roles of predecessors during the process.

Although few in number, some studies have examined successor development in long-standing family businesses. Based on a study of 41 family businesses in the US and Europe that maintained the first or second largest share of the market for more than two decades (the mean age was 104 years), Miller and Le Breton-Miller (2005) found that long-standing families make use of the long tenure of the CEO, which is a characteristic of family businesses, to raise and train the future successor. The owner-CEOs of the sample firms teach their children about their products, brands, culture, history, and mission at home, usually at the dinner table. Another finding was that the development of the successors of these long-standing firms is aided by on-the-job training and mentoring from employees and managers from various ranks according to the level of proficiency of the successor.

Ward (2004) proposed 50 lessons that were identified as important to the survival of family businesses, based on his experience of study and consultation with long-standing family firms around the world. Some of the lessons are related to successor development. His proposals are more formalized and systematic and involve a wider range of family members. For example, he proposed that successor development should start from the early age of the next generation (as young as eight years old) and should include visits to the company site and a gradual assignment of paid work and skill learning programs according to age. He suggests that successor development be carried out by individuals (e.g. grandparents) as well as by organizations (e.g. task forces).

Although Miller and Le Breton-Miller (2005) and Ward (2004) focused on large family businesses, their findings about successor development in long-standing family businesses are important to the present study. It is also worth noting that they did not focus specifically on successor development but covered a wide range of topics, such as management strategy, succession, governance of family and business, and estate planning.

Some studies of the succession process sampled a broad range of firms that included long-standing family businesses as well as newer firms. Handler (1990) investigated 32 organizations in the second to the fifth generations and revealed a mutual role adjustment process between predecessors and successors. The model was developed as a four-stage process, where successors started as novices and developed into leaders while the predecessors gradually decreased their involvement in the management. Cater and Justis (2009) advanced Handler's proposed model. They studied six small family businesses (aged 33 to 140 years) to relate six factors influencing the development of successors to a four-stage model that illustrated a process in which successors as students developed into leaders of the family business. These factors are positive parental relationships that were built on early exposure to the family business and positive advocacy about the business, long-term orientation, cooperation among siblings, acquiring knowledge via mentoring with a parent, and the successor's understanding about his or her role as a manager.

As discussed above, only a limited number of studies investigated successor development in long-standing family businesses, and few of them targeted long-standing SMEs.

METHODOLOGY

We looked for a research participant through purposeful sampling. Tamura Sake Brewery was chosen based on the second author's research network and because it met the following criteria to fit our research focus of investigating a long-standing family-owned SME:

1.   Family-owned company that has remained in operation for more than 100 years.
2.   Small- or medium-sized enterprise.

Tamura Sake Brewery is a Japanese sake brewery that was founded in 1822. The number of employees is approximately 20, including the CEO, manufacturing staff (brewers), marketing personnel, and clerical workers. See Table 7.1 for demographic information about the company.

Tamura Sake Brewery is classified as a family business for the following reasons. First, the current CEO regards the business as a family business. Second, the owner-CEO intends to pass the business down to the next generation. Third, a single family has been involved in the management of the company for sixteen generations. Although there is currently only one family member who is actively involved in the management, usually two members of the owner-family serve as the CEO and the senior managing director.

Table 7.1   Profile case: Tamura Sake Brewery

Interviewee	Current business	Year of foundation	No. of employees	Annual sales
Hanjuro Tamura Position: CEO, the 16th (since 2008) Entered in 1973 Age: 55	– Sake brewery; – Real estate agency; – Franchise store	1822	20	Approx. JPY 200M (=Approx. $2M)

Data Collection

The current data was collected via a semi-structured interview using an interview guide. The interviewee was the current and sixteenth CEO, named Hanjuro Tamura. The first and the third authors conducted the interview on September 24, 2014. Because the second and the third authors had known the interviewee previously through a research experience, we had a good rapport with the interviewee. The interviewee was very welcoming and willing to share his experience, which allowed us to investigate his thoughts in-depth. The interview lasted approximately two hours and twenty minutes. A follow-up telephone interview was conducted on February 5, 2015 by the first author to confirm our understanding and to ask additional questions. Though the follow-up interview was not recorded, the researcher took notes and revisited them immediately after the interview.

To achieve the objective of this study, the researchers inquired into what Hanjuro wants to pass on to his successor and what led him to that thought – an experience, a person, or something else.

Research Design

The current study is designed as a single-case study because Tamura Sake Brewery is a representative case (Yin, 2009) of long-standing family-owned SMEs. It can be considered a representative case because (1) Tamura Sake Brewery has continued for nearly 200 years since 1822, (2) its main business is sake brewing and the sake-brewing industry has the largest number of centuries-old family businesses (Goto, 2009), and (3) it is a small business.

Data Analysis

The authors employed the coding procedure suggested by Corbin and Strauss (2008). There are two phases of coding, i.e. open coding and axial coding.

Open coding aimed to capture lower-level concepts or themes that indicated things that the interviewee wants to pass on to the successor and the influences on his thinking. Then, the authors grouped the emergent concepts into higher-level categories that consist of lower-level concepts that share properties and dimensions in the same domain. Table 7.2 lists the emergent categories, concepts/themes, and some representative accounts.

Table 7.2 Categories, concepts and representing accounts

Categories	Concepts	Representative accounts
Treating employees well and with respect	Treating employees well	• [my father] treated people [or the employees] extremely well. • I learned how important it is to treat people well. Therefore, indeed, I keep it in my mind. It's about treating people, ah, I mean, to treat employees well. • I suppose my family always cared about making the brewers' job pleasant and let them produce good sake. I suppose my family has valued it for a long time. ... • Therefore, I understood how important it is to treat the employees well. ... In a way, he was compassionate. My family must have continuously put a value on it [treating the employees well]. Therefore, I thought I should continue to value it for years to come.
	Treating employees as equal to family members	[During World War II,] although our family ate rice mixed with a lot of wheat, my father provided the brewers with white rice. Even though our family ate less white rice and more wheat.
Maintaining mutual trust with the local community through socially responsible practices	Maintaining mutual trust with the local community	• I swear to myself not to betray the trust. • I mustn't betray the trust [with the local community].
	Mutual trust with the community	• ... we have a sense of trust with the community. Likewise, the community trusts us. We, sake breweries, have come along with the local community. We came along because of the trust relationship with the community. As a result, while the community trusted us, we contributed to the community. Sometimes they helped us. We have lived in this way. (Accounts by chairman of another brewery, quoted by Hanjuro)
	Social act to the benefit of the community	• ... in the face of this life-or-death matter, we should not mind losing our own wealth because we have owed the community for a long time and have come along with the region. ... It's worth doing [donating a large amount of money]. (Accounts by chairman of another brewery, quoted by Hanjuro)

Long-term orientation	Anticipation	Well, I think about things in centuries by centuries. I think about things at least 50 years ahead. I always think about things based on how today's decision will end up in the next generation.
	Transgenerational sustainability intention	• ... we have to pass on Tamura Sake Brewery to the next generation. • I want to show my son what it meant to 'pass it on for generations.'
Individual-level influence	Learning from predecessor	I heard a story like this [from my father].
	Watching an example (visually)	• I felt so impressed by my father at that time. • ... [my father] treated people [or the employees] extremely well. So should I, I thought. Honestly, I was so impressed.
	Learning from external key actor (orally)	I learned from the chairman of X brewery.
	Role of non-family senior manager: Feedback	• For example, the bantoh may say [to my son], 'You are getting better, sir.' • 'That way is not acceptable in the Tamura family, sir.'
Societal influence	Strong bonds with the community	As you see, we have been located here and done our business [for a long time]. Not only I myself, but also all members of our company in the previous generations had connections with the local community. As a result of such circumstances, we have a sense of trust with the community. Likewise, the community trusts us.

FINDINGS

The interview revealed that transmitting values to his successor is the most fundamental issue in developing the next generation and strongly emphasized the importance of this throughout the interview.

We produced 11 concepts via open coding. Those themes were grouped into five categories via axial coding (see Table 7.2 for the coding results). Three categories represent values that the incumbent CEO wants to pass on to his successor. The nature of each value is described in the column labeled 'Concepts.'

'Individual-level influence' in the values category refers to a means of transmitting the CEO's values. The individual-level influence has several dimensions (predecessor, non-family senior manager, and external key actor) and properties (orally and visually).

'Societal influence' refers to a society-level factor that shapes the CEO's values.

Before looking at each theme, we should explain why the incumbent CEO put the highest priority on passing on his values. As the following accounts indicate, Hanjuro thinks that it is possible to acquire content-specific skills later. However, generosity and compassion for other people are essential to the successor being able to successfully manage the company.

> I think you can acquire know-how for doing business later.
>
> If you can sense the grief of another person and feel compassion for him or her, you can be a CEO, even if you don't understand economic theories.

In the following text, we discuss the findings.

Treating Employees Well and With Respect

The first value that Hanjuro Tamura wants to pass on to his successor is 'treating employees well and with respect.' This refers to respecting non-family employees as individuals and treating them as equal to family members.

When we asked Hanjuro to tell us about his learning experience relative to this value, the first experience he recalled was an event in which he felt impressed by his father's behavior: as he said, 'Though I rarely admired my father, I felt so impressed by him at that time.' The story was described in episode 1 in the opening case.

As the following accounts indicate, Hanjuro learned from that experience about the importance of treating the employees with great respect.

In that sense, [my father] treated people [or the employees] extremely well. So should I, I thought. Honestly, I was so impressed.

I learned how important it is to treat people well. Therefore, indeed, I keep it in my mind. It's about treating people, ah, I mean, treating employees well.

Hanjuro narrated another story in which his father told him to instill the value of treating the employees as equal to family members.

During World War II, people did not have enough rice to eat. People ate wheat mixed with a little bit of rice. However, the brewers came from a rice-producing region and they could have eaten white rice had they still been living back home. The following account best describes how Hanjuro's father treated the brewers even better than he treated family members.

Although our family ate rice mixed with a lot of wheat, my father provided the brewers with white rice. Even though our family ate less white rice and more wheat.

Therefore, I understood how important it is to treat the employees well. . . . In a way, he was compassionate. My family must have continuously put a value on it [treating the employees well]. Therefore, I thought I should continue to value it for years to come.

Hanjuro explained the underlying reason:

That's because [the employees] are the ones who made this [the products or the brand], not the CEO. Therefore, I suppose my family always cared about making the brewers' job pleasant and letting them produce good sake. I suppose my family has valued it for a long time . . .

This value was transmitted to the successor (Hanjuro) from his predecessor (Hanjuro's father) both visually and orally. As described above, Hanjuro learned his father's value of respecting the employees when he observed the way his father treated the employees. In addition, the predecessor told the successor about the value.

Maintaining Mutual Trust with the Local Community through Socially Responsible Practices

The second value was to maintain a mutual trust relationship with the local community.

[W]ell, what I want to teach is, definitely, nothing about know-how in doing business. It's definitely a philosophy. It's definitely, in my case, about our role in the community, the local community. We want to respond to the expectations of the community. Then, I want them to have even greater expectations of us. . . . That will build trust. That will build trust, I think. Yes. I mustn't betray the trust, which doesn't come from the quality of our sake, whether it tastes good or bad.

The following accounts indicate that Hanjuro's value of maintaining mutual trust with the local community was affected by the firm's strong bonds with the community, which were built on the long-term relationship between Tamura Sake Brewery and the community.

> Particularly, old-established businesses or companies, especially in the sake brewing industry, have been continuing for a very long time and are rooted in the local community. Therefore, the relationship between the community and us is so strong. As you see, we have been located here and done our business [for a long time]. Not only I myself, but also all members of our company in the previous generations had connections with the local community. As a result of such circumstances, we have a sense of trust with the community. Likewise, the community trusts us. I swear to myself not to betray the trust.

Hanjuro explained that the mutual trust with the local community could be developed through non-commercial activities. For example, he explained in the follow-up interview that he would like to play a role in preserving the traditional local custom, such as the local festivals, making the best use of the historical documents that Tamura Sake Brewery owned.

Hanjuro described the motivation behind this value as a 'sense of mission' and confirmed it in the follow-up interview.

The most critical moment that led him to understand the importance of maintaining trust with the local community was when Hanjuro listened to the chairman of another nearby sake brewery, described in episode 2 in the opening case.

In episode 2, the chairman of the other brewery told Hanjuro that sake breweries should act for the benefit of the community, thereby maintaining the mutual trust between the two entities. To that end, he told Hanjuro that he should donate a lot of money and that they should not mind losing their own wealth. This account of the chairman represents the theory. The chairman persuaded Hanjuro to contribute to the larger community, or Japan, seeing himself as a member of that larger community. The chairman argued that, from that perspective, there was no difference between contributing to the distant area and to the local community.

He confirmed that he would like to instill in his successor the value of spending money for the benefit of the community.

As noted in the mini case, the value of maintaining mutual trust with the local community was transmitted orally, from the chairman of the other brewery to Hanjuro.

Long-term Orientation

The third value is to have a long-term orientation. It refers to acting, planning, and making decisions based on the anticipation of their consequences in the future.

> Well, I think about things in centuries by centuries. I think about things at least 50 years ahead. I always think about things based on how today's decision will end up in the next generation.

Hanjuro told us that he would like his son to think like that.

Hanjuro learned the value of long-term orientation by watching his father make decisions. About 15 or 20 years ago, when the company replaced the wood of its building with new wood. Hanjuro's father bought expensive wood because he thought it would last for 100 years. He thought the cheaper one would deteriorate more quickly and would cost the future generation. Hanjuro admired that his father 'saw value in its sustainability to 100 years.'

The Role of the Non-family Senior Manager

This subsection is related to one of the individual-level influences on the values, or the means to transmit the values.

When the interview turned to Hanjuro's idea about how to train the next-generation member, he stressed the role of the *bantoh* in assisting him in nurturing the successor. Bantoh refers to a veteran manager whom a CEO trusts the most. The current bantoh has served the Tamura family since the generation of Hanjuro's grandfather.

> Although all I know is about the generation of my father and that of my grandfather, and of course we have made sake since before, I think it always comes down to a bantoh. There was a good bantoh. The bantoh, who has served the Tamura family for three generations, including my generation, is still alive.
>
> It's so hard to make it without the assistance of such a person [i.e. a bantoh].

Another expected role of the bantoh is to give meaningful feedback to the successor.

> For example, the bantoh may say [to my son], 'You are getting better, sir.'

What are requirements to being a good bantoh? Living with the family he or she serves, a bantoh should understand everything about the family and the family business. The next account indicates that Hanjuro expected the bantoh to understand his belief in transgenerational sustainability, as well as the family's bonds with the local community.

> The bantoh needs to understand my philosophy, such as we have to pass on Tamura Sake Brewery to the next generation. Besides, [he should also understand] what the Tamura family means to the community.

Hanjuro was referring to the values that have been identified and discussed in the current chapter. Having a rich understanding of Hanjuro's values ensures that bantoh can assist the incumbent CEO in passing on the values to the successor. A bantoh provides constructive advice and appropriate feedback to the successor from the viewpoint of a veteran. For example, the bantoh may say to the successor, 'That way is not acceptable in the Tamura family, sir' to correct the successor's decision and guide him in the right direction. By the term 'that way,' he referred not only to the tactic of managing the business, but also to his beliefs and values relative to doing business. In this way, the bantoh instills the values of the owners in the successor.

After identifying and analyzing the values, we designed a model that illustrates the relationship between the values of the successor and the factors that shaped those values in the value system of the successor (Figure 7.1). We viewed the interviewee as a successor. That means his values represent the values of a successor. Then we considered how his values were shaped.

Based on the discussion above, we ascertained the influences on the values of the interviewee. As explained at the beginning of this section, we generated individual-level influences (or the means of transmission) and societal influence. The influences are considered independent variables against the values of the successor (the dependent variable).

Regarding the individual-level influences, values were transmitted from the predecessor or the external key actor (the chairman of another brewery) by watching example behavior or listening to individuals. Values were also transmitted from the non-family senior manager (bantoh) via his feedback. These aspects of transmission were illustrated as the arrows in the Figure 7.1.

The individual-level influence category was split into two dimensions – within the family business (predecessor and non-family senior manager) and the external key actor.

The societal influence category (strong bonds with the community) affected the formation of the value (maintaining mutual trust with the local community).

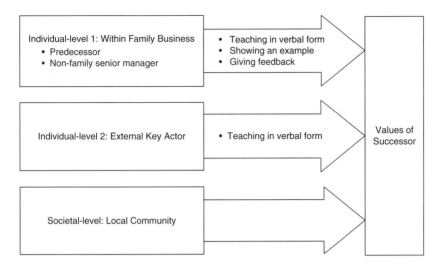

*Figure 7.1   The general model illustrating a development of successors'
values*

DISCUSSION

This chapter investigates key issues in developing a successor to a long-standing small family business in Japan. Based on a semi-structured interview with the incumbent CEO of a small sake brewery in Tokyo, Japan, the study aimed to reveal what the incumbent CEO most wants to pass on to his successor.

The major findings are as follows: First, the present study suggested the importance of value transmission in developing a successor to a long-standing family firm. Second, the study also identified the nature of those values. Third, the study explored factors that affected the development of the values in the value system of the incumbent CEO. Finally, this study provided evidence to support the importance of having a non-family senior manager to nurture the next generation.

Values seem important in developing a successor because they can be a standard for guiding actions as well as for influencing others' values (Rokeach, 1968: 160). A number of studies have suggested the importance of values in long-lasting family businesses. For example, Ward (2004) argued that passing on a value system is essential for long-standing family businesses. Aronoff and Ward (2011) listed 12 benefits of values in successful family businesses. Among them are the following: values create a foundation of organizational culture, values exemplify a framework for decision-making, and people-centered values make employees feel respected and motivated to remain in the organization longer, and they nurture a sense of purpose among the employees. Marques et al. (2014) found that values of 12 CEOs of Spanish family firms had a positive effect on engagement in CSR for the workplace (e.g. employee welfare) and for community.

It is also beneficial to share values among organizational members. Miller and Le Breton-Miller (2005) found that values of the family shape the mission that unites employees as if they belong to the same 'community,' in successfully long-standing large family firms in the US and Europe. Shared values were also related to the job satisfaction of family members (Khanin et al., 2012) and succession planning in family-owned SMEs (Motwani et al., 2006).

As these studies suggest, values are a critical element for continuity and the organizational outcomes of family businesses. Given that a family's values are influenced by the values of the owner-CEO, it is worth noting that the CEO of the current study placed the highest priority on passing on his values to the future successor.

Why did the CEO place emphasis on values in the first place? He explained that the successor can learn and acquire content-specific skills and knowledge later. This finding is consistent with the literature on successors' attributes. Integrity and commitment were rated as the most important attributes for successors in studies in Canada (Chrisman et al., 1998) and India (Sharma and Rao, 2000), while content-specific skills, such as marketing/sales skills, financial skills/experience, and strategic planning skills were rated lower.

The Nature of the Values that are Important for Successors

The current study revealed three values that the incumbent CEO wants to pass on to his eldest son. They are as follows: (1) treating employees well and with respect, (2) maintaining mutual trust with the local community through socially responsible practices, and (3) having a long-term orientation.

The first value identified is treating employees respectfully and as equal to family members. Long-standing large family firms in the US and Europe, too, have generosity toward their employees (Miller and Le Breton-Miller, 2005). However, whereas Miller and Le Breton-Miller (2005) pointed to specific investments for employees in terms of training and benefits, the current study just found a more general attitude toward the employees. The interviewee mentioned respect and gratitude toward the employees for their devoted service.

In order to achieve the second value, maintaining mutual trust with the local community, the incumbent CEO of this study argued that he would contribute to the community through social practices. Existing studies have suggested that long-standing large family businesses tend to engage in philanthropy and pro bono work (Miller and Le Breton-Miller, 2005; Ward, 2004).

The third value is having a long-term orientation. The CEO explained in the interview that he tended to make decisions based on his anticipation of their consequences about 100 years ahead. Thinking with a long-term perspective is a major characteristic of family businesses. Family firms were found to rate statistically higher than non-family firms in terms of long-term orientation (Brigham et al., 2014). Long-term orientation was also found to be a factor influencing successor development (Cater and Justis, 2009; Miller and Le Breton-Miller, 2005).

However, other studies on values of long-standing family businesses have suggested a different picture. The top-rated values were honesty, credibility, quality, and hard work by centuries-old family businesses in Finland (Koiranen, 2002), Spain, Italy, and France (Tápies and Fernández-Moya, 2012). These values were not identified in the current study, but one, credibility, may be related to 'trust with the local community' in this study. The French sample presented some similarities to the current study. 'Mutual respect' and 'trust' were ranked relatively high (the fourth and the seventh place, respectively) (Tápies and Fernández-Moya, 2012). However, values regarding social responsibility were not ranked high in these studies, indicating a clear difference with the current study. Future studies are needed to investigate the influence of national culture on the difference in the values of family businesses across countries.

The current finding about values advances knowledge about socio-emotional wealth and the non-financial goals of family businesses. The existing studies have argued that concern for organizational reputation is a major objective for a family business to preserve its socio-emotional wealth (Berrone et al., 2012; Naldi et al., 2013). In addition, a family's concern for reputation is predicted to affect the business' pursuit of non-financial goals (Zellweger et al., 2011).

The current study partly supports these arguments. The incumbent CEO of this study exhibited a strong desire to maintain mutual trust with the local community by doing more social good than is expected, indicating his desire to pursue a non-financial goal. He is also somewhat concerned about the reputation of the family business within the community. However, obtaining a reputation is not his major reason for contributing to society. Instead, the CEO is driven by genuinely altruistic motives to give back to the local community. He described his emotion as a sense of mission. This finding indicates that there may be another factor affecting the motive of a family business to be devoted to society. Future studies are needed to investigate the altruistic nature of the social practices of family businesses.

Transmission of Values

The current study provided evidence about the means of transmitting an incumbent CEO's values to the successor. As displayed in Table 7.2, the current study identified three individual-level ways to transmit values: being taught orally by the predecessor or other key actor, observing someone's behavior that represents the value, and receiving feedback from a non-family senior manager.

These findings are consistent with the literature. The current study revealed that values were transmitted to the next generation when the interviewee watched example behavior (Cadieux, 2007; Tápies and Fernández-Moya, 2012; Ward, 2004) or listened to the stories of the senior generation (Parada and Viladás, 2010; Tápies and Fernández-Moya, 2012).

The current study also revealed that a non-family senior manager instilled values via feedback. The existing studies of long-standing family businesses support the current findings about the role of senior managers. In long-standing large family businesses, the next generation learns not only skills but also values from senior colleagues and managers assigned as tutors or mentors for the successor (Miller and Le Breton-Miller, 2005).

Limitations

The data of the current study is not sufficient to examine the relationship between the values of the focal CEO and the longevity of the family business. However, as discussed in this section, there are many similarities with other studies focused on long-standing family businesses, implying a relationship with corporate continuity. Future studies need to further test or explore this relationship.

Another limitation of this study is its generalizability. Future studies need to investigate in two directions.

First, because the current study relied on the evidence of a single case, it remains unclear whether the current findings can be applied to the other companies, even though they are in the same industry.

The second direction is related to the size of the business. In the current study, the focal company placed a substantial emphasis on its bonds with the local community because the local region is the main market. Approximately 90 percent of sales come from the local area. Such circumstances, together with the long history (nearly 200 years) of the business in the same location, drove the focal company to devote itself to the local community.

What if the business becomes larger? If the business becomes larger and if the scope of the business expands, the intensity of its relationship with the local community may decrease. The company may act not only for the benefit of the local community, but also try to meet the expectations of other markets. Then, would the company still seek to maintain trust with the local community by means of socially responsible behavior? It is true that large family businesses are engaged in philanthropy for the local community (Miller and Le Breton-Miller, 2005; Ward, 2004). However, there remains room to investigate how a change in the size of a business affects the relationship between the family firm and the local community as well as the values of the family.

ACKNOWLEDGEMENTS

We are grateful to Dr Pramodita Sharma and the editors for their support and permission to publish this study. We wish to thank the two reviewers for their critical reading of the manuscript and their insightful and constructive comments. Without their guidance and persistent support, this chapter would not have been possible. We would like to express our gratitude to Mr Hanjuro Tamura for his participation in this study. Finally, we would like to thank Editage (www.editage.jp) for English language editing.

REFERENCES

Aronoff, C.E. and Ward, J.L. (2011). *Family Business Values: How to Assure a Legacy of Continuity and Success.* New York, NY: Palgrave Macmillan.

Barach, J.A., Gantisky, J., Carson, J.A., and Doochin, B.A. (1988). Entry of the next generation: strategic challenge for family business. *Journal of Small Business Management*, 26(2): 49–56.

Berrone, P., Cruz, C., and Gomez-Mejia, L.R. (2012). Socioemotional wealth in family firms: theoretical dimensions, assessment approaches, and agenda for future research. *Family Business Review*, 25(3): 258–279.

Brigham, K.H., Lumpkin, G.T., Payne, G.T., and Zachary, M.A. (2014). Researching long-term orientation: a validation study and recommendations for future research. *Family Business Review*, 27(1): 72–88.

Cabrera-Suárez, K. (2005). Leadership transfer and the successor development in the family firm. *The Leadership Quarterly*, 16: 71–96.

Cadieux, L. (2007). Succession in small and medium-sized family businesses: toward a typology of predecessor roles during and after instatement of the successor. *Family Business Review*, 20(2): 95–109.

Cater, J.J., III and Justis, R.T. (2009). The development of successors from followers to leaders in small family firms: an exploratory study. *Family Business Review*, 22(2): 109–124.

Cater, J.J., III and Justis, R.T. (2010). The development and implementation of shared leadership in multi-generational family firms. *Management Research Review*, 33(6): 563–585.

Cheng, J.C.Y., Ho, F.H.C., and Au, K. (2013). Transgenerational entrepreneurship and entrepreneurial learning: a case study of Associated Engineers Ltd in Hong Kong. In Sharma, P., Sieger, P., Nason, R.S., Gonzalez, L., A.C. and Ramachandran, K. (eds), *Exploring Transgenerational Entrepreneurship: The Role of Resources and Capabilities* (62–87), Cheltenham, UK and Northampton, MA, USA: Edward Elgar Publishing.

Chrisman, J.J., Chua, J.H., and Sharma, P. (1998). Important attributes of successors in family businesses: an exploratory study. *Family Business Review*, 11(1): 19–34.

Corbin, J. and Strauss, A. (2008). *Basics of Qualitative Research: Techniques and Procedures for Developing Grounded Theory* (3rd edn). Los Angeles, CA: Sage Publications.

Goto, T. (2009). *Sandai, hyakunen tsuburenai kaisha no ruru*: [Principles in companies that will survive for more than three generations, or for longer than one hundred years]. Tokyo, Japan: Purejidento.

Goto, T. (2012). *Famili bijinesu: Shirarezaru jitsuryoku to kanousei* [Family business: Unknown capabilities and potential]. Tokyo, Japan: Hakuto-shobo.

Handler, W.C. (1990). Succession in family firms: a mutual role adjustment between entrepreneur and next-generation family members. *Entrepreneurship Theory and Practice*, 15(1): 37–51.

Khanin, D., Turel, O., and Mahto, R.V. (2012). How to increase job satisfaction and reduce turnover intentions in the family firm: the family-business embeddedness perspective. *Family Business Review*, 25(4): 391–408.

Koiranen, M. (2002). Over 100 years of age but still entrepreneurially active in business: exploring the values and family characteristics of old Finnish family firms. *Family Business Review*, 15(3): 175–187.

Marques, P., Presas, P., and Simon, A. (2014). The heterogeneity of family firms in CSR engagement: the role of values. *Family Business Review*, 27(3): 206–227.

Miller, D. and Le Breton-Miller, I. (2005). *Managing for the Long Run: Lessons in Competitive Advantage from Great Family Businesses*. Boston, MA: Harvard Business School Press.

Motwani, J., Levenburg, N.M., Schwarz, T.V., and Blankson, C. (2006). Succession planning in SMEs: an empirical analysis. *International Small Business Journal*, 24(5): 471–495.

Naldi, L., Cennamo, C., Corbetta, G., and Gomez-Mejia, L. (2013). Preserving socioemotional wealth in family firms: asset of liability? The moderating role of business context. *Entrepreneurship Theory and Practice*, 37(6): 1341–1360.

Parada, M.J. and Viladás, H. (2010). Narratives: a powerful device for values transmission in family business. *Journal of Organizational Change Management*, 23(2): 166–172.

Rokeach, M. (1968). *Beliefs, Attitudes, and Values: A Theory of Organization and Change*. San Francisco, CA: Jossey-Bass.

Sardeshmukh, S.R. and Corbett, A.C. (2011). The duality of internal and external development of successors: opportunity recognition in family firms. *Family Business Review*, 24(2): 111–125.

Sharma, P. and Rao, A.S. (2000). Successor attributes in Indian and Canadian family firms: a comparative study. *Family Business Review*, 13(4): 313–330.

Tápies, J. and Fernández-Moya, M. (2012). Values and longevity in family business: evidence from a cross-cultural analysis. *Journal of Family Business Management*, 2(2): 130–146.

Ward, J.L. (2004). *Perpetuating the Family Business: 50 Lessons Learned from Long-Lasting, Successful Families in Business*. New York, NY: Palgrave Macmillan.

Yin, R.K. (2009). *Case Study Research: Design and Methods* (4th edn). Los Angeles, CA: Sage Publications.

Zellweger, T.M., Nason, R.S., Nordqvist, M., and Brush, C.G. (2011). Why do family firms strive for nonfinancial goals? An organizational identity perspective. *Entrepreneurship Theory and Practice*, 37(2): 229–248.

PART III

Structure and next generation leader preparation

8. Family's decision in venture creation for next generation leaders: the role of trust across two generations in the case of diversification

Leilanie Mohd Nor, Christian Lechner, Mohar Yusof, Barjoyai Bardai and Siri Roland Xavier

MINI CASE STUDY: MOFAZ GROUP

> My top priority now, is to retire. But I have broken my promise. I said I want to retire at 65, but I am already 69. This is not right. I want time for myself. I want to pass the business over to my children.
> (Haji Mohamed Fauzy Abdul Hamid)

In January 2015, Haji Mohamed Fauzy Abdul Hamid (Fauzy) marked his 40th anniversary as the founder and owner of MOFAZ Group. MOFAZ evolved from a small retail shop that used rice sacks as partition and furniture for its distribution office to a giant conglomerate that managed diversified businesses of automotive, international and domestic trading, aviation, marine, services and hospitality, green technology, motor sports, advertising as well as wellness and well-being sectors.

In the 1970s, Fauzy spent thirteen years working with Nestlé before he decided to resign and set up his own venture. He envisioned himself to be a distributor. With USD 10,000 from Nestlé as part of the dealership arrangement, Fauzy embarked on becoming the first Malay retailer and one of the most successful distributors for Nestlé Malaysia. Starting up was not easy. Soon after, with the assistance of the Malaysian government for start-ups, Fauzy bought his first shop lot at Taman Tun Dr. Ismail, which he proudly owned up to this day.

In the early 1980s, Fauzy was one of the pioneer Malay entrepreneurs with an approved permit for importing cars. By the late 1980s, he ventured into the marine business, and made history when he became the first and only dealership in Malaysia for Bayliner Boats, USA. Although Malaysia was not a boating society, MOFAZ Group became the number one dealership in the world for selling 360 boats in its first year of operations.

Soon after, he set up a flying academy in Langkawi, which led to the birth of MOFAZ Air and MOFAZ Air Academy. During this time, Fauzy resided in Dallas for a few years, and saw how Southwest Airlines, the no frills airline, was taking off in the US aviation industry. In 1993, he decided to set up AirAsia. However, in 2002, due to some challenges faced by AirAsia, Fauzy's business partner, DRB-HICOM's (a leading Malaysian conglomerate company) shares were sold to Tony Fernandes, who then, ten years later took AirAsia to become the leading no frills airline in the world. Looking back, Fauzy was happy that the vision he had in mind materialized,

> My vision was a no frills airline. Their timing was right. They had Internet marketing and all other forms of digital marketing – there was none at my time.

Members of the Malaysian public and petrol-heads were familiar with the name MOFAZ as franchise dealers of well-known imported vehicle brand names such as Honda, Mercedes Benz and Suzuki as well as the leading 'Complete Built Up' (CBU) car trader of imported premium cars from Japan and Europe. Conveniently located at a bustling Damansara area of Kuala Lumpur, MOFAZ main headquarters faced the busy Damansara-Puchong highway where vehicles which passed by that freeway could get a good view of the sophisticated building with its spacious showroom displaying a full range of the latest Honda models and up-class models of fast cars such as Ferrari, Lamborghini and Porsche (see Figure 8.1).

MOFAZ Group continued to grow with new ventures, especially its latest initiative with Circle K, a US-based company, which Fauzy had acquired the license for Malaysia and targeted to open 500 outlets by 2018. Unlike other Circle K franchises in the world, the Circle K outlets in Malaysia operated on a *Halal* concept. Moreover, MOFAZ was targeting Malaysians, local graduates and senior citizens to work for them in the stores. The organization planned to contribute to the nation through Circle K by reducing unemployment among local graduates and likewise provide investment opportunity for those in the golden age.

The Fauzy family was the sole owner of this business. His three sons have their own distinct roles in managing the MOFAZ Group. Fauzy had always encouraged his family to set up their own ventures, too. For example, in 2009, he supported his eldest son, Ferhan, to launch the *Halal* Subways in London, in addition to managing the Group's European automotive market.

Source: www.mofaz.com.

Figure 8.1   MOFAZ group key milestones

> Every new venture will be set up in their own (the Fauzy family) capacity. Once it is successful, it will be absorbed into the company. So, only successful companies are absorbed to the group. For the Subway business, it was the family's own personal investment. (Adit Rahim, Head of Corporate Communications, MOFAZ Group)

Fairuz, the middle son, was in motor sports. He became the first Malaysian to break the world's lap record set by racing legend Ayrton Senna at the Donnington Park Circuit, UK. MOFAZ significantly contributed a giant step in steering Malaysia into the global racing limelight by managing their very own carting circuit as well as providing support for local racing talents to make it onto the world stage through their international motor sports team, MOFAZ Racing. Fauzy pioneered driver development and evolution programs for motor sports in the country, especially Formula One. MOFAZ seized the opportunity created by its participation in the World Series to promote products, services and brands, at all World Series venues. Fauzy had encouraged Fairuz to take on the challenge to create a driving academy, leveraging on his experience as a professional racing driver upon his return from UK, where he was trained.

176 Next generation leaders for transgenerational family enterprises

Farriz, the youngest son, was leading the automotive and property businesses of the Group in Malaysia. He joined the MOFAZ Group in 2009 and worked his way up from being a car salesman to Vice President. Described by his father as a driven and hardworking individual, Farriz spoke fondly of his father's decision in property development:

> The best example is this area. People used to criticize him for buying that land. It's the vision he has. He believes in his ventures, he knows he can manage it, and because he is confident with his decisions, I feel I am learning so much from him by just observing how he does things. (Farriz, MOFAZ Group)

Fauzy wanted to create a culture of openness, and willingness to take calculated risks. But at the same time, he wanted to build a 'no blame' workplace where employees are confident in their choices, but also learn from their mistakes. On the other hand, this also meant that they bore the responsibility for what they did. Responsibility of employees and managers were central issues for him. Thus, at the MOFAZ Group, employees were provided with equal opportunities for individuals to progress within the business.

Fauzy also embraced technology readily to communicate with his employees:

> He (Fauzy) gets feedback from everyone, every member of the MOFAZ Group family, and they will have an avenue to say what they think about it. Fauzy is very open to suggestions and feedback from employees. He will ask them to put themselves in his shoes and think how to do it. And he likes to bounce ideas back and forth. He does not breed a yes-man. (Adit explained)

In addition to knowledge sharing, family was the 'soul' in the MOFAZ Group. There were a lot of informal sessions with everyone over lunches at the cafe. Fauzy took time to learn about their interests, their children, their families, and their difficulties. The employees at the MOFAZ Group were closely knitted. Twenty to thirty percent of the employees had been with the company for more than thirty years and many of their children also came to work for the MOFAZ Group.

Fauzy was already in his late 60s; he wanted to retire and pass the business over to his children. Fauzy's decisions to further explore into new business opportunities had always been discussed among family members. Given the fact that the MOFAZ Group was highly diversified, Fauzy wanted to ensure that his three sons (and his nine-year-old daughter, Falysha) were able to pursue their interests and dreams, too. He felt that the business could be managed either by his children or professionals. Fauzy was confident that the creation of the 'Supreme Council' which he set up three years ago was able to carry out the responsibilities of managing the MOFAZ Group. The Supreme Council met once a month discussing important operational issues and was represented by Farriz and nine CEOs of selected subsidiaries.

Fauzy was guided by three principles he held dearly in life: (1) to raise children to the right religious path; (2) to follow 'Sedekah' – the act of giving charity – as much as you can afford; and (3) to transfer your knowledge so as to multiply it. The following three simple lines guided his life:

> When I commit, I fulfill; When I promise, I deliver; When I have my aim, I must achieve it.

Discussion Questions

1. Analyse and compare how trust was developed between family members, and between the family and employees.
2. Diversification has been Fauzy's strategy from the inception of the family business. How has this influenced his three sons in creating ventures? Discuss.

INTRODUCTION

This chapter examines how the family influences entrepreneurial outcomes in the context of a successful family business in Malaysia, the MOFAZ Group. The main focus is on the founding entrepreneur, within a business group (Lechner and Leyronas, 2009), and his multiple activities ('portfolio entrepreneurship') in order to exploit new opportunities through diversification, how he functions as an entrepreneur, the dynamics of his family environment, and how he makes and arrives at decisions.

We focus specifically on trust in family firms and its effect on diversification decisions, particularly across two generations, that is, the founding and second generation of the MOFAZ Group. Trust can be defined as the positive expectation that an actor will not behave opportunistically and to the willingness of an actor to be vulnerable to another actor (Mayer, Davis, and Schoorman, 1995). Kinship is characterized by interpersonal trust and thus family firms are considered to be governed by such trust (Corbetta and Salvato, 2004). Trust within family members of the same or across generations, and between the family and the non-family employees, are important drivers to understand how family firms perform (Karra, Tracey, and Phillips, 2006).

Given the low survival rate in transgenerational entrepreneurship, the family members' ability to make sound decisions together is crucial (Tisue, 1999). Understanding how trust is developed between family members, between family and non-family members and how it impacts decisions about firm diversification as a mode of firm development could thus help to increase our understanding of transgenerational success. Hence, the key research question of this study is, 'How does trust act on diversification decisions within a family business?'

The unique make-up of the family, and the lack of research that can tailor to specific situations in the orientation of the role of trust in the decision-making process, justifies a qualitative study that allows also to take into account multiple interactions between family members across generations and with the employees and to explore dynamic process of trust building within organizations. Moreover, research in family business management is still in its early stages in Malaysia. Hence, this study fills the lacuna in the discipline particularly in explaining the relationship between trust and decision-making in venturing into new business.

This chapter focuses on a family business case which highlights two key elements. First, the founder's decision in venture creation. Second, it centers around trust as a key pillar that binds the two generations in a family business embarking on a diversification strategy. The next section is an overview of the literature, followed by the methods and case selection. Then, findings are shared and discussed. Limitations, future research possibilities, lead to the conclusions.

GUIDING LITERATURE

Social relations are the context in which economic activity is embedded (Granovetter, 1985; Grabher, 1990; Granovetter, 1992). Social relations might be seen as a mechanism that installs trust (Granovetter, 1985, 1992). Trust can be understood as the expectation that the other actor in a dyad will not exploit one's vulnerabilities and that the overall outcome of a relation will benefit both parties (Ring, 1997; De Laat, 1997; Steier and Muethel, 2014). 'Reduced to its basics, trust involves a belief that the other person will be honest. Trust is warranted if the belief is true' (Casson and Cox, 1997: 179).

Stronger forms of trust involve uncertainty (Ring, 1997). Trust can be built by mutual commitments through relation specific investment that creates inter-dependencies (De Laat, 1997; Hakansson and Snehota, 1995); mutual commitments require however some form of initial unwarranted trust in the other partner, some optimism in the success of the inter-firm relation (De Laat, 1997). Therefore, this form of actor bonding is both an outcome and pre-condition of trust (Hakansson and Johanson, 1992).

Trust might be also seen as path-dependent, based on experience (Gulati, 1998). The questions 'who do we trust?' and 'what do we trust them with?' have also an experience or knowledge component (McAllister, 1995). The reputation of an actor in terms of quality of activities but maybe more important in terms of behavior (De Laat, 1997; Casson and Cox, 1997) might be understood 'as-if-warranted' trust.

An even stronger form of trust seems to be personal based trust rather than knowledge based trust (McAllister, 1995). This form of trust is based on the identification of common values and on the affection with the other actor; these effects are reinforced by culture and kinship (Lewicki and Bunker, 1996; McAllister, 1995). Steier and Muethel (2014) postulated that interpersonal trust has five dimensions namely integrity, consistency, ability, benevolence and openness and argued that institutional trust in family firms mirrors benevolence-based trust.

Generally, there is the assumption that family firms are particularly built on trust (Corbetta and Salvato, 2004). In a family setting where by definition the family members have strong social ties, trust in the next generation involves both a personal and a competence component. On the interpersonal side, if trust will be warranted to the children, it will be stronger than for outsiders; the same might apply to distrust, that is, there might be a tendency to judge trustworthiness at the extremes (both positive and negative). While generally, trust building between actors is seen as moving from calculated to competence based to finally interpersonal trust, it might be necessary to treat interpersonal and competence based trust as parallel and distinct components. However, little is known about the development of competence based trust in family firms. This involves questions and the development of interpersonal and competence based trust across generations, between family members and between family members and non-family employees.

Past studies suggested that entrepreneurs may embark on portfolio entrepreneurship due to growth aspirations, wealth and risk diversification, value maximization and providing career opportunities to family members (Ram, 1994). Portfolio entrepreneurship is regarded as the resultant of creative entrepreneurial activity through entrepreneurial diversification (Rosa, 1998; Lechner and Leyronas, 2009). Interestingly, portfolio entrepreneurship is especially prevalent in family firms due to decisions made in a dynamic family context, time horizon of family firms (Zellweger, 2007) that opens up the opportunity to various ventures being created within the family web to generate income and stability for their families.

Zellweger, Nason, and Nordqvist (2011) argued that across time, families exhibit a significant level of entrepreneurial activity, in terms of rearrangements of the portfolio of activities through founding activity, mergers, acquisition and even divestments. Even though there might be various reasons and ways for diversification, in exploring the connection between trust and motivation in affecting decision-making in creating new ventures, this chapter focuses on two types of motivation within a family business context, that is, motivation for finding a place for the family, and, motivation for business growth.

METHODS

Qualitative Research as the Appropriate Method

Given the unexplored role of trust in diversification decisions of family firms, the complex nature of different forms of trust from a process perspective, a qualitative approach to investigate why and how questions appears appropriate. Though the grounded theory recommends that a literature review is completed at the beginning of the study, as is the norm for most scholarly research (Charmaz, 2006), the challenge, however, is to think critically, and not to have preconceived beliefs. Alternatively, Glaser and Strauss (1967) suggested that as part of theory formation, the literature review is carried out after data collection has begun, so as to prevent preconceived ideas.

In this study, the literature review is carried out before data collection, as it is necessary to understand family business issues, outline what is known of family business, highlight the gaps in knowledge of family business decision-making, and focus the study in the context of a family firm's diversification, particularly, in the creation of new ventures. In this sense, literature is guiding towards the areas to explore in order to generate new theoretical propositions.

Case Selection

The case selected for this study is chosen to ensure the effort drawn from this activity is theoretically a useful case, that is, those that replicate or extend theory by filling conceptual categories. As Pettigrew (1998) illustrated, it makes sense to work within the limited number of cases where the process is 'transparently observable'. MOFAZ Group was selected based on:

1. Annual sales turnover.
2. Innovativeness towards products or process.
3. Transgenerational entrepreneurship.

Table 8.1 Selection criterion for MOFAZ Group

Type of firm / Description	
Firms	MOFAZ Group
Industry	Automotive, Trading, and Properties
Sales turnover (2013)	More than USD 200 million per annum
Innovativeness towards products or services	Diversifying into property and Halal food businesses
Transgenerational entrepreneurship	First generation passing on to second generation
Ventures created in the past 3 years	Halal Subway franchise in the UK Property Management Business

Table 8.1 provides details on the selection criterion for MOFAZ Group.

We interviewed Fauzy, the founder, his youngest son, Farriz, and a long-serving non-family manager, Adit, who is a confidante of the founder. Each interview ran between 40 and 90 minutes and was recorded. Two new ventures were identified which were created in the past three years namely the first Halal Subway franchise for the UK and a property business involving the development of a township comprising residential and commercial property units.

In this study, the richness, depth and dynamics of family business research led to approaches such as observation on site, interviews, conversations during social gatherings with the founder, family members and non-family members, data collected in past research, public-content articles found, and other relevant documentation were collected, to provide stronger substantiation of construct and propositions and to promote high levels of synergy (Eisenhardt, 1989; Eisenhardt and Graebner, 2007).

Personal interviewing sessions took place at the offices of the respondents. All the respondents had earlier requested for a copy of the interview questions to be sent to them. Hence, the interview schedule was emailed to them two weeks prior to the appointment dates. The interview schedule was designed to provide semi-structured interview questions. It was meant just to guide the interviews so that the sessions did not stray or deviate into unrelated areas. For each interview session, we started with a brief introduction to the respondents on the purpose and objective of the interview. For Farriz and Adit, they were also informed of the earlier interview which the researcher had with Fauzy.

FINDINGS

Development of Trust between Family Members

In this study, we found that 'trust' develops between family members as a result of Fauzy's ongoing efforts of laying the foundation through informal meetings (even meetings at dinner tables) or social gatherings for the family, which in turn encourage communication, openness and respect among family members. To ensure that family members understood his vision, philosophy, aspiration and purpose of doing business, Fauzy believed that trust is the key. He said:

> In life, the one golden rule you need to have and understand is to learn how to trust. If you don't learn how to trust, you yourself are the crook, because you don't trust yourself, and you don't trust other people. If you learn how to trust, you trust other people, then, you too can be trusted. If you have doubt in every human being, please take a close look at yourself and think why?

We identified that there is high interpersonal trust between family members in this case, particularly between the founder and the second generation leaders. For instance, Farriz's perception of his father's attitude and practices include:

> I think, his (Fauzy) top priority is family, it is not his work. He is family first, then, work second. We never fail to have dinner every night together, even though he comes home late, at 9:30pm, or if there is no big workload, he comes home, every single day, at 8:00pm. And we will all have dinner.

The above is in line with LaChapelle's (1997) contention that relatively low and high trust in family businesses is created and maintained by the attitudes, leadership practices, and interpersonal relationships of family members, who serve as a primary constellation of role models (based on family histories, norms and values) for those who are involved in the organization. In addition, leadership practices also create and reinforce relative trust or mistrust in the organization, and identified effective communication processes, involvement in decision-making and approaching trust-building as a proactive and reinforcing process.

Development of Trust between Family and Non-family Members

In this case, we also found that there is high trust between family and non-family members. The trust which has been developed between family members has also seeped into the firm level which affects the employees.

Adit, a non-family manager, spoke of the trust among family members and employees as well as commitment level among family members and employees:

> When he (Fauzy) makes something successful, he will really make it happen. He will go down to the ground, and really push the cards. So, the commitment level is always 100 percent throughout.

In addition, Adit said:

> We are fortunate enough to be groomed by him (Fauzy), either directly or indirectly. So, we tend to not just be a typical staff, but to inculcate a culture that this company is a family. If one person is hurt, everyone gets hurt. One person knows about it, everyone knows about it. One because it is founded by an entrepreneur and headed by an appointee. It is not easy to follow his pace. Seventy-five percent of the time, I am with him handling events. It amazes me how he could go on and on and on, like an Energizer Bunny, and we want to call it a day.

Further, to demonstrate the level of commitment that Fauzy and his family have for the well-being and interest of employees, below is an excerpt of Fauzy's expression. It is interesting to see here how he regarded MOFAZ Group as home.

> [T]he golden rule is, you don't pay to get glamour. For me, my pocket is to pay my responsibilities first, that's my responsibility, above all. Charity begins at home. So, I must be able to pay the salary of my staff, about 600 under my wings. And each of them have an average of four in their household, and that is my responsibility, all 2,400. They all need to eat. If I pay them, they get to eat. Let's settle for that. The rest will come later. When you have got that in mind, and you do things with sincerity. Of course, I sacrifice a lot of things, like, I do not play golf, because I cannot appreciate hitting the ball, walk in the sun, wear the gloves . . . unless you have other motives.

Clearly, there is the overriding role of the founding entrepreneur in nurturing trust. But the founder's reputation also crosses over to the next generation leaders. The mediating role of the founder between the family and the employees, is important because it might reduce the risk of blind faith and familism (Cruz et al., 2010; Sundaramurthy, 2008) since the founder will need to respect expectations of both family and non-family members.

How Trust Affects Diversification Decision Within MOFAZ

MOFAZ Group is a highly diversified company with approximately fifty subsidiaries, with core businesses in automotive and property investment. Over two decades, the family firm expanded into property development, hospitality, health care management, and food and beverage. Being a large private group, wholly owned by the family and professionally-managed, decisions related to venture creation and diversification are made at the strategic level through two structures: the 'Exco' which consists of family members only, and, the 'Supreme Council' which consists of ten members, namely Farriz, a second generation leader and nine CEOs of subsidiary companies.

Fauzy, the founder, chairs the Exco but does not sit in the Supreme Council, although he comes in as an observer at times. Fauzy spoke of Farriz who is put in charge of the overall operations in Kuala Lumpur and currently groomed to lead the company:

> Farriz handles the business here alone, and the business is very spread out. . . . But, we have other things we are doing. We have put in place what needs to be done for the next level, for the group. This will take one to three years. We are already planning that, hence the formation of the Supreme Council, of which Farriz is the chair.

Farriz explained the strategic decision-making process:

> The Supreme Council meets once a month. I sit in all the meetings. I don't sit on the Exco . . . on the Exco is all family members. I see all of them at home. This business is 100 percent owned by the family, I see them every day. So, Exco is just formality. We do sometimes, discuss work at home. If there is a third party involved, then it goes to the board.

In the subsequent subsections we examine and answer the question of how trust affects diversification decisions within the MOFAZ Group. In the decision-making process, we identified three things which were affected by trust, namely speed of the process, motivation for the venture creation and mode of the new ventures.

Trust Affects Speed

Speed of the decision-making process is seen to be 'faster' because decisions are made among family members, often at informal meetings such as at their dinner tables, or social gatherings. In the MOFAZ Group, what goes to the board is a matter of formality.

Speed was clearly seen at MOFAZ Group. Adit reiterated:

> It is never quick or fast with Fauzy. It will usually be deliberated very very carefully. He gets feedback from everyone, every member of the MOFAZ Group family, and they will have an avenue to say what they think about it. Fauzy is very open to suggestions and feedback from staff. He will ask them to put

themselves in his shoes and think how to do it. And he likes to bounce ideas back and forth. He does not breed a yes-man. We go into any business with informed decisions, running, we never walk. Because we value our time, and do not want to second guess our decisions as they are well thought out.

It was evident that decision-making at the MOFAZ Group was deliberate yet fast because of Fauzy's ability to foster trust in the family and between the family and employees. This enabled Fauzy to attain the commitment of family members and employees (at the 'operational level') in embarking on creating ventures (at the 'performance' level).

Trust Affects Motivation

In this study, we found a connection between trust and motivation. We explored the understanding of motivation in the context of the MOFAZ Group, by unearthing Fauzy's motivation when creating the two new ventures – the Halal Subway franchise and the property business. When we asked why he made the decision and what the priority was for him, Fauzy's answer was:

> That's why I created the Supreme Council. It is now in its third year. I don't attend that meeting anymore. Because if I attend, it becomes my meeting. But now, it is run and managed without me. When we iron out our financials, they will have their own resources to manage themselves for their own. Say, you need x-amount to manage. They need that amount with this average income. The balance is yours. So, they have a sense of belonging of the business. Now, it is already happening. My children are also in the Supreme Council, where they want, they go. They are the shareholders.

When Adit's perceptions about Fauzy's motivation were asked, he said:

> This is a family business. He (Fauzy) will consult his family because it is not just about investment of funds, but always about him having to release his time to travel, if need be, to promote his business. There are a lot of sacrifices he will have to make. He will consult his family first.

It is interesting to find that the founder's motivation is to find a place for the family. Interpersonal trust of the founder increases the motivation to find a place for family members but what does 'find a place mean'? It means also – as the case indicates – to find a place where the family members are motivated to perform. This implies that the founder trusts the next generation leaders to acquire the necessary competences because they are highly motivated or that they have already acquired some of the competences and are willing to acquire the missing ones, resolving thus the problem of an incomplete trust process that would start and end with interpersonal trust in a family setting compared with non-family members. Mutual motivation for the new venture, that is, finding a place for the family, is thus creating some form of competence based trust based on motivation.

Trust Affects Mode of New Venture

Mode of new venture describes how the venture is managed upon its formation. Business ventures can either be managed by a family manager, or by a non-family manager. How and why this is decided upon is dependent on the trust level at the family level and firm level. In the case of the MOFAZ Group, its new ventures (one core business and one non-core business) are managed by family managers, namely the family's second generation leaders. Ferhan, Fauzy's eldest son, manages the Subway franchise outlets in the UK (unrelated diversification) while Farriz manages the property business in Kuala Lumpur (related diversification).

Adit described the management of the non-core business:

> It is headed by Ferhan. When he was based here (in Kuala Lumpur), he was the VP Automotive. But then he decided to venture into Europe because he sees it as a challenge for him to fortify and strengthen the MOFAZ brand there. We have been in Europe for the past 20 years, prevalently in motor sports. But out of the need for Halal food at the track when we go racing, that also cultivated the requirement of having our catering or food outfit. . . . So, Ferhan decided to go into convenient food, i.e. sandwiches, Ferhan discussed that at length with his father. And the opportunity arises for him to open the first all-Halal Subway in Northampton.

The fact that either options of choosing family or non-family members for diversification have important signaling effects. While finding a place for the family based on motivation already creates some form of competence based trust between family members, the potential choice of non-family members increases also the competence based trust that non-family employees can place on the family members. That means, interpersonal trust leads through the type of diversification to competence based trust between the family members but also between the family and employees. In this sense, the unrelated diversification activities away from the core business might be better received inside the firm since both employees and family members can find unique opportunities based on competence trust.

The implication of this finding is far reaching: as employees need to 'earn' interpersonal trust through a process that starts with calculated trust and subsequently competence based trust, it is crucial that family members need to acquire also some form of competence based trust but not as an intermediary step for interpersonal trust (which already exists) but as a credibility trigger to assure trust among employees across family generations. This can be done through education but also through motivation based diversification. That is, new activities where the next generation family members can prove their competence and trustworthiness vis-à-vis the employees, who will then continue to be supportive of the family.

DISCUSSION

This study explores and examines the development of trust between family members, development of trust between family members and non-family members, and, how trust affects diversification decisions of the MOFAZ Group. Initially, when we conducted the interview sessions, the responses we received gave the impression that the diversification decisions were based on seizing opportunities they saw before them. But, when asked further, the participants started to talk about the future and development of the next generation. And, when further probed about the top priority in creating these ventures, Fauzy, in particular, began to share his hopes and dreams of:

> What they want *for* the family, rather than what they get *from* the business.

Hopes and dreams for the family. These were the top priorities when the founder was creating ventures.

1. The hope that the next generation will take over the business, yet, ensuring that the children's dreams are also met.
2. The dream of continuously having a harmonious family institution, even after the founding generation is long gone.

But, putting one's hopes and dreams across and having the next generation and the extended family understand the philosophy behind all these, is intricate; a challenge all by itself. Having to extend these hopes and dreams to the firm level is crucial and difficult, but it can be done if one is true to oneself. Based on the findings of this case, we found trust between family members to be a key factor for the family business to attain a bigger meaning in exploring the family's hopes and dreams. The family's decision and motivation in creating ventures is influenced by the trust built among family members and employees. This is seen to be inculcated by the founder and conveyed effectively to his three sons, in preparing them to take the MOFAZ Group to greater heights.

This case study has theoretical implications. Trust in family firms is multi-faceted and concerns not only the family across generations but also the non-family employees. The trust built between the founding entrepreneur and employees cannot easily be transferred across generations since trust is relationship based. Interpersonal trust between the founding entrepreneur and the employees create one of the distinct social capitals in organizations. In this sense, interpersonal trust between the founding entrepreneur and other family members – especially across generations – is a first positive signal to the employees who trust the founding entrepreneur.

Three types of trust are the calculated, competence, and interpersonal trust, with the latter being the strongest form. While family members may develop interpersonal trust through interactions in the family domain, it is not obvious for employees to simply accept this trust across generations of the family. Thus, while employees needed to move from competence based to interpersonal trust, the MOFAZ case suggests that next generation family members must earn a base level of competence trust of non-family employees to be viewed as credible leaders.

This finding not only explains why family firms may embark on unrelated diversification to find a place for the family, but also why such decisions might be accepted more easily by the non-family employees who have contributed significantly to the development of the core business, thereby earning competence based trust. In essence, trust-building across family generations and between employees driven by the founding entrepreneur are important for organization development. In the case of diversification, they drive the speed of decision-making, motivation and mode of diversification.

LIMITATION AND FUTURE RESEARCH

By design, this chapter focuses on a single case which can also be considered as its main limitation as the findings and conclusions cannot be generalized. Hence, in a future publication, we plan to increase the number of cases and conduct cross-case analysis to examine whether the findings of this study are robust in other large family businesses with at least two generations involved in the business.

This study has produced several interesting findings and insights, and the application of interpersonal trust and competence based trust in the context of diversification decisions for a large family firm. These findings could be useful in guiding the development of next generation leaders and transgenerational entrepreneurship of family businesses. Perhaps future research could determine whether these factors could be distinguishing factors between family business and non-family business.

Further, the contention of this study needs to be explored further in more depth. In a strict business setting, it is assumed that trust-building is a process that starts with calculated trust moving to competence based trust and culminating in interpersonal trust, while in a family setting trust starts with interpersonal trust, that is, from the opposite. We could even argue that competence based trust might be absent; if competence considerations are completely ignored, then research findings reporting detrimental familism are not surprising (Cruz et al., 2010; Sundaramurthy, 2008).

CONCLUSION

This study has uncovered the role of trust in the decision-making process of a successful and diversified entrepreneurial family enterprise and how the motivation for the second generation family members and leaders to create and lead or manage new ventures became a critical component of the process. The opening case demonstrated the MOFAZ Group's strategy to proliferate and constantly diversify into many different businesses in the past 10 years, from automotive, to properties, international and domestic trading, hospitality and services, wellness and well-being, and, green technology. The chapter discusses two major diversification decisions of substantial investments by the MOFAZ Group.

The study explained the decision-making process in the venture creation and the reasons why the family made such a decision when creating ventures. The motivation to find a place for the next generation leaders in the business, the speed of decision-making, the mode of new ventures by which they were formed and managed, and, most importantly the influence of the perceived trust within the family and among the family and employees that connects all the elements and components of the decision-making process.

The research answered the question of 'how does trust act on diversification decisions within a family business?' With this contribution to theory and practice, leaders of family businesses, their families and stakeholders, policymakers and other stakeholders are able to enhance their understanding of the decision-making process undertaken by the business owner when they venture into new businesses. The drive towards organizational growth, profitability and wealth creation of these family businesses is not limited to financial investments but are also motivated towards fortifying family legacy across generations.

REFERENCES

Casson, M. and Cox, H. (1997). An economic model of inter-firm networks. In Ebers, M. (ed.), *The Formation of Inter-Organizational Networks* (174–196). Oxford: Oxford University Press.

Charmaz, K. (2006). *Constructing Grounded Theory: A Practical Guide Through Qualitative Analysis.* London: Sage Publications.

Corbetta, G. and Salvato, C.A. (2004). The board of directors in family firms: one size fits all? *Family Business Review,* 17(2): 119–134.

Cruz, C.C., Gomez-Mejia, L.R., and Becerra, M. (2010). Perceptions of benevolence and the design of agency contracts: CEO–TMT relationships in family firms. *Academy of Management Journal,* 53, 69–89.

De Laat, P. (1997). Research and development alliances: ensuring trust by mutual commitments, in Ebers, M. (ed.), *The Formation of Inter-Organizational Networks* (146–173). New York: Oxford University Press.

Eisenhardt, K.M. (1989). Building theories from case study research. *Academy of Management Review,* 14(4): 532–550.

Eisenhardt, K.M. and Graebner, M.E. (2007). Theory building from cases: opportunities and challenges. *Academy of Management Journal,* 50(1): 25–32.

Glaser, B.G. and Strauss, A.L. (1967). *The Discovery of Grounded Theory: Strategies for Qualitative Research.* Chicago: Aldine Publishers.

Grabher, G. (1990). On the weakness of strong ties: the ambivalent role of inter-firm relations in the decline and reorganization of the Ruhr. WZB, Wiss.-Zentrum Berlin für Sozialforschung.

Granovetter, M. (1985). Economic action and social structure: the problem of embeddedness. *American Journal of Sociology,* 91(3): 481–510.

Granovetter, M. (1992). Problems of explanation in economic sociology, in Nohria, N. and Eccles, R. (eds), *Networks and Organizations: Structures, Form and Action* (25–56). Boston: Seite feht.

Gulati, R. (1998). Alliances and networks. *Strategic Management Journal,* 19: 293–317.

Hakansson, H. and Johanson, J. (1992). A model of industrial networks, in Axelsson, B. and Easton, G. (eds), *Industrial Networks: A New View of Reality* (28–34). London: Routledge.

Hakansson, H. and Snehota, I. (1995). *Developing Relationships in Business Networks.* London: Routledge.

Karra, N., Tracey, P., and Phillips, P. (2006). Altruism and agency in the family firm: exploring the role of family, kinship, and ethnicity. *Entrepreneurship Theory and Practice,* 30: 861–878.

LaChapelle, L.K. (1997). The role of trust in leadership and continuity of family-owned businesses. PhD Dissertation in Organizational Behavior, Union Institute Graduate School.

Lechner, C. and Leyronas, C. (2009). Small-business group formation as an entrepreneurial development model. *Entrepreneurship Theory and Practice,* 33(3): 645–667.

Lewicki, R. and Bunker, B. (1996). Developing and maintaining trust in work relationships, in Kramer, R. and Tyler, T. (eds), *Trust in Organizations: Frontiers of Theory and Research* (114–139). Thousand Oaks, CA: Sage Publications.

Mayer, R.C., Davis, J.H., and Schoorman, R.D. (1995). An integrative model of organizational trust. *Academy of Management Review,* 20: 709–734.

McAllister, D.J. (1995). Affect-and cognition-based trust as foundations for inter-personal cooperation in organizations. *Academy of Management Journal*, 38(1): 24–59.

Pettigrew, T.F. (1998). Intergroup contact theory. *Annual Review of Psychology*, 49: 65–85, retrieved from http://dx.doi.org/10.1146/annurev.psych.49.1.65 (accessed May 25, 2015).

Ram, M. (1994). *Managing to Survive: Working Lives in Small Firms*. Oxford: Blackwell.

Ring, P.S. (1997). Processes facilitating reliance on trust in inter-organizational networks, in Ebers, M. (ed.), *The Formation of Inter-Organizational Networks* (113–145). Oxford: Oxford University Press.

Rosa, P. (1998). Entrepreneurial process of business cluster formation and growth by 'habitual' entrepreneurs. *Entrepreneurship Practice and Theory*, 22(4): 43–61.

Steier, L. and Muethel, M. (2014). Trust and family businesses, in L. Melin, Nordqvist, M., and Sharma, P. (eds), *The Sage Handbook of Family Business* (498–513). London: Sage Publications.

Sundaramurthy, C. (2008). Sustaining trust within family businesses. *Family Business Review*, 21: 89–102.

Tisue, L. (1999). Facilitating dialogue and decision-making in a family business. PhD Dissertation in Education, the University of Tennessee, Knoxville, USA.

Zellweger, M.T. (2007). Time horizon, cost of equity capital, and generic investment strategies in firms. *Family Business Review*, 20(1): 1–15.

Zellweger, M.T., Nason, R.S., and Nordqvist, M. (2011). From longevity of firms to transgenerational entrepreneurship of families: introducing family entrepreneurial orientation. *Family Business Review*, 20(10): 1–20.

Other Sources

http://www.mofaz.com.
http://en.wikipedia.org/wiki/Fairuz_Fauzy.
http://www.fashionwiredaily.com/first_word/news/article.weml?id=2917.
http://www.financialexpress.com/news/mittal-daughterinlaw-snaps-up-escada/ 538199.
http://www.drb-hicom.com/.

9. Family social capital, transgenerational learning and transgenerational entrepreneurship

Maria Teresa Roscoe, Adriane Vieira and Denize Grzybovski

MINI CASE STUDY

'Is my son ready to take over the company? What are his advantages over an external CEO?' With these questions in mind, Patrícia Braile Verdi, the president of Braile Biomédica (BRAILE) recalls the events of the last five years.

Patrícia's father, Dr Domingo Braile (76) is an award-winning surgeon, professor and self-taught engineer and he is regarded as an icon in the medical industry. His scientific research background prompted him to found BRAILE and to create and develop technologies and products in the field of cardiovascular surgery. Dr Braile led the business for over 30 years but advancing age and health problems forced him to step down from the company's management. In 1992, at her father's request, Patrícia left her career as a lawyer and professor and joined the family business as administrative manager. After a financial crisis in 2009 Patrícia succeeded her father as president.

BRAILE's activities have historically been financed with equity. Recently the company had to resort to private bank loans to settle some debts, generating instability. In spite of receiving various offers from multinational organizations, the family chose to perpetuate the company within the family. Patrícia knew she would need help to resolve the company's financial problems and keep the flame of innovation alight. The best way forward seemed to be to professionalize management and reorganize operations.

To boost business efficiency the family decided in 2010 to enroll all its members in the 'Partnership to Develop Shareholders and Entrepreneurial Families' program at Fundação Dom Cabral. In 2012 they decided to structure a more qualified board of directors, keeping only two family members in management positions (Patrícia as president and her brother-in-law, Walter Sternieri Junior, as commercial director). In 2013, they contracted with a well-known consulting company and hired an executive director from the market.

The new vision involved terminating the manufacture of products with low volumes of sales, and cutting personnel expenses. A new product portfolio was proposed and a new sales strategy was adopted. Even employees with over 30 years of service with the company were retrenched. After an intense five years Patrícia needs to decide on the course of succession.

Patricia was preparing to turn to the market for a new president to replace her when her son, Rafael, mentioned in a family meeting that he would like to be involved with the family business. Dr Braile had fostered his grandson's interest in machine building and Rafael went on to study mechanical engineering at the University of São Paulo. Upon graduation, he hired a coach and developed his career plan. In the first half of 2014, Rafael studied business innovation at Harvard University, along with his cousin, Giovani, who took courses in genetics and biotechnology. Rafael is currently working as a trainee in an Italian multinational that operates in the oil and gas sector in Brazil. His plan is to take an MBA course in the United States and come back to work in the family business.

Patrícia was surprised by Rafael's interest, as he had never expressed, in such a categorical manner, his wish to participate in the family business. Now she wonders what to do. Should she remain as the company president until her son is ready to take over (which would mean she would have to keep postponing her academic career)? Should she hire a new CEO and have the company go through yet another transition in the future? Would Rafael be prepared to follow in his grandfather's footsteps, and give continuity to the family business by focusing on product innovation?

INTRODUCTION

This chapter aims to clarify the relationship between family social capital and transgenerational learning and entrepreneurship. Family social capital (FSC) consists of the personal relationships that family members develop between themselves and with internal and external stakeholders, through a history of familial interactions (Hoffman, Hoelscher, and Sorenson, 2006). This notion of FSC helps illuminate how family businesses become entrepreneurial (Cisneros, Chirita, and Deschamps, 2014).

According to Grzybovski (2007), transgenerational learning (TL) is a cognitive process that results from the overlapping of generations and that enables continuity through knowledge retrieved by new generations. This process generates questions regarding the subjects brought into debate during social interaction, including the issue of the family's presence in the management of the business. An understanding of learning in the family business is linked to the generation system, in which the family's vertical movements (for example, behavior standards and family legacies) are replicated in different generations and represent transgenerational entrepreneurship.

Habbershon, Nordqvist, and Zellweger (2010: 1) define transgenerational entrepreneurship (TE) as 'the processes through which a family uses and develops entrepreneurial mindsets and family influenced capabilities to create new streams of entrepreneurial, financial and social value across generations.' TE shifts the focus of the analysis from the organization to the family, allowing understanding of how the family business lifespan tends to be longer than that of any individual (Zellweger and Sieger, 2010; Zellweger et al., 2012; 2013).

The succession process necessarily involves entrepreneurial learning (Hamilton, 2011) and TE (Sharma et al., 2014; Cheng, Ho, and Au, 2014). Therefore, the authors assumed that TE covers the development of the heirs' entrepreneurial leadership through social practices found in the family business environment.

The question guiding this research was: What is the influence of family social capital (FSC) on transgenerational learning (TL) and transgenerational entrepreneurship (TE)? The research rests on two propositions, namely that (1) the greater the family business's capacity to create social capital, the greater its capacity to promote TL; and (2) that TL positively influences the grooming of heirs to become entrepreneurs. Thus, FSC and learning favor TE.

Guided by these propositions, the authors analyzed the history of the Brazilian company Braile Biomédica from its inception in 1973 until 2014, when the family was preparing the third generation to take over the business. The core concepts used in this study are outlined, along with the methodology, a summary of the key events in the company's history, and discussion of the data. In conclusion, we present the implications for further research and business practice.

CONCEPTUAL FRAMEWORK

Family Social Capital (FSC)

What distinguishes family businesses from other types of enterprise is the influence of family relations on the ways that the business is managed, structured, and transferred to successive generations. The literature on social capital describes the advantages of family relationships for a family business (Hoffman, Hoelscher, and Sorenson, 2006; Chua, Chrisman, and Sharma, 1999).

FSC creates value because it develops connections between individuals through relationship networks built within the family that strengthen with time (Salvato and Melin, 2008). The ties found in family social structures differ from those in non-family organizations and communities, because they are stronger, more intense and longer-lasting (Hoffman, Hoelscher, and Sorenson, 2006).

One cannot hire or import FSC; it is something that exists within the family relationship. In addition, the nature of family relationships is very important because the presence of negative feelings can put the business at risk. On the other hand, family relationships can be a trump card when feelings of trust and cooperation exist (Sorenson and Bierman, 2009).

Ties are the relational bonds existing among the role players and can be measured by the degree of network cohesion and the flow of resources (such as money, time, affection and information) between individuals. Strong ties are characterized by high levels of intimacy and proximity among family members, whereas weak ties are characterized by relationships that involve less investment of time, emotion, intimacy and reciprocity (Granovetter, 1974).

However, weak ties are just as important as strong ties and a competitive advantage can be gained by alternating them. Individuals who share strong ties usually participate in the same social circles, while individuals who share weak ties are configured as a social network, connecting across different groups and breaking the configuration of 'isolated islands' of tie clusters. Weak ties are key to disseminating innovation, because they are networks comprised of individuals with different experiences and backgrounds (Granovetter, 1974, 1983).

Considering the relationships between family members and stakeholders, Andrade et al. (2011) proposed that the equilibrium between strong and weak ties in family business is essential. The strengthening of strong ties creates 'familiness' (Chrisman, Chua, and Steier, 2005; Habbershon, Williams, and MacMillan, 2003), while weak ties broaden the trust among role players.

FSC is limited to unique issues in family relationships, including structural and relational components. The structural components refer to 'network ties' and their communication channels. The relational components concern the family rules and include: collective confidence, identity, moral infrastructure, obligations, expectations, and reputation. Family norms provide the social control necessary for the family business.

These norms determine acceptable behaviors and common belief systems, which allow family members to communicate their ideas and experiences and share a strategic vision and guiding normative values (Hoffman, Hoelscher, and Sorenson, 2006; Sorenson and Bierman, 2009).

The quality of the social capital the family creates depends on the quality of relational capital. Therefore, the family business may create more or less social capital, according to the family's structural and functional characteristics (Chrisman, Chua, and Sharma, 2005). FSC is developed to improve relational capital, but it is also a source of competitive advantage (Arrègle et al., 2007). This advantage is due to the diversity of competencies and strategic leadership among family members (Farington, Venter, and Boshoff, 2012), which reveal the existence of two dimensions in the formation of social capital: one internal and the other external. The internal dimension favors family members (Farington, Venter, and Boshoff, 2012; Cisneros, Chirita, and Deschamps, 2014), while the external dimension favors society as a whole, as the resources appropriated by the family are also important to the sound coexistence of the family business and its stakeholders (Salvato and Melin, 2008).

Transgenerational Learning (TL)

FSC considers the environment (family and company) in which it is produced as a 'site of practice-based knowledge' (Hamilton, 2011). Moreover, it serves as a basis for the construction of a learning type specific to family business: transgenerational learning (Grzybovski, 2007). If the family's objective is to recognize the family aspect of the company, the knowledge created should be considered from a social perspective, with attention to cultural and historical contexts (Hamilton, 2011). The knowledge created by the family should reflect the transgenerational characteristics of family members (succession).

The concept of the generational system uses systemic theory as a framework developed by psychologists and applied in family therapy. It is described by two sets of movements. The first comprises vertical movements (patterns, myths, secrets, family legacies) and horizontal movements (life cycle transitions). The second set encompasses developmental movements (births, marriages, deaths) and unpredictable movements (early death, chronic disease) (Carter and McGoldrick, 1989).

The vertical movement is considered transgenerational (Carter and McGoldrick, 1989) and, at its intersection with the horizontal movement, increases the stress within the system due to changes in the family life cycle (Simionato-Tozo, 2002). The stress that appears at a certain transition point in a family life cycle, for example the birth of a child, may reappear at any other point, and can change the family dynamics.

In this sense, understanding the generational system involves recognizing the metamorphosis that the family experiences as the relationship patterns between generations change, owing to the physical and emotional maturity of family members (Carter and McGoldrick, 1989). The stages of a family life cycle are not predetermined, but are constructed through a systemic analysis of the family structure. This analysis is made by mapping the separation and belonging movements within the family life cycle and transgenerational history. Relationship changes between generations result from the generational system dynamics. These changes reshape other organizations that are part of the same social group, including the family business.

Because companies are not always able to solely produce all the activities of a value-chain they are required to establish relationships with other organizations (Au et al., 2013). In Brazil, the process of technology transfer between companies and universities (outside transactions) is part of a public policy to foster the creation of innovation centers, technological parks, business incubators and technological hubs. This public policy aims to boost innovation and expand companies' technological capacity through inter-organizational learning and open innovation. Although this practice is seldom mentioned in family business research, it encourages innovation in traditional companies and prompts youngsters to establish innovative companies, or to create spin-offs from other relatives' ventures (usually parents or grandparents).

Transgenerational Entrepreneurship (TE)

Although entrepreneurship is usually associated with the creation of new companies (Schumpeter, 1934), it is not restricted to it. Entrepreneurship is linked to the organizational learning process and to knowledge transfer between generations (Souza, 2005; Hamilton, 2011; Brazeal and Herbert, 2000). According to Motta (1999) and Souza (2005), learning is not simply accumulating information. It concerns the awakening of a critical mindset and the capacity to create, change and expose the organization to new mindsets. Therefore, entrepreneurship makes the company's creative process a collective (Steier, 2007), localized (Hamilton, 2011) and transgenerational action (Cheng, Ho, and Au, 2014).

Steier (2007) draws attention to the process of creating new companies and highlights the close relationship between entrepreneurship and family legacy. Families serve as an important source of resources (economic, affective, educational, and relational). Sharma et al. (2014: 1) note that 'families are engines of economic activity around the world'; their ventures influence the economy for generations, suggesting the existence of a process through which knowledge is passed from generation to generation. The authors consider that this manner of analyzing entrepreneurship in family businesses shifts the analytic fulcrum from the individual (the entrepreneur) to the family, which may develop its own heir capacity-building program (intra-entrepreneurship) for different generations (transgenerational entrepreneurship).

TE is a process through which the family influences its members into developing an entrepreneurial mindset, so that that they can produce knowledge with financial and social value for successive generations (Habbershon, Nordqvist, and Zellweger, 2010). The incoming generation should be prepared to create, change and innovate (Motta, 1999), be capable of reading the 'familial sub-narrative' and be able to explore the family as a 'rich repository of resources' (Steier, 2007: 1106).

METHODS

This research uses a qualitative approach, as a function of (1) the nature of the data collected (behaviors and perceptions) and (2) the researcher's role in conducting the investigation. The investigative approach adopted was based on case study research (Yin, 2009). The criteria for the choice of subject were that the company should have existed for over 20 years, be legally defined as a large enterprise (according to Brazilian legislation) and have second-generation family members in its executive. The company chosen was Braile Biomédica (BRAILE).

Primary data was collected mainly by means of semi-structured interviews. This sort of interview values the presence of the researcher and, at the same time, offers an environment in which the respondents can feel free to express their views. All interviews were recorded and transcribed in full. For data consistency, all interviews were conducted by a single researcher. Secondary data was collected from BRAILE's corporate website and from magazine articles and reports about this family business. Data analysis involved all researchers. The Gioia single-case analysis method was adopted (Reay, 2014), guided by the thematic content analysis technique (Mozzato and Grzybovski, 2011).

Table 9.1 lists our respondents. The interview process started in 2013. In 2014, the authors resumed contact with the company to update data.

Table 9.1   Profile of the interviewees

Name	Position	Date
David Peitl	Production Director	23/10/2013
Walter Sternieri Júnior	Commercial Director	23/10/2013
Rafael Braile Cunha	Heir	23/10/2013
		09/10/2014
Eric Mifume	Administrative-Financial Director	23/10/2013
Maria Cecília Braga Braile	Board of Directors	23/10/2013
Patrícia Braile Verdi	President	23/10/2013
Domingo Marcolino Braile	Founder	10/10/2014
Marcelo Rodrigues	Executive Director	10/10/2014

THE CASE

Introduction

BRAILE is a health care company that manufactures cardiovascular, biological solutions, electro-medical, endovascular and oncology products. Over 450 items are produced at the company's plant in São José do Rio Preto, in the State of São Paulo. The company was founded by the cardiovascular surgeon and professor Dr Domingo Braile. The founder's daughter, Patrícia Braile Verdi, who is a lawyer and professor with a master's in Philosophy of Law, is the current president of the family business.

BRAILE has approximately 360 employees and creates around 200 indirect jobs in Brazil and abroad. The company has enjoyed growing revenues every year offering products designed for the domestic market. BRAILE's products are currently exported to over 25 countries. To maintain financial sustainability, BRAILE aims to increase exports, improve internal controls and consolidate its position in the Brazilian market.

This case focuses on the challenges faced by the second generation in professionalizing management and in preparing the third generation to give continuity to this entrepreneurial family's legacy. Consideration of the motives that prompted the founding of BRAILE, and the manner by which learning and innovation became an essential part of the business, help provide a better understanding of the company and its culture.

Recognition of an Opportunity

In 1957, Dr Braile moved to São Paulo to study medicine at the University of São Paulo (USP), the most recognized university in Brazil. Between 1959 and 1962, Dr Braile joined the team that organized Professor Euryclides Zerbini's Artificial Heart Workshop. Professor Zerbini was the first surgeon to perform heart transplantation in Latin America. The need for machines, pipes and fittings prompted Professor Zerbini to set up an experimental workshop in the Hospital das Clínicas. This early career opportunity had a great influence on Dr Braile's professional life.

Upon graduation in 1963, Dr Braile returned to his hometown, São José do Rio Preto. In that same year, he performed heart surgery with extracorporeal circulation, which, at that time, was a very rare procedure in Brazil. Dr Braile went on to help create and implement over 20 medical services in Brazilian hospitals, in which he also held leadership and preceptor positions. As a pioneer in the field, he was invited to demonstrate surgical techniques throughout Brazil, as well as in countries like India, Japan and China. In the educational area, Dr Braile was a professor, researcher, and administrator, based primarily at the São José do Rio Preto School of Medicine.

In 1973, Dr Braile, in partnership with other surgeons, created a company called Instituto de Moléstias Cardiovasculares (IMC) – literally, the Institute of Cardiovascular Diseases. The company was created to manufacture machines and equipment for heart surgery procedures and to continue Dr Braile's research work. At that time, high import duties in Brazil restricted access to imported products and equipment, making entrepreneurship a matter of necessity.

The founding mission statement of Dr Braile's company, to inspire and nurture innovation, encapsulated the identity of the company and initiated the launch of large quantities of quality products for the advancement of heart surgery in Brazil. In 1977, they started making biological heart valves and bovine pericardium grafts, designed for cardiovascular surgery. In 1985, the company began producing cardiac pacemakers and esophageal stimulators for the study and control of arrhythmia. In 1988, they began making membrane oxygenators for the heart–lung system.

In 1992, the partnership was dissolved. After the equity and assets were apportioned, Dr Braile kept the plant, despite much debt pending liquidation, and changed the company name to Braile Biomédica S.A. As of 1998, BRAILE began developing products for use in treatment of aortic artery diseases and in oncological therapies. In 2008, in line with the trend toward minimally invasive surgeries, the company began the research and development of a biological valve for catheter-borne implantation (stents), the

'Inovare Transcatheter Valve', which was awarded the 'Inova Award' by ABIMO, in April 2012. In 2013, BRAILE launched its transapical valve, which has already been awarded two prizes, and also began studies to use stem cells in cardiac surgical procedures.

The 'Ties' of the Innovation and Learning Process

BRAILE has survived for 41 years, in a fiercely competitive market dominated by multinational corporations, due to two factors. The main factor is the high regard in which professionals in the clinical and academic environment hold Dr Braile. The second factor is Dr Braile's knowledge and experience, which enable him to influence the behavior of his peers and convert entrepreneurial attitudes into entrepreneurial behavior.

It was his father's mentoring that developed Dr Braile's entrepreneurship. These lessons were, in turn, conveyed to his daughters and grandchildren:

When I was 14, my father took me to a repair shop and had me dismantle an engine. . . . What we always tried to do was to develop our children and grandchildren's curiosity. Be inquisitive! Dismantle things! (Dr Braile)
From childhood, my grandfather placed me inside the different sectors of the business to get to know the manufacturing processes. He would put me to build steam machines with him. Or to dismantle a radio and put it back together. He inspired my interest in engineering. (Rafael)

The company's first products were designed to meet the needs of surgeons. To this day, doctors are considered as partners in BRAILE's 'open innovation' philosophy, as they are on the front line at conferences, clinics, hospitals, universities and research centers, and can share updated and privileged information.

Dr Braile introduced the principles of 'teaching hospitals' into the company, effectively turning the family business into a 'company-school'. Most research was equity-funded, but the company also relied on grants from research supporting institutions at the federal and state level.

He is a researcher, and you can see the research bias in this company. Everything we do here generates a thesis or publication, and for him this is of essential importance. (Walter)

For some time, the company was not concerned with filing patents to protect innovations. Consequently, no subsequent funds were plowed back into research and development. The business focus was always on innovations that improved Dr Braile's medical practices. Innovation was not seen as a resource that should generate revenue. Such behavior is common in the early years of family businesses, because the growth of the business rests on the founder's creativity and the support of family and friends. However, the informal processes used in the formative years of the business are usually the cause of crises in the following stages of the organizational life cycle. In the past, internal and external partnerships for product research and development were informal. However, in the current competitive environment, partnerships must be formalized and R&D must yield financial returns.

Dr Braile found in his daughter the technical support he needed. While he kept managing the innovation and learning processes, Patrícia took care of the administration of the business. However, in order to perpetuate BRAILE, it was necessary to professionalize management, redesign processes and continue grooming the next generation to take over the family business.

Family, Succession and Leadership

Dr Domingo Braile (73) and Maria Cecília (73) married in 1962. The couple had two daughters, Patrícia Braile Verdi (50) and Valéria Braile Sternieri (49). Maria Cecília was a professor at the State University of São Paulo, with a doctorate in Education. She serves on BRAILE's board of directors. Valéria is a cardiologist. She was the company vice-president from 2009 to 2012 and sits on the board of directors. Patrícia holds a bachelor of Law and a master's in Philosophy of Law. She had a successful career as a lawyer and law professor before joining BRAILE.

The third-generation members are still very young. Rafael (23) and Luiza (16) are Patrícia's children; Sofia (20) and Giovani (17) are Valéria's (see Figure 9.1). Rafael graduated as a mechanical engineer from the University of São Paulo. Giovani and Sofia Braile are both medical students, while Luiza is still at high school.

In 1992, after the company buyout, Dr Braile asked Patrícia to help him reorganize BRAILE. She worked for many years as the company's administrative manager and became president at the height of a financial crisis that erupted in 2009. In 2010, the family enrolled all its members in the 'Partnership to Develop Shareholders and Entrepreneurial Families' (PDA) program at Fundação Dom Cabral (FDC) to begin the professionalization of the company's management. In 2012, they restructured BRAILE's board of directors. The only other family member who remained in office was Walter, Valéria's husband, who was responsible for marketing and sales.

In 2013, the family hired a company to provide broad-scope consultancy services covering governance, succession, product portfolio, segmentation,

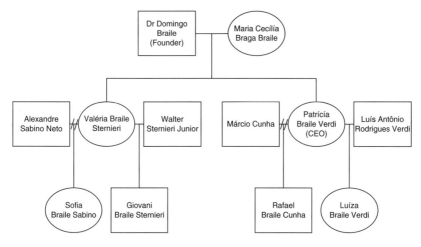

Figure 9.1   Braile family genogram

and the redesign of the sales and production areas. The family believed that this process was necessary, both to ensure the company's growth and professionalization and to fulfill their dream of seeing BRAILE becoming the leader in the domestic market and a benchmark in the international market.

Initially, 30 employees were dismissed and many others were reassigned to the holding company, which was created to promote the separation between the family ownership and management subsystems. It was decided to discontinue low-sales products, which depended almost exclusively on the demand from professionals in Dr Braile's network. The sales department was segmented and production processes were substantially reviewed to obtain product certifications and grow exports.

The family's main concern involved the renegotiation of debt with creditor banks. Return on equity had been negative in 2011 (−3.05 percent), positive in 2012 (7.87 percent) and negative again in 2013 (−1.06 percent). The financial consultant retained by the company became increasingly involved in implementing strategic actions. His extensive experience, with private banking and mergers and acquisitions, prompted the decision to hire him in 2013 as financial director, with chief executive status. He was also tasked with regulating the relations between family and business, and establishing new rules for the Shareholders' Agreement. However, the pressure he applied to keep the family away from the company caused a great deal of discomfort, which culminated in his dismissal.

First and second generation members expected that the company would be perpetuated within the family, so that the third generation could join the business as shareholders or managers. The family decided to outsource a CEO and groom the third generation members to be the business' future leaders.

> We learned how important succession planning is. Rules and planning are necessary to assure the company has a future. The family is the center of everything, and must be preserved. (Patrícia)

Dr Braile's four grandchildren (third generation members) are very close and keep constant social contact. Both Rafael's and Giovani's career choices were influenced by their grandfather. This way, Dr Braile ensured the link between engineering and medicine would remain in the family.

Rafael developed an interest in business management as an undergraduate, and took many economics and management courses. He did internships at BRAILE and at a company operating in the agricultural sector. Upon graduation, Rafael moved to São Paulo, where he attended a coaching program and drafted his career plan. As part of the third generation preparation process to manage the family business, Rafael and Giovani spent the first half of 2014 at Harvard University where they took short-term courses. Giovani took courses focused on genetics and biotechnology, while Rafael studied business innovation. They attended lectures together and participated in a product development project, under the sponsorship and guidance of guest companies, including some from the health sector.

Rafael reiterated his admiration for Giovani and his wish that they both take on BRAILE's leadership in the future. Rafael is currently working for an Italian multinational oil and gas corporation, and intends to return soon to the USA to complete an MBA program. Sofia began studying medicine in 2014, and Luiza is expected to follow the same path. Both sit on the board of heirs, and may develop a greater interest in the company's management in the future.

Dr Braile welcomed Rafael's and Giovani's complementary studies as a dream come true. However, he also expects them to proceed with their studies, since all first and second generation family members hold master's or doctoral degrees. When Dr Braile gave his name to the company, he wanted it to remain in the family, not as an obligation but rather as the result of desire, curiosity, genuine entrepreneurship and merit.

> We wanted Rafael to work in another company to establish an understanding of business. The day he decides to come back, he will have amassed great knowledge, so that he can be respected as an engineer rather than as a shareholder. (Dr Braile)

In July 2014, the company hired Marcelo Rodrigues to become executive director. He proposed new changes. To give continuity to the process of financial reorganization he implemented further personnel cuts (involving approximately 40 dismissals), reduced operating costs and renegotiated the bank debt. These changes turned the negative financial scenario around in three months. Moreover, the company started to enjoy sales growth and a positive cash flow once again. Marcelo also replaced the operations and sales directors and reduced these positions to managerial level. He assumed the responsibility of helping prepare the third generation for business management. A board of heirs was established, convening once a month to discuss emerging issues.

Patrícia is very optimistic about the changes and confident in the recovery of the synergy between family and business:

> I think I have done what I promised myself I would do. People should know when it's time to leave. (Patrícia)

DISCUSSION: THE INFLUENCE OF FAMILY SOCIAL CAPITAL ON TRANSGENERATIONAL LEARNING AND ENTREPRENEURSHIP

The Family Business' Ability to Generate Social Capital Increases With its Ability to Promote Transgenerational Learning

Analysis of the data confirms that the greater the family business's capacity to yield social capital, the greater its capacity to promote TL. In addition, the greater the capacity of the family business to promote synergy among strong-tie networks and weak-tie networks, the greater its capacity to promote TL.

Notably, it is through strong ties that values, contents and tacit knowledge are conveyed, enhancing learning and TE (Hoffman, Hoelscher, and Sorenson, 2006; Sorenson and Bierman, 2009; Andrade et al., 2011). Strong ties are key to developing future generation leaders and ensuring continuous innovation. Weak ties, in turn, strengthen learning and innovation among internal and external stakeholders (Arrègle et al., 2007; Salvato and Melin, 2008). However, the most important point is that weak ties enhance the interdependent relationships between members of the entrepreneurial family through transgenerational movements (Grzybovski, 2007; Zahra, 2012; Sharma et al., 2014).

The case study shows that the web of weak ties was enhanced by the principle of 'open innovation' (Au et al., 2013) of Dr Braile's 'company-school', without being restricted to internal organizational dynamics. On the other hand, the grandchildren were imbued with the family legacy at a young age through content delivery strategies adopted by their grandfather. Hence, the family legacy is built upon a strongly tiered network instilled by 'children's play' in the early years of the grandfather–grandchildren relationship.

The challenge for the second generation, Patrícia and Valéria, is to understand their father's legacy and how they can expedite the transition between the generations. The challenge facing the third generation involves incorporating the creative and innovative potential inspired by their grandfather while ensuring the company's profitable future in a competitive business environment.

Building the incoming generation's technical capacity is an interesting way of professionalizing management, as the members of an entrepreneurial family tend to preserve the company's organizational identity and strive for non-financial objectives (Zellweger et al., 2013). This is what Sharma et al. (2014) referred to as intangible resources, within their concept of transgenerational entrepreneurship.

External professionals find it difficult to comprehend the dynamics of a family business because, from an outsider's perspective, the family is permeated by conflicting emotions, particularly when the dynamics are analyzed outside the context of the generational system. Hamilton (2011) has proposed that, in family businesses, learning happens through social interactions and is embedded in everyday practices, which are reproduced and transformed over time.

However, the outside professional's perspective becomes necessary, to focus attention on critical managerial issues such as the return on investment that should be factored into R&D projects. It is imperative for the survival of the family business to organize, align, and promote synergy between production and sales, without ignoring the organizational learning process that is responsible for the company's high product innovation level, which is the trademark of Dr Braile's management.

Transgenerational Learning Helps Prepare Heirs to Become Entrepreneurs

The analysis of the interaction between strong and weak ties allows us to examine the influence of social capital upon learning, as well as the relationship between learning and the development of entrepreneurial leadership. This brings us to the second proposition, namely that the construction of a transgenerational learning network positively influences the grooming of heirs to become entrepreneurial leaders (Sharma and Chrisman, 1999; Sharma, 2004; Cheng, Ho, and Au, 2014).

The life cycle of BRAILE was characterized by growth through creativity in its first stage and growth by direction (based on process standardization, operational efficiency and a functional organizational structure) in the second stage, in accord with Greiner's (1972) model. Dr Braile's entrepreneurial behavior in the product innovation process (the first stage) also determined what happened in the second stage, when his daughter, Patrícia, took over, restructuring internal processes and guiding the company towards new developments. In this case, the family provided the company resources which in turn enriched the collective family resources ('familiness') (Chrisman, Chua, and Steier, 2005; Habbershon, Williams, and MacMillan, 2003).

In BRAILE's case, the relationship between first and second generation women in the family is very strong. However, the founder's capacity to influence the third generation is notably stronger, especially with regard to the grandchildren's professional choices (engineering and medicine) and entrepreneurial mindset, as reflected in their affinity for experiential learning. However, the inclination of the two grandsons, especially Rafael, regarding the family legacy is the desire to perpetuate the business as envisioned and founded by Dr Braile. The critical events affecting the family, especially the grandfather's health (an unpredictable horizontal movement) reveals a grandson committed not only to the family business but also to his own professional accomplishment. Grandchildren do not only follow their grandparents' or parents' determinations, but pursue their own wishes and will to lead, influencing the behavior of those around them.

The analysis of the relationship between transgenerational learning and entrepreneurship also shows that, even when passing the baton from one generation to the next was unplanned, entrepreneurship can manifest in successive generations. The learning network, built by the family through its social capital, allows the development of leaders through successive generations (Grzybovski, 2007; Zellweger and Sieger, 2010; Sharma et al., 2014).

The important thing, in these contexts, is the successor's understanding that his or her role is to smooth the transition for the third generation. Families are strengthened when members understand and accept their differences and do not allow possible sorrows and frustrations between two generations to affect the incoming generations. This improvement in the way the family deals with emotions is as important as the more objective and rational aspects of the succession process, related to managerial competencies.

With each transgenerational transition in the family business management, the acquired knowledge is retrieved, revised or adapted by the new generations, creating a continuous innovation cycle. Innovation is

Figure 9.2   The influence of family social capital on transgenerational learning and entrepreneurship

a means to develop and implement new ideas (Van de Ven, Angle, and Poole, 2000), but can also lead to renovation, prompted by engaging new family members and making the necessary adjustments to keep the family entrepreneurial spirit (Au et al., 2013).

The entrepreneurial spirit, leadership profile and innovative capability of one or more family members are just a few of the legacies that may have been incubated by business families without them realizing it. Analysis of vertical movements in the generational systems allows us to understand the transgenerationality of events and the dynamics and behavior of entrepreneurial family members at a specific moment in its history. It is also apparent that the process contains intangible resources that explain business longevity, the development of third generation leaders and of product and service innovations. These are rooted in the bonds between the founder, his children and his grandchildren around a collective and, above all, entrepreneurial, action.

In summary, the notion of family social capital allows an under-standing of how family businesses become entrepreneurial. This is how social capital is linked to transgenerational learning and entrepreneurship (Hoffman, Hoelscher, and Sorenson, 2006; Zahra, 2012; Sharma et al., 2014) (see Figure 9.2).

CONCLUSION

The purpose of this study was to examine the relationship between family social capital and transgenerational learning and entrepreneurship. The two propositions presented and addressed in this chapter have both proven valid, based on the data analysis. The study demonstrates that (1) the capacity of the family business to create social capital influences its ability to promote transgenerational learning; and (2) that its capacity to promote synergy between strongly or weakly tied networks generating social capital correlates with its capacity to promote transgenerational learning and innovation.

The study shows that entrepreneurship can be resumed by successive generations. Critical events in the generational system (early death, chronic ailment) of the entrepreneurial company not only cause changes in the family life cycle, but prompt patterns, myths, secrets and family legacies to reappear in management decisions. It is incumbent upon the first generation to prepare family leaders while in their early years, so that they feel responsible for maintaining the family legacy in the third generation.

Another contribution of this study concerns the ways in which transgenerational learning and transgenerational entrepreneurship are facilitating factors in the choice of a third generation leader. However, their occurrence depends on the level of 'familiness'. Transgenerational entrepreneurship does not occur at a moment in history; rather, it is an ongoing process throughout an entire lifetime, starting with the person who first tutored the third generation.

This study also shows that the elements of family social capital are born in the family generational system and radiate across the organization and the community, affecting the dynamic between the family business and its internal and external stakeholders.

LIMITATIONS

This research is not without limitations. The qualitative study of one Brazilian case does not allow inferences to be made as to whether or not the results would also apply in other countries. However, it differs from other research methods by allowing an in-depth analysis of the context and history of the entrepreneurial family. This in-depth analysis was key to discuss the theme of transgenerational entrepreneurship. To test the capacity to generalize the research findings (Yin, 2009), the authors propose that further research be done to develop a learning continuum at the transgenerational level and to introduce entrepreneurship as one of the categories to be analyzed.

REFERENCES

Andrade, D.M., Lima, J.B., Antonialli, L.M., and Muylder, C.F. (2011). The family social capital impact in practices of learning, change and innovation in entrepreneurial family businesses. *African Journal of Business Management*, 5(33): 12819–12828.

Arrègle, J., Hitt, M.A., Sirmon, D.G., and Very, P. (2007). The development of organizational social capital: attributes of family firms. *Journal of Management Studies*, 44(1): 73–95.

Au, K., Chiang, F.F.T., Birtch, T.A., and Ding, Z. (2013). Incubating the next generation to venture: the case of a family business in Hong Kong. *Asia Pacific Journal Management*, 30: 749–767.

Brazeal, D. and Herbert, T. (2000). The genesis of entrepreneurship. *Entrepreneurship Theory and Practice*, 23(3): 29–45.

Carter, B. and McGoldrick, M. (eds) (1989). *The Changing Family Life Cycle: A Framework Therapy*. Boston: Allyn & Bacon.

Cheng, J.C.Y., Ho, F.H.C., and Au, K. (2014). Transgenerational entrepreneurship and entrepreneurial learning: a case study of Associated Engineers Ltd in Hong Kong, in Sharma, P., Sieger, P., Nason, R.S., Gonzalez, A.C., and Ramachandran, K. (eds), *Exploring Transgenerational Entrepreneurship: The Role of Resources and Capabilities* (62–87). Cheltenham, UK and Northampton, MA, USA: Edward Elgar Publishing.

Chrisman, J.J, Chua, J.H., and Sharma, P. (2005). Trends and directions in the development of a strategic management theory of the family firm. *Entrepreneurship Theory and Practice*, 29(5): 555–576.

Chrisman, J.J., Chua, J.H., and Steier, L. (2005). Sources and consequences of distinctive 'familiness': an introduction. *Entrepreneurship Theory and Practice*, 29(3): 237–247.

Chua, J.H., Chrisman, J.J., and Sharma, P. (1999). Defining the family business by behavior. *Entrepreneurship Theory and Practice*, 23(4): 19–39.

Cisneros, L., Chirita, M.G., and Deschamps, B. (2014). The role of social capital in succession from controlling owners to sibling teams, in Sharma, P., Sieger, P., Nason, R.S., Gonzalez, A.C., and Ramachandran, K. (eds), *Exploring Transgenerational Entrepreneurship: The Role of Resources and Capabilities* (110–127). Cheltenham, UK and Northampton, MA, USA: Edward Elgar Publishing.

Farington, S.M., Venter, E., and Boshoff, C. (2012). Elements in successful sibling teams. *Family Business Review*, 25(2): 191–205.

Granovetter, M.S. (1974). The strength of weak ties. *American Journal of Sociology*, 6: 1360–1380.

Granovetter, M. (1983). The strength of weak ties: a network theory revisited. *Sociological Theory*, 1: 201–233.

Greiner, L. (1972). Evolution and revolution as organizations grow. *Harvard Business Review*, 50: 37–46.

Grzybovski, D. (2007). *Plataforma de conhecimento e aprendizagem transgeracional em empresas familiares*. Doctoral dissertation, Doctor of Business Administration, Federal University of Lavras, UFLA, Brasil.

Habbershon, T.G., Nordqvist, M., and Zellweger, T.M. (2010). Transgenerational entrepreneurship, in Nordqvist, M. and Zellweger, T.M. (eds), *Transgenerational Entrepreneurship: Exploring Growth and Performance in Family Firms Across Generations* (1–38). Cheltenham, UK and Northampton, MA USA: Edward Elgar Publishing.

Habbershon, T.G., Williams, M.L., and MacMillan, I.C. (2003). A unified system perspective of family firm performance. *Journal of Business Venturing*, 18: 451–465.

Hamilton, E. (2011). Entrepreneurial learning in family business: a situated learning perspective. *Journal of Small Business and Enterprise Development*, 18(1): 8–26.

Hoffman, J., Hoelscher, M., and Sorenson, R. (2006). Achieving sustained competitive advantage: a family capital theory. *Family Business Review*, 19(2): 135–145.

Motta, P.R. (1999). *Transformação organizacional: a teoria e a prática de inovar.* Rio de Janeiro: Qualitymark.

Mozzato, A.R. and Grzybovski, D. (2011). Análise de conteúdo como técnica de análise de dados qualitativos no campo da administração: potencial e desafios. *Revista de Administração Contemporânea*, 15(4): 731–747.

Reay, T. (2014). Publishing qualitative research. *Family Business Review*, 27(2): 95–102.

Salvato, C. and Melin, L. (2008). Creating value across generations in family-controlled businesses: the role of family social capital. *Family Business Review*, 21: 259–276.

Schumpeter, J.A. (1934). *The Theory of Economic Development*, published in German (1912), 1st edition in English: Cambridge, MA: Harvard University Press 1934, also: Cambridge, MA: Harvard Economic Studies, volume 46, London: Oxford University Press.

Sharma, P. (2004). An overview of the field of family business studies: current status and directions for the future. *Family Business Review*, 17: 1–36.

Sharma, P. and Chrisman, J.J. (1999). Toward a reconciliation of the definitional issues in the field of corporate entrepreneurship. *Entrepreneurship: Theory and Practice*, (spring): 11–28.

Sharma, P., Sieger, P., Nason, R.S., Gonzalez, A.C., and Ramachandran, K. (eds) (2014). *Exploring Transgenerational Entrepreneurship: The Role of Resources and Capabilities.* Cheltenham, UK and Northampton, MA, USA: Edward Elgar Publishing.

Simionato-Tozo, S.M.P. (2002). *O ciclo de vida familiar: um estudo transgeracional.* Doctoral dissertation, Doctor of Psychology, University of São Paulo, USP, Brazil.

Sorenson, R.L. and Bierman, L. (2009). Family capital, family business and free enterprise. *Family Business Review*, 22(3): 193–196.

Souza, E.C.L. (2005). Empreendedorismo: da gênese à contemporaneidade, in Souza, E.C.L. and Guimarães, T.A. (eds), *Empreendedorismo além do plano de negócio* (3–20). São Paulo: Atlas.

Steier, L. (2007). New venture creation and organization a familiar sub-narrative. *Journal of Business Research*, 60(10): 1099–1107.

Van de Ven, A.H., Angle, H.L., and Poole, M.S. (eds) (2000). *Research on the Management of Innovation: the Minnesota Studies.* New York: Oxford University Press.

Yin, R.K. (2009). *Case Study Research: Design and Methods.* Los Angeles: Sage Publications.

Zahra, S.A. (2012). Organizational learning and entrepreneurship in family firms: exploring the moderating effect of ownership and cohesion. *Small Business Economics*, 38(1): 51–65.

Zellweger, T. and Sieger, P. (2010). Entrepreneurial orientation in long-lived family firms. *Small Business Economics Journal*, 1: 1–18.

Zellweger, T.M., Kellermanns, F.W., Chrisman, J.J., and Chua, J.H. (2012). Family control and family firm valuation by family CEOs: the importance of intentions for transgenerational control. *Organization Science*, 23(3): 851–868.

Zellweger, T.M., Nason, R.S., Nordqvist, M., and Brush, C.G. (2013). Why do family firms strive for nonfinancial goals? An organizational identity perspective. *Entrepreneurship Theory and Practice*, 37(2): 229–248.

10. Parenting and next gen development

Alberto Gimeno and Maria José Parada[1]

MINI CASE STUDY

It was a sunny day of February 2015 and Mrs See was thinking about her closest competitors who were facing a major succession crisis in taking their firm from the second to the third generation. On reflection, she thought that most of the problems they were facing had to do with the way the members of the next generation behaved toward the family business, their lack of commitment, inability to adapt, and lack of cohesion. What most surprised her about the younger members of the family was their sheer frivolity. They frittered away most of their time racing around in sports cars and living it up. Worse still, the parents allowed them to do whatever they liked. 'After all, the parents did not see eye to eye, the father was away most of the time and the mother indulged her children's every whim,' Mrs See told her husband. Then she thought: 'I think we have done a good job in bringing up our children. Luckily they seem to have learnt that effort and hard work and, a down-to-earth approach to life is what counts, no matter how rich you are.'

Metal Inc. is a Spanish family business based in Barcelona. Founded in the early 1950s, the business is making a transition from the third to the fourth generation. The company is successful and a leader in the infrastructure sector at both the national and the international levels. The main growth and internationalization was driven by members of the third generation who are now in their sixties.

Mrs See (62) grew up in a humble family, whose main values were hard work and giving back to the community. These values were steeped in all members of her generation. Mrs See brought up her own children to value the same things. She got married and never stopped working even when her children were born. They admired their mother. Her aging parents often praised her efforts to look after her children, the business, and them. The balance between Mrs See and Mr See was also a key element in making their children part of the family business. Indeed, the children remember how they were subtly socialized within the family business from their earliest years.

Mrs See has three children, Rita (38), James (35) and Maria (32). The way Mrs See brought her children up determined the path her kids followed in their professional and personal lives. Mrs See is a competent CEO who, together with her brother, has grown their family business from €50 million to €2,000 million in annual sales in the last 25 years. From small beginnings as a local firm, it has expanded to become a leading company in its field and has a worldwide presence. Mrs See has played a vital role in developing staff and other resources in the company. Supporting her entrepreneurial brother, she has always taken care of both her family and the business.

She insisted that her children look for the best schools in their fields. She explains how she tried to teach her children the value of hard work and to be good at whatever they did. She recalls:

> I remember sending my kids to work in the family business at a young age. This was very important to me because I wanted them to grasp that all jobs require effort and that hard work leads to success. . . . I am pleased that they have all made the most of what they have learnt.

All of them graduated in their chosen fields. The eldest daughter studied biotechnology and she works in this field. She did not feel pressured to study anything related to the family business. She has become an expert in her field. While she is not really interested in managing the family business, now that she is married and has children she is starting to think more about the family business from an owner's perspective. James has also succeeded in his professional field. After studying business at the New York University (NYU), he got a senior position in finance in a top company in New York. After a couple of years, his mother asked him to join them in the family business because a management post had become vacant. He has now been working in the family business for over six years and has been promoted three times. The youngest daughter has finished her marketing studies abroad. She has been working for the family business for over six years in various business units, supervising the Marketing department in each unit. All three children of Mrs See are married and the oldest one has two children.

The See family has forged strong bonds over the years. Mrs See takes every opportunity for family gatherings – Sunday lunch, sailing holidays in the summer, Christmas. When her children and nephews grew older, she started a family council to create another forum for discussing family issues and for socializing within the family business. For her, building bonds is of the utmost importance in furthering her children's business development. The next generation members see their mother as a caring and strong-willed individual who is always ready to help them in difficult times:

> I also remember when I wanted to quit and change work, my mother telling me that she was there and that whatever I needed, I could count on her. Just her hugs were enough to feel that this was going to work.
> For me it was clear that I had to go to NYU, as it was the best school for my studies. This is something I learnt from my mother. What I really appreciate though is how she supported me in the decision to go abroad and helped when she saw I had doubts about where to head after graduating. (James)

Discussion Questions

1. How has Mrs See influenced her children in their development?
2. To what extent did her parenting style affect their commitment to the family business?

INTRODUCTION

Family business literature is starting to consider the family dimension, going beyond the 'return on investment' approach (e.g. Sharma and Salvato, 2013). So far, the family has been considered as a homogeneous unit of analysis particularly from the economic standpoint though less so from sociological and historical perspectives. Studies on household economies in bourgeois middle-class families and Roman families reflect this perspective.

In the family business field family is considered a unit that is inextricably linked with the business and the focus is on issues and dilemmas that emerge as a consequence of this overlap (Sharma, Melin, and Nordqvist, 2014). The heterogeneity of the family and family business is often neglected (Corbetta and Salvato, 2004; Nordqvist et al., 2014). Usually, this level of analysis follows a similar logic to microeconomics. The business is treated as a 'black box' that responds in specific ways to different competitive, regulatory or macroeconomic situations. The system of incentives, information flows and expectations determine the behavior of the businesses. This level of analysis was useful for understanding the behavior of businesses in general but did not necessarily explain the behavior of a specific firm; hence the need to take a much closer look at specific aspects and dimensions of the business. This has been the approach adopted by business schools that study businesses from the inside, their organization, human relations, and decision-making processes, etc.

Higher resolution is needed in examining the family when considering the family business. Despite the importance of families in the family business field, few efforts have been made to define and/or measure the 'family' variable (Pearson et al., 2014). In addition, the behavior of family businesses in general has been mostly understood by thinking of the family as a unit for furthering the socio-emotional wealth of its members (e.g. Gomez-Mejia et al., 2007), much as an economist would say that the behavior of a company is explained by shareholder maximization of returns. Therefore at this broad level, family business may be understood as a dialectic relationship between maximization of returns and socio-emotional wealth.

This level of analysis, however, does not necessarily help in understanding the behavior of a specific family business in much the same way as the competitive context does not necessarily explain the behavior of a specific company. One needs to delve deeper in the understanding of the business family to gain a better grasp of the family business dynamics. As Sharma et al. (2014) suggest, the family variable is critical given that the family shapes the values that influence the attitudes and behavior of its members.

In dealing with next generation involvement in the business, succession has been extensively studied from the business perspective, trying to understand what explains its success. Hence, planning (Carlock and Ward, 2001), family protocols (Aronoff and Ward, 1996) mentoring (Boyd et al., 1999) and governance (Steier and Miller, 2010) have been extensively researched. The underlying yet usually unstated assumption of this research is that families are all the same, at least thereby neglecting the heterogeneity arising from the type of family involved.

Family business literature has also emphasized the importance of specific behaviors of next generation family members – the importance of being entrepreneurial (Steier, 2001), commitment to the business project (Sharma and Irving, 2005), education (Ibrahim et al., 2004) and skills (Sharma and Rao, 2000). Yet, limited effort has been made in understanding how younger generations are brought up and how this affects both the company and individual family members. There is a large literature supporting the importance of contextual factors, mainly parenting, as the main influence on child behavior (Maccoby, 2000).

Covering this gap in the literature and following recent calls to tackle heterogeneity of family businesses and focus on the family as the unit of analysis (cf. Sharma et al., 2014) we stress that family business dynamics are highly dependent on the way each family works (Corbetta and Salvato, 2004; Nordqvist et al., 2014). How families exercise their parenting role may be one of the key aspects to understand family members' behavior toward their businesses. The research question we seek to answer is: How do parenting styles impact the development of adaptability and cohesion in next generation family members? To understand this, we draw upon the well-established concept of parenting in the developmental psychology and some of the widely accepted models that explain the main ways in which it is exercised.

PARENTING STYLES

Various styles of parenting have been identified. The most widely accepted model explaining parenting styles was developed by Baumrind and first presented in her seminal work of in 1966. She differentiates between the two dimensions of parenting: 'demandingness' and 'responsiveness'. Demandingness refers to 'the claims parents make on children to become integrated into the family whole, by their maturity demands, supervision, disciplinary efforts and willingness to confront the child who disobeys' (Baumrind, 1991: 61–62). The dimension of responsiveness describes 'the extent to which parents intentionally foster individuality, self-regulation, and self-assertion by being attuned, supportive, and acquiescent to children's special needs and demands' (Baumrind, 1991: 62). Responsiveness has been also labeled as autonomy by other authors (Doret et al., 2013). While demandingness is associated with instrumental competence and behavioral control, responsiveness is associated with social competence and psycho-social functioning (Darling, 1999). These two dimensions generate a grid of four parenting styles, three of which – authoritative, authoritarian, and permissive – were first identified by Baumrind (1966). Later, Maccoby and Martin (1983) introduced the fourth style – uninvolved parenting (Figure 10.1).

We are interested in how parenting affects the development of the business family and therefore the business. Empirical research in the four models can help understand family dynamics in the business families.

Authoritative parents are both demanding and responsive. 'They monitor and impart clear standards for their children's conduct. They are assertive but not intrusive and restrictive. Their disciplinary methods are supportive, rather than punitive and they want their children to be assertive as well as socially responsible and, self-regulated as well as co-operative' (Baumrind, 1991: 62). These parents tend to develop control over their kids through negotiation and explanations. They could be described as 'conversational parents.'

Authoritarian parents are very demanding and directive, but not responsive. 'They are obedience- and status-oriented, and expect their orders to be obeyed without explanation' (Baumrind, 1991: 62). This kind of parenting emphasizes obedience, respect for authority, and order; and can be described as 'hierarchical-controlling parents.'

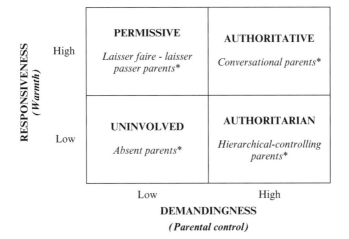

Sources: Baumrind (1966) and Maccoby and Martin (1983); *Authors.

Figure 10.1 Parenting styles

Permissive parents are more responsive than they are demanding. They are 'nontraditional and lenient, do not require mature behavior, allow considerable self-regulation, and avoid confrontation' (Baumrind, 1991: 62). This parenting style emphasizes self-regulation and exploration of the kids without previous definition of limits. Such parents tend to use reason and manipulation but not hierarchy to manage their children; and can be described as 'laissez faire – laissez-passer parents.'

Uninvolved parents are detached, lax and cold, lacking the nurturing component of parenting. Interaction with the child is either lacking or negative (Levendosky and Graham-Berman, 2000; Out et al., 2009). This parenting style is characterized by non-interaction of the parents with the kids. We could describe them as 'absent parents.'

Parenting Styles and their Influence in the Family Business

In order to understand the impact of parenting style in business family behavior, we study nine business families that represent the three main parenting styles. We avoid the disengaged style because, as previously stated, it is very infrequent in business families. Based on the empirical research on parenting styles, we make propositions on the kind of family business dynamics that could emerge.

Authoritative style
Authoritative parenting leads to more socially skilled offspring than non-authoritative parenting (Baumrind, 1991; Weiss and Schwarz, 1996; Miller et al., 1993). Research indicates that this parenting style tends to generate positive educational outcomes as better social skills (Baumrind, 1989, 1993; Fagan, 2000), development of self-esteem (Carlson, Uppal, and Prosser, 2000), academic success (Steinberg, Dornbusch, and Brown, 1992a; Steinberg et al., 1992b), less problem behavior in developmental phases (Darling, 1999) and better psychological health (Reiss et al., 1995). Offspring who received such parenting are not only more likely to act as competent managers but also to be more capable of advancing their careers outside the family business. They are more likely to possess greater social skills and an ability to reach agreements with other family members and be emphatic to the needs of others. It is thus quite likely that this parenting style may develop the best conditions for creating a competent business family, based more on the interdependence among their members than the dependence among them. The greater the level of autonomy conferred by this style, the greater the chances of introducing innovation and transformation in the family business.

Authoritarian style
Authoritarian parents tend to establish a clear, ordered environment for the next generation, with clear rules that have to be followed (Baumrind, 1991). This style tends to foster children and teenagers that get quite fairly good academic results and who 'toe the line' but who have lower self-esteem, lower social skills, and are more prone to depression (Darling 1999). In contrast to the authoritative parenting style, this style fosters continuity but tends to lead to a lack of instrumental competence. The autonomy fostered by this style is more likely to lead to greater independence in terms of career paths. The bonding to the company is more likely to be based on the attraction of the business and its projects than the legacy of and loyalty to earlier generations. It seems likely that this parenting style leads to companies that are more likely to be professionally managed and incorporate governance systems based on 'checks and balances' in which power is split between the management and governance hierarchy.

   This has contradictory effects on the next generation's autonomy. On the one hand, kids tend to pursue ideals that are more similar to those of their parents, than the ones fostered in an authoritative parenting style. This decreases self-control by reducing the number of choices but at the same time it increases the child's scope of control by introducing a higher commitment to a specific family legacy (Doret et al., 2013). This style focuses on following the traditional paths, hindering autonomous thinking and self-regulated individuality, autonomy and internal motivation to achieve (Lamborn et al., 1991; Lepper and Greene, 1978; Steinberg et al., 1994).

Authoritarian parenting style likely develops different business family dynamics. Instrumental competence and self-control not only tend to develop competent professionals for the business but also individuals who are capable of developing by themselves.

Self-control combined with limited social skills is likely to lead to rigid attitudes that can hinder family agreements. It is quite likely that such families develop a 'business first' approach, that combined with instrumental competence may yield good business results for a while.

The respect for the legacy, the higher conformism to rules and hierarchies that this style generates makes it more likely that offspring will enter the business to carry on the family tradition. This can spark rivalry between family members to fill the positions or rivalry among the older generation and each member tries to favor his or her progeny. These next gen managers would be more likely to follow the business path blazed by the previous generation, and be less innovative than those brought up in the authoritative style.

The authoritarian style would make it hard to embrace a family council (which is based on conversation and mutual consent). Authoritarian parents are not wont to justify their decisions and their children lack the socials skills to approach difficult conversations. Parents tend to approach family relationships from their position at the top of the family pecking order and loathe passing the baton to the next generation.

In our experience, it is not uncommon to find youngsters that were brought up by very authoritarian parents to seek escape from parental authority by studying abroad, studying something that makes them non-candidates for the family business (studying agriculture in a family with an engineering business, for instance), entering groups that separated them from the business (meditation groups in India, religious groups, and so on) or even through mental illness. In fact, Shelton, Frick, and Wootton (1996) associate greater levels of child psychopathology with both the authoritarian and the permissive parenting styles.

It seems plausible that this parenting style tends to the development of more unipersonal management practices in which the owning manager is the center around which the firm's management revolves.

Permissive style

Permissive parents tend to allow substantial self-regulation but do not necessarily demand mature behavior. Confrontation with the next gen tends to be avoided, which gives the children a great degree of freedom (Baumrind,

1991: 62). The offspring of such parents perform worse at school and display more problem behavior. On the other hand, they have better social skills, higher self-esteem and are less prone to depression (Darling 1999).

Permissive styles tend to foster social skills but weak instrumental skills. It tends to develop egocentrism and poor self-control, which will likely make it hard to reach a family consensus. This supposes some restriction to the private interests of the various individuals. This style is likely to generate 'family-first' approaches.

The dominance of individual needs would make it hard to create proper family council dynamics. It is therefore likely that family councils would focus on the negotiation of the various individual interests, with little consideration being given to common or business interests.

Business tends to be seen as a source of family welfare (wealth, prestige, entertainment). As such, business needs are given scant consideration, there is little commitment to the success of the business project and the owners are likely to disregard the interests of other stakeholders. Family interests tend to invade business spheres.

Uninvolved style

The classification was developed to study parent–child relationships and it has been extensively used in the study of adolescents (Glasgow and Dornbusch, 1997). Kotchick and Forehand (2002) highlight the importance of the context in which parenting occurs.

The Uninvolved Style (low in both responsiveness and demandingness), tend to generate less competent children and adolescents in all fields. In our research and practical experience, we have very seldom found this model of parenting. Some tendency can be found in business founders, due to the high demands made by the business. In such cases, the parental presence tends to be the spouse or the grandparents but even so, there tends to be some level of involvement.

FAMILY WEALTH AND COMPLEXITY

Parenting styles and its effect on next gen development can be better grasped when incorporating contextual factors. In our cases, we identified two main variables that explain the outcome of each parenting style. These two contingent factors are family wealth and family complexity.

Family wealth is important because it determines the degree of economic freedom of the individual. So we observed that the impact of parenting was different according to the wealth of the family. We can define high wealth families as those in which family wealth can provide the family members with enough income to provide the family with a good living (as defined by the family in question). Poorer families would be those in which the family wealth cannot provide a good living for the family. This means that family members have to shift for themselves to earn a decent living.

Members of wealthy families do not have to rely on their individual activities to maintain their standard of living. They have what one could define as economic freedom. By contrast, members of poorer family business cannot rely only on the family business alone to give them the standard of living they seek. They have to get extra income from their individual activities to maintain their standard of living. In that sense, they have little economic freedom.

Family complexity is another variable that we identified as explaining the differences in the impact of parenting. We define family complexity as the number of persons, their diversity and the variety of relationships that make up the family (Gimeno et al., 2010).

Family complexity defines the range of possibilities that family members have in relation to their business. In this sense, greater family complexity means that the family members have to share and to agree their decisions with more family members. It also means that their individual professional possibilities toward the business are mediated with more individuals and that also their individual impact on the business is lower.

METHODS

To study how parenting affects next gen development, we have relied on qualitative research in order to glean in-depth information and create possible meaningful explanations (Stake, 1995). We rely on the STEP Methodology (cf. Nordqvist and Zellweger, 2010) analyzing in-depth case studies undertaken for various projects and that have been followed over long periods. This aspect is important as longitudinal studies allow for history to surface. We followed these cases for between 4 and 10 years, depending on each business family.

The Spanish companies used in this study were deliberately chosen to depict each parenting style based on two main dimensions: Level of wealth and level of family complexity. Purposive sampling allowed us to choose cases likely to show the features and/or processes we were interested in (Patton, 1990).

We interviewed an average of six family members per company. Pseudonyms are used throughout the chapter for confidentiality purposes.

In total, we chose nine cases, which could be placed in each dimension related to parenting style, family complexity and family wealth.

CASES AND FINDINGS

We have seen that the different parenting styles have an influence on the development of offspring (Maccoby, 2000) and they will obviously also have an impact on the offspring of the business families. The first observation was that we could quite clearly recognize the different parenting styles in the cases we were reviewing and also confirmed that the behavior patterns proposed by the empirical studies were also observed. At the same time there was a great variety in the effect of these behavior patterns in the various cases. We also saw that these differences could be explained by two different factors – family wealth and family complexity.

This framework of high and low wealth and high and low family business generates four possible scenarios, yet the lack of data within the fourth category led us to focus on only three of them. By reviewing our records and trying to allocate them in the different parenting styles, we found that we had no cases that could be clearly put in the 'uninvolved' category. Accordingly, we do not address this parenting style in our study.

We therefore looked at the three remaining parenting styles in the three contingent situations of wealth and family complexity (see Figure 10.2). We illustrate all nine possibilities with a case that allows us to draw up some propositions on the consequences of a given parenting style in given circumstances of wealth and family complexity. As the issues mentioned are highly sensitive, we use pseudonyms to avoid any possible identification.

Parenting Style	Contingent Circumstances		
	High F. Wealth **High F. Complexity**	**High F. Wealth** **Low F. Complexity**	**Low F. Wealth** **High F. Complexity**
Authoritative	Fam A	Fam D	Fam G
Authoritarian	Fam B	Fam E	Fam H
Permissive	Fam C	Fam F	Fam I

Figure 10.2   Parenting style and contingent circumstance

HIGH WEALTH AND HIGH FAMILY COMPLEXITY

Family A: Authoritative Parenting

Family A is both wealthy and complex, and brought up its children with an authoritative parenting style. The father spent a lot of time and effort to building up the company and so could not spend as much time on the kids as he would have liked. He has a close relationship with his offspring and they greatly admire their father. Father and mother played traditional roles, the father being the breadwinner and the mother running the household.

Both father and mother took an active part in local social activities. Some of them were shared with their kids, who continued them when they grew up.

The upbringing of the offspring (now in their fifties) was fairly successful. All have university degrees and some of them also have an MBA. The succession process was relatively smooth, with the father working with the kids in the company, gradually handing over the business to them.

In this process, a family council was created, which allowed them to solve the two main critical issues that they had to face. The first one was the father's gradual retirement from management of the company. The company was facing difficult times and the kids wanted to make changes that the father disliked. This raised the thorny question of which generation's opinion should prevail (in fact, what generation was in power). This issue was addressed thought conversation between them. As a result, of this 'conversational process' the company was able carry out the strategic changes that were needed. Far from being damaged in the process, family relationships were strengthened. The family was proud of having risen to making the changes needed even though they were far from easy.

A second major challenge for this family has been the process of retiring family members from management positions in the company to board positions. The retirees triggered the process after arriving at the conclusion that management positions should not be permanent ones and that the company needed different management profiles.

This tricky moment in the family business history was overcome by family consensus, supported by both the Family Council and the board of directors. Family members are currently represented on the board of directors but not elsewhere in the company. This process faced the siblings with many issues concerning social prestige, self-esteem, financial security, occupational activities, and so on.

The transition process in ownership has been also agreed. Most of the shares have been transferred to the next generation, and there is an agreement as to the stake retained by the previous generation.

This process was difficult but they tackled it sensibly, transforming the company by both exploiting and maintaining family unity.

Family B: Authoritarian Parenting

In Family B, parenting was exercised in an authoritarian style. The roles of the two parents were very clear, the father ran the business and the mother was the home-maker and brought up the kids. Unlike in Family A, conversation between parents was less open; both respected the other's areas of influence, which did not overlap.

The children were expected to excel at what they did whether it be studies or sport. Most of them followed the pattern that their parents suggested, getting business-related degrees, two of them an MBA.

One of the kids struck out in a direction other than expected by her parents and was thus cast in the role of 'the black sheep of the family'. Her life was an 'alternative one'; she did not get a degree, failed to make a 'decent living' (by her parents' lights) and even entered into dependencies.

This kid – a girl – made her parents suffer. They did all they could to get her back on 'the right path' with psychiatric support. This eventually paid off. She now lives in the countryside and has a family of her own. The company has given her a constant source of income and continues to do so. The amount of money she receives is an allowance given by the father on which she is wholly dependent.

The father continues to be active in the company, despite his age. The succession has been established, identifying which of the kids is 'best' to run the company. This created a non-explicit competition between them, each of whom does his or her best to please the father.

One of the kids failed in his tasks in the family business and this led him to being separated from the business activities. This led to a rift between his family and the family firm.

The other two kids working in the family business competed to show that each one of them was best-fitted to run the company. The outcome was that one of them was chosen by the father as best meeting his performance demands. The son who won the race acted on the same lines as his father, replicating the autocratic model his father had successfully developed. This made the other brothers feel there was no future for them in the company and they left, feeling deeply aggrieved. The family management succession was thus a painful affair. The issue of ownership succession remains open and the stakes are high, given that the firm is worth a great deal. These issues have not been openly discussed between the generations, even though it is on everyone's mind. The offspring are waiting to see what the father decides but he is in a quandary and finds all of the options unsatisfactory. In any event, he had to choose one in order to draw up his will. His wife helped him take a decision but she is distressed at the way the company has caused ructions in the family.

Family C: Permissive Parenting

Family C owns a fairly large family business, which is managed by non-family professionals. Each of the three branches of the family sits on the board of directors, which runs the firm with the help of some external directors.

Each branch also has its own family office, which manages the investments of the respective branch.

Parenting was of the permissive kind. Parents and kids have been close. The family made the children's well-being its priority. The parents were inordinately proud of their children but pretty undemanding. The kids were given the impression that the sky was the limit because of who they were rather than what they were.

Nowadays the younger generation of cousins is in its thirties. They have followed different career paths. Some have become successful managers in various companies; others act as managers in their family offices, while another group spends its time socializing and living it up.

The family relationship has been very good in the past. Today it is still very good but now that the parents are growing old, the new generation will be faced with hard issues.

The parents are perfectly aware that their kids vary in their ability to deal with business issues and are at a loss as to what they should do to keep both the family and business together.

The next generation is also having difficulties in establishing fruitful conversations on the decisions that have to be made. Almost all of them see themselves as capable of representing the family on the board of directors and of making the right decisions on the family office investments. Those that have the requisite skills have no doubts about their ability to run the company. Unfortunately, those lacking such skills are unaware of their short-comings simply because they have never been professionally challenged.

The family members have strong social skills so talking about such issues comes easily. The problem arises from the fact that they find it hard to reach a common understanding of the issues given that family members have taken different paths through life.

To ensure the continuity of the business, the parents have empowered the next generation members to prepare themselves as board members. This means members of the younger generation have the older generation's 'seal of approval' but are not necessarily seen as fit to run the company by their siblings.

HIGH WEALTH AND LOW FAMILY COMPLEXITY

Family D: Authoritative Parenting

Family D is a high wealth, low complexity family that adopted an authoritative parenting style. The family comprises the founder, his wife and two kids (a son in his early thirties and a daughter in her late twenties).

As is common with founding entrepreneurs, the father has worked and traveled extensively while the mother stayed at home. Her father was also an entrepreneur, which meant she was aware of business needs which helps her advise her husband. The mother's narrative explains her husband's absence from home in terms of sacrificing time with the family to build up the firm.

The founder has also shared his business initiatives with his kids since their teenage years. This encouraged them to be part of the business from an early age. The eldest boy has been directly involved in the company since he was 19, when he began university studies in the field that was the core activity of the family group. After his graduation, he took an MBA, with the idea of leading the business.

When the father saw that the son was able to run the company (on turning thirty), he retired from the management position to the board of directors. He says that his son has a more risk-taking attitude than him and this makes him worry. Nevertheless, the son enjoys his father's support.

The daughter did not study in a family business-related field but after a couple of years of work experience in which she informally shared family business life, she decided to take an MBA and enter the firm. She trusts her brother and vice versa. She wants her brother to continue running the business in the same way and she wants to enter the firm to lead some of the supporting activities. Although she has not worked in the business apart from a few spells in the summer, she has shared strategic decisions concerning the group with her father, brother and (to a lesser extent) her mother.

Management succession has worked out well. To tackle the issue of ownership succession, the father is thinking of openly discussing the matter with his wife and the kids so that all four can agree on a fair settlement.

Family E: Authoritarian Parenting

Family E also belongs to the high wealth and low complexity group and brought up the children in an authoritarian way. This case is different because the parenting style the divorced couple exercised over their two girls was related to the experiences they themselves had with their respective parents.

The girls' father is the second-generation member of a business family. His father (the founder) brought him up under the authoritative style. He was quite successful in getting his management degree and entered the company, where he replicated the founder's management style based on centralization, control and a low degree of trust in the management teams.

He had to shoulder responsibility for running the company in his early twenties when his father (the founder) died. He had clear ideas about what to do and 'took the bull by the horns.' The business throve under his management.

He got married and had two daughters whom he brought up in the same authoritarian style that had been inflicted on him. His daughters reacted badly and became emotionally distant from their father.

He got on poorly with his wife. The mother was much warmer towards the girls but did not forge a common approach to parenting with her husband. This distance grew until the marriage ended in divorce.

The girls continue to respect their father but there is little warmth in their relationship with him. For them, their father's life revolves around the company and they come second. They are interested in money the company makes for them but have no other attachment to the firm. Indeed, they emotionally reject the company. They spent a couple of summers working in the company but they chose to study in a non-related field of their business and have no interest in working in the firm. Both are blazing good careers in different fields.

For them, the company belongs to their father. When they are together, they do not speak about the business because they are not interested in it and the father does not know how to generate this interest. The father finds the situation frustrating but has come to accept it.

Family F: Permissive Parenting

Family F is also a simple, wealthy one that adopted a permissive parenting style. The founder of the company and his wife adopted fairly 'traditional' roles. He focused on building up the company and she looked after their two girls.

The father was the breadwinner and the mother led a fairly independent life with lots of non-business social activities. The couple seemed to live parallel lives.

Each parent seemed to try to forge stronger bonds with their daughters by making them take part in their own lives. The mother did so by giving the girls a taste of local social life. The father did so by familiarizing the girls with the business.

Both girls got good degrees and their father invited them to join the company, earmarking them posts that they would feel comfortable with. The downside of this cozy arrangement was that this did not help them develop their management skills. Nevertheless, the company helped bond father and daughters. When the two girls got married, the sons-in-law were also offered posts in the company.

Ill health has now forced the father to retire and the daughters now realize that they have not developed the skills to lead the company, even though they are trying to make a go of it. They have been clever enough to build up a team of good managers to make up for their own shortcomings.

LOW WEALTH AND HIGH FAMILY COMPLEXITY

Low family wealth usually refers to small or medium-sized companies. If this is combined with a family with high complexity, it means that the family wealth does not allow the various family members to rely on the company to make a decent living.

Family G: Authoritative Parenting

Family G has low wealth and high complexity. The family has brought up the children in the authoritative parenting style. The father and the mother had five kids.

The father worked as a manager in a large company and when the kids were young, he decided to form his own company and exploit the experience gained in his previous job. His wife gave him moral support but was not directly involved in the business.

The company throve and the family had a comfortable lifestyle. The five kids did well. Four of them got university degrees. The one who did not (he disliked studying) was invited to join the company and work for his parents.

Soon afterwards, the company ran into trouble and was forced to file for bankruptcy. This put the father under a lot of stress. He had a heart attack and died.

The son who had worked with his father then set up a new company that largely drew on the intangible assets of the old one (knowledge, reputation, networks, and so on). The ownership of the new company was split equally between the five siblings because they thought it was what their father would have wanted.

The son who had joined the old company was the driving force behind the new one. His siblings tried to help him but they had their own careers.

On a couple of occasions, one of his siblings temporarily joined the company to help him deal with a given problem.

The managing brother asked the siblings to boost his stake in ownership given that he was the one making the business grow. They understood his demand that he should have a majority stake in the firm. They all struck a bargain whereby the managing brother got a majority stake and was free to manage the small company as he saw fit and as a steward for the minority shareholders. In our view, the managing brother will eventually buy out the minority shareholders and become sole owner.

Family H: Authoritarian Parenting

Family F also falls within the low wealth, high complexity group. The founder of the company was a fairly dominant person who had a clear division of roles with his wife. They had five children, two boys and three girls.

The company was a traditional company working in the agricultural sector. The father inherited the land and bought more acreage while he was in charge of the business.

The father felt that the two boys should work with him in the company. This also applied to girls, although they could turn the offer down if they so wished.

The kids got a fairly tough, traditional education along Victorian lines. Displaying emotions was strongly discouraged and the stress was on doing well. The eldest boy managed to escape parental control. At the age of 18, he got a foreign scholarship and left home to study abroad. He then became an entrepreneur.

The youngest brother stayed with the father and tried to meet his demands and rise to his expectations. Two of the three girls worked with the father as well but much fewer demands were made of them than the boy. This 'gender discrimination' made life much easier for them. The youngest daughter got a university degree and pursued a career outside the family business.

When the father died, he left the ownership split equally between the siblings. All five of them decided to continue together and lend support to the brother who had stayed with his father. The rejection of their father's authoritarian style was so great that they promised to decide everything by consensus and treat each other as equals.

The company yields low dividends but for the siblings, it is a good excuse to meet and be together. They are thinking now how to bring the next generation into the business and have created a family council to do so.

For them the business is more a social family activity than a commercial venture. Bitter memories of their tough father make them avoid differences and conflict. Consensus and agreement is what drives the family business. They avoid transformation and modernization of the business because the firm's mission is to bind the family rather than make profits.

Family I: Permissive Parenting

Family I is the last one in this low wealth, high complexity group. The founder of the company, as was the case with almost all the other firms considered here, spent his time building up the business, while his wife was mainly in charge of the business.

Both father and mother took great care of their four children. Three of them worked with the father, while the fourth one pursued his path after graduating from university. The company made enough money to provide a living for the four families (the parent's one, and those of their offspring).

When the father died, the business continued growing. Ownership was shared between the three kids, and they paid a monthly sum to their mother.

Some years later, the company was going through tough times and there were disagreements among the siblings. The business could not support the three families and a family conflict arose about who was best suited to run the firm, who should leave, and where the blame for the company's woes lay.

Of the five, two had made reaching agreement particularly difficult. In our view, only one of them was capable of maintaining his standard of living if he were to leave the firm. The other two who were more inclined to reach agreement did not recognize that they needed him to turn the business round and that this would mean breaking with the relationship between equals that had sustained the company hitherto. In the end, they proved too conceited to see the changes needed. The company was declared bankrupt and was closed.

CONCLUSIONS AND IMPLICATIONS

Parenting styles seem to greatly influence the development of younger generations and, therefore the behavior of that generation and how it behaves towards the business. This ownership, regardless of whether it is juridical or psychological, is exercised in different ways according to how the offspring have been brought up.

Parenting styles affect the offspring's relational and instrumental resources as the family literature states but our study suggests that the way they relate to the business and between themselves may also vary, thus affecting the family's skills in interacting with its business.

This impact of parenting on family behavior can be understood by applying the Circumplex Model (Olson, 2000), a widely accepted model in the family field. This model analyzes families according to two main descriptive variables (cohesion and flexibility), and an instrumental one (communication).

Cohesion is the 'emotional bonding that family members have towards one another' (Olson, 2000: 145), differentiating four levels of cohesion: disengaged, separated, connected and enmeshed. According to the Circumplex Model, the extreme levels of cohesion would be dysfunctional. Very low cohesion (disengaged) means that family members do their own thing, with limited attachment or commitment to their family (Olson, 2000: 145), while the very high commitment (enmeshed) there is too much consensus within the family and too little independence (Olson, 2000: 146).

Flexibility is the amount of change in its leadership, role relationships and relationship rules (Olson, 2000: 146) that the family can incorporate. Flexibility is also scaled in four levels: rigid, structured, flexible and chaotic. According to the model, extreme flexibility levels tend to be dysfunctional. The extreme low (rigid) is because decisions are imposed by a controlling individual and extreme high (chaotic), because of the erratic or limited leadership and unclear roles.

Business families are more demanding than non-business families in terms of striking a balance between flexibility and cohesion. Such a balance is needed to develop relationships with the appropriate degree of change (flexibility) and levels of togetherness, balancing group cohesion with individuality. This means striking the right balance of role change, leadership, discipline, and change in opinions, mindsets and attitudes over time. Family flexibility is required to ensure the business can adapt while keeping the values and mission clear.

The same can be said about cohesion. The right balance of group identity, closeness, loyalty and dependence has to be struck. The owning family has to maintain a level of closeness that allows them to agree on a common business project, while also giving individuals sufficient scope to fully develop their potential.

This need for balance is likely to become more important as a family's wealth and complexity increase. High family complexity will easily break rigid families, create serious disorder in the business in the case of chaotic families, lose the mission in disengaged families and generate conflict in enmeshed families.

Wealth also creates a greater need to strike the right balance. Rising

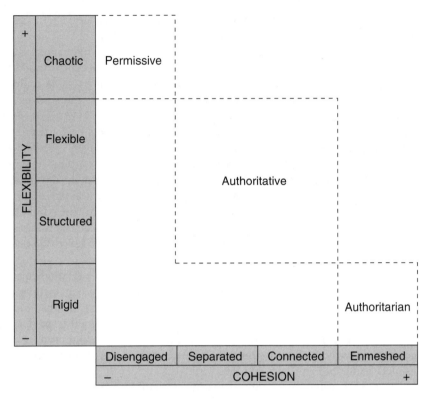

Figure 10.3   Olson's model adapted by authors

wealth may exacerbate domination in rigid families, spur rivalry in chaotic families, accelerate disengagement in disengaged families and frustration in enmeshed families.

Therefore business families need to be more balanced in terms of both flexibility and cohesion (see Figure 10.3). Our research suggests that parenting style affects both flexibility and cohesion. Permissive styles would lead to chaotic families, in terms of flexibility, and disengaged families, in terms of cohesion.

The family literature states that permissive parenting tends to develop social skills and a great degree of freedom but does not necessarily foster instrumental competence and maturity (Doret et al., 2013). This is mirrored in the business family in various ways, because the power they have towards the company requires a higher level of maturity than in non-business families. Problems tend to emerge when the older generation loses its ability to effectively manage the company.

The business also requires strong management skills and acquiring these can be more difficult for offspring brought up by permissive parents.

All three cases show behaviors of a younger generation with some or most members finding it hard to empathize with the business and the other family members' needs, and see the situation in a self-centered way. This may be the result of a lack of skills, making it difficult to grasp the complexity of the business decisions and the need to take the feelings, needs and circumstances of others into account.

This may explain why: (1) Family C has difficulties in recognizing the skills of its members and in choosing the ones needed by senior managers; (2) why the next gen in Family F has no relationship to the business other than as a source of income; (3) Family I plunges into crisis when there is a mismatch between the real world and family members' high opinion of themselves.

By contrast, authoritarian styles would lead to rigid families, in terms of flexibly and enmeshed families, in terms of cohesion.

All three had business-first approaches that could apparently strengthen the business. In all three cases, the weak encouragement provided by this parenting style created difficulties in adapting the family reaction to the business needs.

Family research shows that this parenting style generates instrumental competence, but not necessarily self-esteem and relational ability (Darling, 1999). This limitation in the possible family reactions may be a minor misfortune for non-business families but can be a serious handicap for business ones.

The business forces the family to maintain bonds that require certain empathy, altruism and interpersonal abilities, and these attitudes and capacities are not strongly developed by this parenting style. This may explain why: (1) Family B suffered a crisis between the siblings in the succession process, which may imperil the company's survival; (2) in Family E, the next generation was wholly detached from the business; (3) Family H lost its entrepreneurial capability in order to create a cozy atmosphere that contrasted with the father's harsh, authoritarian style.

Authoritative families would be the parenting style that is most conducive to striking the right balance in both dimensions. According to the Circumplex Model, this balance is struck through a third dimension – communication. This is one of the characteristics of the authoritative model, that we label as 'conversational style' in order to stress this communicational capacity.

Our study supports the idea that the authoritative parenting style seems to be the best one for developing a business family. The business confronts the family with different demands that require both relational and instrumental skills, which are better developed by authoritative parenting. This parenting style develops greater ability by family members to reach functional agreements in the light of varying circumstances – which in our study were represented by wealth and family complexity.

All three authoritative families that we studied were able to make major changes in their family business through a conversational process. Family A was able to withdraw itself from management positions, Family D was able to push through an entrepreneurial succession and Family G was able to let the manager brother dominate the business and its ownership. All three major changes were of great importance to proper running of the business and are likely to be key to their future success.

Implications and Future Research

This study reflects the importance of both 'demandingness' and responsiveness in business families. Weak development of either or both of them may have a fairly negative impact on both the business and the family. This highlights the importance of parenting in the family business. Different lines of research emerge for further research.

All cases present a relationship between baby-boomer parents and offspring belonging to Generation X or Millennial in a western context. Exploring the impact of belonging to a specific context (cultural and generational) on the impact of parenting styles could shed light on how generational issues play a role.

Another question that arises from the cases is the importance of fraternal relationship (between siblings). In our study, this seems to be linked to the parental style. Thus, in Case A, the authoritative parenting style seemed to allow the development of a stronger fraternal relationship, whereas in Case B, the authoritarian parenting style seems to have hindered such a relationship. Understanding how fraternal relationships are built in the light of the parenting style might expand knowledge on how to manage parenting and fraternal relationships within the family business.

It also seems that the marital relationship has an impact on the parenting style and its effects. We have seen some similar situations (in which the father was often absent and the mother running the family) that had different results. The differing outcomes seem to be a result of a different relationship between the couple – something that would also open an interesting line of research.

Another possible research line would be the prevalence of a patriarchal versus a nuclear family model and its impact on opting for a specific parenting style. This research also suggests some possible relationships in this direction.

Gender seems also to be an issue, especially with regard to the authoritarian style. The cases show some discrimination against women in this style, which paradoxically, saves them from the parental authority, giving the women greater freedom than men.

Another interesting line of research emerges from studying the influence of different parenting styles in different nuclear families inside a complex family. It seems that this could explain some of the relational difficulties that often arise between different branches of the family.

Our study also opens the study of how parenting influences the business family, described through the Circumplex Model. Further research is needed on how parenting styles affect more the specific dimensions of the flexibility and the cohesion of the business family.

Finally, delving deeper into the impact of parenting style on specific family business practices would open new avenues for research. The main ones would be to examine how parenting style affects: (1) commitment to/ detachment from the business; and (2) the development of a governance structure. It would also be worth looking at how parenting style influences the prevalence of personal interest and project over a common one and the ability to broach difficult issues through frank conversations.

NOTE

1. We are very thankful to Pramodita Sharma for her insightful comments that helped us expand widely the conceptual scope of this chapter.

REFERENCES

Aronoff, C.E. and Ward, J.L. (1996). *Governance: Maximizing Family and Business Potential*. Marietta, GA: Family Enterprise Publishers.

Baumrind, D. (1966). Effects of authoritative control on child behavior. *Child Development*, 37: 887–907.

Baumrind, D. (1989). Rearing competent children, in Damon, W. (ed.), *Child Development Today and Tomorrow* (349–378). San Francisco: Jossey-Bass.

Baumrind, D. (1991). The influence of parenting style on adolescent competence and substance use. *Journal of Early Adolescence*, 11(1): 56–95.

Baumrind, D. (1993). The average expectable environment is not good enough: a response to Scarr. *Child Development*, 64(5): 1299–1317.

Boyd, J.H., Upton, N.B., and Wirenski, M. (1999). Mentoring in family firms: a reflective analysis of senior executives' perceptions. *Family Business Review*, 12(4): 299–309.

Carlock, R.S. and Ward, J.L. (2001). *Strategic Planning for the Family Business*. New York: Palgrave.

Carlson, C., Uppal, S., and Prosser, E.C. (2000). Ethnic differences in processes contributing to the self-esteem of early adolescent girls. *The Journal of Early Adolescence*, 20(1): 44–67.

Corbetta, G. and Salvato, C. (2004). The board of directors in family firms: one size fits all?, *Family Business Review*, 17(2): 119–134.

Darling, N. (1999). Parenting style and its correlates. ERIC Clearinghouse on Elementary and Early Childhood Education Champaign IL. ED427896.

de Ruyter, D.J. and Schinkel, A. (2013). On the relations between parents' ideals and children's autonomy. *Educational Theory*, 63(4): 369–388.

Fagan, J. (2000). Head start fathers' daily hassles and involvement with their children. *Journal of Family Issues*, 21(3): 329–346.

Gomez-Mejia, L.R., Haynes, K.T., Nunez-Nickel, M., Jacobson, K.J.L., and Moyano-Fuentes, J. (2007). Socioemotional wealth and business risks in family-controlled firms: evidence from Spanish olive oil mills. *Administrative Science Quarterly*, 52(1): 106–137.

Ibrahim, A.B., Soufani, K, Poutziouris, P., and Lam, J. (2004). Qualities of an effective successor: the role of education and training. *Education and Training*, 46(8/9): 474–480.

Gimeno, A., Baulenas, G., and Coma-Cros, J. (2010). *Family Business Models: Practical Solutions for the Family Business*. London: Palgrave Macmillan.

Glasgow, K.L. and Dornbusch, S. (1997). Parenting styles, adolescents' attributions, and educational outcomes in nine heterogeneous high schools. *Child Development*, 68(3): 507–529.

Kotchick, B.A. and Forehand, R. (2002). Putting parenting in perspective: a discussion of the contextual factors that shape parenting practices. *Journal of Child and Family Studies*, 11(3): 255–269.

Lamborn, D.S., Mounts, N.S., Steinberg, L., and Dornbusch, S.M. (1991). Patterns of competence and adjustment among adolescents from authoritative, authoritarian, indulgent, and neglectful families. *Child Development*, 62: 1049–1065.

Lepper, M.R. and Greene, D. (1978). Overjustification research and beyond: toward a means–end analysis of intrinsic and extrinsic motivation. In Lepper, M.R. and Greene, D. (eds), *The Hidden Costs of Reward* (109–148). Hillsdale, NJ: Erlbaum.

Levendosky, A.A. and Graham-Berman, S.A. (2000). Behavioral observations of parenting in battered women. *Journal of Family Psychology*, 14(1): 80–94.

Maccoby, E.E. (2000). Parenting and its effects on children: on reading and mis-reading behavior genetics. *Annual Review of Psychology*, 51: 1–27.

Maccoby, E.E. and Martin, J.A. (1983). Socialization in the context of the family: parent–child interaction. In Mussen, P.H. (ed.) and Hetherington, E.M. (volume ed.), *Handbook of Child Psychology: Vol. 4. Socialization, Personality, and Social Development* (4th edn, 1–101). New York: Wiley.

Miller, N.B., Cowan, P.A., Cowan, C.P., Hetherington, E.M., and Clingempeel, W.G. (1993). Externalizing in preschoolers and early adolescents: a cross-site replication of a family model. *Developmental Psychology*, 29: 3–18.

Nordqvist, M. and Zellweger, T. (2010). A qualitative research approach to the study of transgenerational entrepreneurship, in Nordqvist, M. and Zelleweger, T. (eds), *Trangenerational Entrepreneurship: Exploring Growth and Performance in Family Firms across Generations* (39–57). Cheltenham, UK, and Northampton, MA, USA: Edward Elgar Publishing.

Nordqvist, M., Sharma, P., and Chirico, F. (2014). Family firm heterogeneity and governance: a configuration approach. *Journal of Small Business Management*, 52(2): 192–209.

Olson, D. (2000). Circumplex model of marital and family systems. *Journal of Family Therapy*, 22: 144–167.

Out, D., Bakermans-Kranenburg, M.J., and van Ijzendoorn, M.H. (2009). The role of disconnected and extremely insensitive parenting in the development of disorganized attachment: the validation of a new measure. *Attachment and Human Development*, 11: 419–443.

Patton, M.Q. (1990). *Qualitative Evaluation and Research Methods* (2nd edn). Newbury Park, CA: Sage Publications.

Pearson, A., Bergiel, E., and Barnett, T. (2014). Expanding the study of organizational behaviour in family business: adapting team theory to explore family firms. *European Journal of Work and Organizational Psychology*, 23(5): 657–664.

Reiss, D., Hetherington, E.M., Plomin, R., Howe, G.W., Simmens, S.J. et al. (1995). Genetic questions for environmental studies: differential parenting and psychopathology in adolescence. *Archives of General Psychiatry*, 52: 925–936.

Sharma, P. and Irving, G.P. (2005). Four bases of family business successor commitment: antecedents and consequences. *Entrepreneurship Theory and Practice*, 29(1): 13–33.

Sharma, P. and Rao, S. (2000). Successor attributes in Indian and Canadian family firms: a comparative study. *Family Business Review*, 13: 313–330.

Sharma, P. and Salvato, C. (2013). *Family Firm Longevity: A Balancing Act between Continuity and Change*. Cambridge: Cambridge University Press.

Sharma, P., Melin, L., and Nordqvist, M. (2014). Introduction: scope, evolution and future of family business studies, in Melin, L., Nordqvist, M., and Sharma, P. (eds), *The Sage Handbook of Family Business* (1–23). Thousand Oaks, CA: Sage Publications.

Shelton, K.K., Frick, P.J., and Wootton, J. (1996). The assessment of parenting practices in families of elementary school-aged children. *Journal of Clinical Child Psychology*, 25: 317–327.

Stake, R. (1995). *The Art of Case Study Research*. Thousand Oaks, CA: Sage Publications.

Steier, L. (2001). Family firms, forms of governance, and the evolving role of trust. *Family Business Review*, 14(4): 353–367.

Steier, L. and Miller, D. (2010). Pre- and post-succession governance philosophies in entrepreneurial family firms. *Journal of Family Business Strategy*, 1(3): 145–154.

Steinberg, L, Dornbusch, S.M., and Brown, B.B. (1992a). Ethnic differences in adolescence achievement: an ecological perspective. *American Psychologist*, 47(6): 723–729.

Steinberg, L., Dornbusch, S.M., and Darling, N. (1992b). Impact of parenting practices on adolescent achievement: authoritative parenting, school involvement and encouragement to succeed. *Child Development*, 63: 1266–1282.

Steinberg, L., Lamborn, S., Darling, N., Mounts, N., and Dornbusch, S. (1994). Over-time changes in adjustment and competence among adolescents from authoritative, authoritarian, indulgent, and neglectful families. *Child Development*, 65: 754–770.

Weiss, L.H. and Schwarz, J.C. (1996). The relationships between parenting types and older adolescents' personality, academic achievement, adjustment and substance use. *Child Development*, 67: 2101–2114.

Index

and debt management 192, 203, 205
and family values 129, 138–9, 142
and firm restructuring 202–3, 205
and innovation 192, 199, 207
literature on 104–6
major themes overview 7–9
and organizational transformation
    130–31, 142–3
practical research implications 15–16
of second generation family
    members 100–101, 106,
    110–113, 117, 119–20
and succession 101, 103, 105, 110,
    113, 115, 121, 202–4
and technical capacity of next
    generation 202, 206
transgenerational 101–2, 104–6,
    110–21

quality control systems 111

R&D (Research and Development)
    106, 202, 206
Ramesh, K.P. 76–8, 79–82, 86–7, 88, 90
Ramesh, Kumar 76–8, 80–81, 89
Ramesh, Ravi 76–8, 80–81, 89
Rao, A. S. 164
'regenerative capability' 119
reinforcing capacity of structure 9
relational capital 196
'respect' 77–8, 127, 138, 141, 149, 156,
    158–9, 164–5, 182, 183, 224, 227
'responsiveness' 216–17, 220, 234
retirement 54, 62–3, 65, 80, 81, 173,
    176, 223, 226, 228
'return on investment' approach 214
'rigid flexibility' 231, 232
RO (responsible ownership) 52, 54–6,
    57, 65–7
Rodrigues, Marcelo 199, 205
Rokeach, M. 132, 163
Rose, M. 120

Sáenz, Carolina 61
Sáenz, Don Antonio 61, 67
Sardeshmukh, S.R. 151, 152
secondary socialization 27–8, 43
'Sedekah' 177
See, James 213, 214
See, Maria 213

See, Mrs 212–14
See, Rita 213
self-regulation 216, 217, 219
Senna, Ayrton 175
'separated cohesion' 231, 232
shared leadership 7, 13, 82, 84, 92, 109
    see also collective leadership
Sharma, P. 28–9, 78, 164, 197–8, 206,
    215
Shelton, K. K. 219
'Sindhi' communities 90
situational leadership 84
SMEs (small-and medium-sized
    enterprises) 147, 151, 152, 153,
    154, 155, 163, 164
social relations 178
socialization 27–8, 32–4, 37–8, 42–3,
    45
'societal influence/values' 157, 158,
    162–3
socio-emotional wealth 165
Sorenson, R. L. 132
Souza, E. C. L. 197
Spanish case study
    conclusions 230–34
    family wealth/complexity 220–21,
      223–30
    interviews 221–2
    methodology 221–2
    mini case study 212–14
    parenting styles 216–20, 222–30,
      232–5
    study overview 10–11
speed of decision-making 184–5, 189
Steier, L. 132, 178, 179, 197
STEP (Successful Transgenerational
    Entrepreneurship Practices)
    project 1–2, 57, 101–2, 109,
    120–21, 143, 221
Sternieri, Valéria Braile 202, 203, 206
Stewart, A. 9, 105, 106, 129, 131
Strauss, A. 155, 180
strong ties 195, 205, 208
'structured flexibility' 231, 232
Subway 174–5, 181, 185, 186
succession
    see also continuity
    and collective leadership 76–82, 88
    and Communities of Practice 52,
      54–5, 57–8, 63, 64–6, 67